Brilliant ECDL

James Moran and Victoria Hull

PEARSON

Prentice
Hall

Harlow, England • London • New York • Boston • San Francisco • Toronto
Sydney • Tokyo • Singapore • Hong Kong • Seoul • Taipei • New Delhi
Cape Town • Madrid • Mexico City • Amsterdam • Munich • Paris • Milan

PEARSON EDUCATION LIMITED

Edinburgh Gate
Harlow CM20 2JE
Tel: +44 (0)1279 623623
Fax: +44 (0)1279 431059

Website: www.pearsoned.co.uk

_____

First published in Great Britain in 2006

© Happy Computers 2006

ISBN-13: 978-0-13-197631-3
ISBN-10: 0-13-197631-1

British Library Cataloguing-in-Publication Data
A catalogue record for this book is available from the British Library

Library of Congress Cataloging-in-Publication Data
Moran, James.
   Brilliant ECDL / James Moran and Victoria Hull.
      p. cm.-- (Brilliant guides)
   ISBN-13: 978-0-13-197631-3
   ISBN-10: 0-13-197631-1
      1. Electronic data processing personnel--Certification--Europe. 2. Microcomputers. 3.
   European Computer Driving Licence. I. Hull, Victoira. II. Title. III. Series.

   QA76.3.M649 2005
   005.5--dc22

                                                    2005053923

Microsoft product screen shots reprinted with permission from Microsoft Corporation.

10 9 8 7 6 5 4 3 2
10 09 08 07 06

Typeset in 9/12pt Helvetica Roman by 30
Printed and bound in Great Britain by Bell & Bain Ltd, Glasgow

The Publisher's policy is to use paper manufactured form sustainable forests.

Brilliant Guides

What you need to know and how to do it

When you're working on your PC and come up against a problem that you're unsure how to solve, or want to accomplish something in an application that you aren't sure how to do, where do you look? Manuals and traditional training guides are usually too big and unwieldy and are intended to be used as an end-to-end training resource, making it hard to get to the info you need right away without having to wade through pages of background information that you just don't need at that moment – and helplines are rarely that helpful!

Brilliant guides have been developed to allow you to find the info you need easily and without fuss and guide you through the task using a highly visual, step-by-step approach – providing exactly what you need to know when you need it!

Brilliant guides provide the quick easy-to-access information that you need, using a detailed index and troubleshooting guide to help you find exactly what you need to know, and then presenting each task on one or two pages. Numbered steps then guide you through each task or problem, using numerous screenshots to illustrate each step. Added features include information boxes that point you to related tasks and information in the book, and alert you to relevant expert tips, tricks and advice to further expand your skills and knowledge.

In addition to covering all major office PC applications, and related computing subjects, the *Brilliant* series also contains titles that will help you in every aspect of your working life, such as writing the perfect CV, answering the toughest interview questions and moving on in your career.

Brilliant guides are the light at the end of the tunnel when you are faced with any minor or major task!

Authors' Acknowledgements

Compiled/edited/mismanaged by James Moran, based on manuals written by me, Victoria Hull, Nik Taylor, and Clare Simmons.

This book could not have existed without the hard work, team spirit and good teeth of the Happy Computers and Happy eLearning teams, specifically:

Cathy Busani – for manuals, caring, and being lovely

Victoria Hull – for keeping us eLearning people safe and warm, being fab, and remembering things

Jodie Kearns – for all your help and support, especially with synchronization

Debbie Lampon – for beating the website into shape using "programming", or something

Clare Simmons – for manuals, and knowing the way to San José

Nik Taylor – for more manuals, and being a diamond geezer

Nick Velasco – for hitting the PC when it crashed to make it work

...and Henry Stewart who, thankfully, didn't listen to all the people who said that you could never run a business being nice to the staff, or with a silly name like Happy Computers. Thanks for starting such a great place to work, and employing all of us troublemakers.

Happy Computers (www.happy.co.uk) is a computer training company that believes learning should be fun. It was established to combine technical expertise and excellent training skills with an enjoyable learning environment. In 2001 it was named as IT Training Company of the Year by the Institute of IT Training. In 2003 it was voted by Management Today to be the best company in the UK for customer service. And in 2004 it was named as the best company in the UK for work/life balance by the *Financial Times*. All Happy Computers' training is based around the following age-old principle:

- Tell me and I will forget
- Show me and I will remember
- Involve me and I will understand

Happy eLearning is the online division of Happy Computers, and is the lead supplier of online ECDL training for the NHS and the DWP. Contact us via the website, at www.happyelearning.co.uk

For more details of classroom training contact Happy Computers:

Website: www.happy.co.uk
Email: happy@happy.co.uk
Phone: 020 7375 7300

And seeing as I spent ages fiddling about with putting the pages together, coping with a constantly crashing PC and a deadline of about 12 seconds, I think I deserve a paragraph all to myself. And that was it. Oh well.

Contents

4 Legal Issues   28

MODULE 2 FILE MANAGEMENT

1 The Desktop   33

5   Programs and Printing

3　Functions and Cell References　243

4　Printing Workbooks　251

MODULE 5 DATABASES

3 Forms — 330

MODULE 6 PRESENTATIONS

3 Formatting Slides

6 Graphics

7 On-Screen Shows

Introduction

What is this book for?

This book is designed to teach you everything you need to know to be able to pass the ECDL (European Computer Driving Licence) exam for Syllabus 4. It is aimed at users using Microsoft Office XP, and all screenshots will reflect this. If you are using any other packages, for example Star Office or Lotus, then the screenshots will look completely wrong to you. It is recommended that you use Office XP while using this book. The File Management section of the book is based on Windows XP and above.

How do I use this book?

Open the first page of the book, and read the words from left to right, starting at the top of the page, and working your way down to the bottom. Proceed to the next page, ensuring that the page numbers are ascending as you go along. When you have finished the book, close it.

That's very funny. Now how do I really use it?

As this book is aimed at helping you to pass the exam, you really need to read every scrap of information in it. There is nothing more, nothing less than you need. If you are very confident that you know, for example, how to mail merge, then it should be okay to skip that part. But it is worth checking through just in case – you may know how to mail merge using an Excel data document, but the ECDL syllabus assumes that you know how to do it using a Word data document. So even if you think you know everything, it won't hurt to read everything just in case.

If you know lots of things, but just need to know one particular thing, you can just flick around and pick up the piece of information. Feel free to dip in and out, but some things will require you to know something else first – taking the mail merge example, the section on merging will assume you know how to create a data document and a main document. The book also assumes that you can switch a PC on and off, and can use a mouse.

Instead of just reading the book, try and go through it when you have access to a PC and Microsoft Office. Have a go at anything you learn, or anything you're not sure of – it's the best way to understand it.

BASIC CONCEPTS OF INFORMATION TECHNOLOGY

FILE MANAGEMENT

WORD PROCESSING

SPREADSHEETS

DATABASES

PRESENTATIONS

INTERNET AND EMAIL

CHAPTER 1

Getting Started

What You'll Do

→ Discover Computers

→ Discover the Parts of a Computer

→ Discover Computer Accessories

→ Discover Memory and Storage

→ Compare the Cost and Capacity of Different Memory Devices

→ Discover Software

1.1 Computer Terms

1.1.1 What is a Computer?

A computer is a machine that can run programs to carry out a wide range of tasks. Unlike, say, a calculator, it can be programmed to do more or less anything. However, it can only do what you tell it to do. It cannot take over the planet. Unless you tell it to. And even if you did, it probably wouldn't be able to, because of the cables and things.

1.1.2 The First Computer

The first computer was called the Atanasoff-Berry Computer, or ABC for short, named after its inventors, John Vincent Atanasoff and Clifford Berry. It was made between 1937 and 1942, and was originally designed to solve equations. It was the size of a desk, weighed 700 pounds (50 stone), and contained more than 300 vacuum tubes (a large glass device for converting electricity) and over a mile of wire. It could do one calculation every 15 seconds, which was quite fast in those days.

Later, computers got much bigger, heavier, and more complex. Information was fed into them with punched cards, and bits of them kept popping and exploding. That's why nobody tried to use them on the train on the way to work. As computers became more advanced, they got smaller, faster, more reliable, and less likely to explode. Nowadays they are very small, and never explode at all, unless you fill them up with dynamite, but you should never, ever do this.

1.1.3 Hardware and Software

A computer, and all the physical, solid objects that come with it, is a piece of hardware. If you can touch it or feel it or bang your head on it, it is hardware. Software is the name for programs that run on the computer, or that come supplied with it.

1.1.4 Other Names for Computers

- **PC/Microcomputer:** A computer is usually called a PC – this stands for Personal Computer. Back in the olden days (the 1970s and 1980s) it was called a microcomputer. Just like computers, they've managed to make the words smaller as well.

- **Desktop/Laptop:** The two main types of PC are desktop and laptop. Desktop PCs are used on or near a desk, and consist of a large box base, a screen, keyboard and mouse. Laptop PCs are very small, and contain everything in one small package – they are a lot more expensive than desktops.

- **Mainframe:** This is a large, expensive computer used by, for example, NASA for critical, complex operations like launching the space shuttle.

- **Minicomputer:** Halfway between a mainframe and a normal computer, this is typically used by large companies like banks to keep the business running smoothly.

- **Network Server:** Like a minicomputer, this controls a company network, letting users access company files and communicate with each other.

- **Dumb/intelligent terminals:** A dumb terminal is connected to a network server but can only access it and read/write to it, it cannot do anything on its own. An intelligent terminal can do this and also perform other functions – a normal PC connected to a company network would also be called an intelligent terminal.

- **PDA (Personal Digital Assistant):** This is a small, mobile hand held device that provides computing and information storage and retrieval for personal or business use, often for keeping schedule calendars and address book information handy. Most PDAs have a small keyboard. Some have an electronically sensitive pad you can write on with a special pen.

1.2 Computer Hardware

1.2.1 Computer Types

- **Tower:** A tower-style PC is slightly larger than a normal one, and usually stands on its end. Network servers are usually tower PCs.

- **Desktop:** A desktop-style PC is one that sits flat on a desk.

1.2.2 Parts of a Computer

Outside:

1 Base unit: this is the square box that all the other parts plug into. It contains all the components that make the PC work.

2 **VDU:** The screen/monitor/visual display unit (VDU) is the part of the computer that shows you what is going on, and what you are doing. For example, in a word processing program, you would see the letters you type appearing on the screen.

3 **Keyboard:** This is what you use to type information into the computer.

4 **Mouse:** The mouse is used to point and click on things on the screen – when you move the mouse, a pointer on the screen moves as well. If you press the mouse button while the pointer is on certain icons or buttons, you can run programs or press buttons.

Inside:

■ **CPU:** The CPU, or Central Processing Unit, is the brains of the computer. All the "thinking", calculating and processing is done here. Its speed is measured in megahertz (MHz) or gigahertz (GHz), which measures the amount of complete circuits a signal can travel around the processor in one second, or the millions of simple calculations it can make in a second. If it has a speed of 600 MHz, this means it can do 600 million things in one second. If it has a speed of 2 GHz, then it can do 2000 million (or 2 billion) things in one second.

■ **Hard disk:** The hard disk drive is used to store programs and information. When you save a file, it is saved onto your hard disk.

■ **Floppy disk:** A floppy disk drive is like a hard disk, but with removable disks called floppies or floppy disks. Floppies can be used to transfer small files from one PC to another. Older floppies really were floppy, as they came in soft plastic or card cases. Today's floppies are a bit more sturdy, although the disk itself is very floppy and wobbly, which is why it comes in a strong plastic case.

■ **Memory:** When a program is run, it is loaded into the computer's memory. The more memory a PC has, the more things it can do at one time.

1.3 Computer Accessories

1.3.1 Disks

■ **Floppy disks:** These are used when you need to transfer a small file from one PC to another. If the file is a bit too big, you need something a bit bigger.

■ **Zip drives:** These are another type of floppy drive, that use zip disks instead of floppy disks. Zip disks can hold about 100 times as much as a floppy disk.

■ **CDs:** If you have a CD writer/burner, you can put files on to a CD (Compact Disc), which can hold over 400 floppies' worth of files. A DVD (Digital Versatile Disc) is a higher quality form of a CD, and can hold 6 to 7 times as much as a normal CD.

1.3.2 Backup Tapes

Another way of backing up large amounts of information is a backup tape. This is a magnetic tape, like a video or audio cassette, which has the files streamed onto it. It usually takes a long time, and is only used for large backups. They are sometimes called data cartridges.

1.3.3 Printers

Printers are used to transfer information from the computer onto paper; for example, if you typed a letter in a word processor you would probably want to print it out. Printers come in many different shapes and sizes:

- **Laser:** These are large, expensive printers that work like a photocopier. They usually have very high quality printouts. They would normally be used in busy offices.

- **Inkjet:** These are smaller, cheaper printers that use a little cartridge to spray a jet of ink onto the paper. They are fairly quiet and of good quality, but are not as fast or good as lasers. Most home printers are inkjets.

- **Dot matrix/impact:** The old type of printer uses a ribbon and a print head, like a typewriter. They are very loud and extremely slow. However, they are very cheap to buy. They are rarely used now, but are usually used with pre-printed forms, on continuous rolls of paper.

- **Plotters:** These are used in professional printing shops, and can be used to make signs or fabric designs. They "plot" out the shape on material, which is then cut.

1.3.4 Modems

A modem is a device that allows a computer to connect to a telephone line and access the Internet, send and receive emails, or dial into a computer network. Most PCs have a modem built inside them, but external ones are also available.

1.3.5 Network Cards

A network card is used to link up to another PC or several PCs in a network.

1.3.6 Talking to the PC

Apart from the mouse and keyboard, there are other ways of communicating with your PC:

- **Trackball:** Like an upside-down mouse – it sits on the desk, and you move the ball with your fingers to control the movement of the pointer on the screen.

- **Light pen:** A special pen that lets you draw directly onto the screen, or click on buttons and menus.

- **Touch screen:** Like a normal screen, but with a thin, transparent, touch-sensitive layer of plastic covering it. When you touch a part of the screen, it has the same effect as if you had clicked on that area with a mouse.

- **Joystick:** A knob that can be moved around in any direction. Used mainly for playing games.

- **Scanner:** A scanner is a machine attached to a computer for copying pictures or text. It then sends the copied picture to the computer. It's a bit like a photocopier really.

- **Digital camera:** A digital camera takes pictures just like a normal camera. But instead of having a film which you develop and print, it records and stores photographic images in digital form that can be sent to a computer.

- **Microphone:** Some computers come with internal microphones, with others you can plug in an external microphone. They can be used for recording sounds onto the computer, or to make phone calls via the Internet.

1.3.7 Multimedia

Multimedia is a fancy word for something that uses sound, music, pictures, video and animation. Multi means many. A medium is a thing, like sound or video, that is used to communicate. Multimedia literally means "many types of communication". Most modern PCs are multimedia machines, and need certain things to work:

- **Sound card:** A special controller inside the PC that translates sound into a form the computer can understand.

- **Microphone:** A device that lets you record your voice, or other sounds.

- **Speakers:** The objects that let you hear the sounds and music playing.

- **Scanner (optional):** A bit like a photocopier, this scans your own pictures or drawings into the computer so that you can edit them.

- **Digital camera (optional):** This works like a normal camera, but doesn't use film – instead it lets you transfer the pictures directly into your PC.

1.3.8 Input and Output Devices

All of the above extra bits and pieces are input and output devices. This means that they are used to get information into the PC, or take information out of it.

- An **input** device lets you put information **in** to a PC – a keyboard, mouse, microphone, scanner, digital camera, etc.

- An **output** device takes information **out** of the PC – a printer, a screen/VDU, speakers, etc.

Some items, like floppy disk drives, modems, touchscreens, or external hard drives, are both input **and** output devices – they are used to get information in as well as out of a PC.

1.3.9 What is a Peripheral Device?

A peripheral device is anything which you can attach to the main part of your computer. Some of the accessories we have looked at so far are peripheral devices, such as:

- Printers

- Scanners

- Modems

- Speakers

1.4 | Memory and Storage

1.4.1 RAM

When a computer runs a program, it loads it into its RAM (Random Access Memory). The amount of RAM a computer has affects its performance – the more RAM, the more things it can do, faster. You can read and overwrite the RAM, but everything in it disappears when the computer is switched off.

It works a bit like your own memory – when you eat a packet of crisps, your brain loads up the programs about how to open the packet, how to pick up crisps, how to chew, how to swallow, etc. You don't need those "programs" in your mind all the time, only when they're needed. When you have finished the crisps, your brain "closes" the eating program, and loads up something else.

1.4.2 ROM

ROM (Read Only Memory) contains all of the information that the computer needs to switch itself on, and check that all its systems are working. It cannot be changed or overwritten by you, and keeps its contents even when the PC is switched off.

1.4.3 Hard Disks

A hard disk drive contains a hard, round disk covered in a magnetic layer. Special arms, like record player needles, read and write the magnetic information whenever you run a program or save a file. They don't actually touch the surface of the hard disk – if they did, they would damage it. A hard disk is very delicate and complicated. It is sealed in a hard, airtight case, so that no dust can get in and damage it.

1.4.4 Formatting a Disk

Before you can use a disk to store data, it must be formatted. This prepares it to hold data, and checks it for errors. Usually they are formatted at the factory, but you may find an unformatted one from time to time.

1.4.5 Bits and Bytes

Computer memory and hard disk space is measured in bits and bytes. One bit is the smallest unit, and represents either 1 or 0, depending on its magnetic charge. Eight bits make one byte, which is roughly the space you would need to store one letter of the alphabet. Basically:

> 8 bits = 1 byte
>
> 1,000 bytes = 1 kilobyte (KB)
>
> 1,000 kilobytes (KB) = 1 megabyte (MB)
>
> 1,000 megabytes (MB) = 1 gigabyte (GB)
>
> So 1 GB = 1,000 MB = 1,000,000 KB = 1,000,000,000 bytes = 8,000,000,000 bits

If a PC has 64MB of RAM, it is capable of keeping 64 million letters in its memory at once. If its hard disk had 4GB of space, it could store 4 billion letters.

1,024, not 1,000 bytes in a kilobyte

Actually there are 1,024 bytes in a kilobyte, 1,024 kilobytes in a megabyte, etc. This is because memory is based on a binary system, not based on the number 10 (2, 4, 8, 16, 32 .... 1,024). However, most people use 1,000 because it is easier to multiply and makes life easier.

Let's try to understand this in terms of what you will be using a computer for. Imagine that you produce a file in Word.

- Each character that you type will be roughly one byte

- If you type 3,000 characters to a page then each page will be roughly 3,000 bytes, 3KB

- Let's say that you type 3 pages – your file will be 9,000 bytes, or 9KB

- Imagine that you type 500 pages – your file will be roughly 1,500,000 bytes or 1.5MB

- Now, if you save two 500 page files into the same folder, that folder will be 3,000,000 bytes or 3MB

My file is bigger than that!

Word saves lots of other information along with your file – formatting, tables, etc. These will make the file bigger. Pictures will also dramatically increase the size. Try saving it as a plain text file, to see how big it really is.

1.4.6 Comparing the Capacity of Different Memory Devices

Memory Device	Average Capacity
Hard disk	5GB
Zip Disk	100MB
CD-Rom	650MB – 1GB
Floppy Disk	1.38MB
Data Cartridge	4GB to 200GB depending on length of tape

1.4.7 Comparing the Cost of Different Memory Devices

Memory Device	Average Cost
Hard disk	£50 – £150
Zip Disk	£20
CD-Rom	£0.50
Floppy Disk	£0.10
Data Cartridge	£0.35 per GB

1.4.8 What Should I Consider When Buying a PC?

The performance of the PC depends on various factors. When you are buying a PC, consider the following…

■ **CPU speed:** This is measured in megahertz (MHz) and is usually included in the name of the chip. The higher the number of megahertz, the faster your PC will run. 33MHz used to be considered quite fast, but these days 3GHz (gigahertz) is the norm.

■ **RAM:** This is temporary memory. The more RAM your computer has, the faster it will run. You should look for at least 128MB, more if possible – memory is usually very cheap, and can dramatically improve PC performance.

■ **Hard disk space:** Hard disk space used to be measured in megabytes (MB), and a 200MB hard disk drive used to be a lot. These days the operating system normally takes up at least 200MB, and hard drives come in gigabytes (GB). The more bytes your hard disk has, the better your computer will perform. The average is about 80GB, but the more you have, the better.

■ **Sound card and graphics card:** If you just want to write letters and do your accounts, then these are not important. But if you want to play the latest games or create music, then you will need a decent sound card and a good graphics card. These can be expensive, but you should be able to pick them up for around £50 each.

1.4.9 Volatile and Non-volatile Memory

Volatile memory is memory that loses its contents when the computer is switched off – like RAM.

Non-volatile memory is memory that keeps its contents, even when the computer is switched off – like ROM.

1.4.10 Smart Cards

A smart card is a small card that contains memory and a tiny circuit board, which lets you store personal information and other details. These are usually very small, about the size of a normal credit card.

1.5 Computer Software

1.5.1 What is Software?

Software refers to the programs that are loaded onto a computer. Microsoft Word and Excel are software programs, as is Internet Explorer, and Windows.

■ **Systems software** is the software that runs the computer – this is usually called the operating system. Some common operating systems are Windows, Mac OS, and Linux.

■ **Application software** is the programs that run on the PC. Word and Excel are applications, for example.

1.5.2 Examples of Application Software

Type of Software	What Does it Do?	Examples
Word Processor	Has the same function as a typewriter – for producing letters, reports or other written documents	Word, WordPerfect
Spreadsheet	Lets you perform calculations on a table containing text and figures. Spreadsheets are usually used for budgets, statistics, etc.	Excel, Lotus 1–2–3
Database	Stores information, e.g. the names and addresses of all your clients	Access, FileMaker Pro
Accounting	Lets you analyse finances, do your accounts, organise your company payroll, etc.	Sage, QuickBooks
Desktop Publishing (DTP)	Lets you produce magazines, newsletters, etc.	Quark, PageMaker, Publisher
Web Browsing	Lets you read webpages on the Internet	Internet Explorer, Firefox, Netscape, Safari, Opera

1.5.3 The GUI

Older operating systems, like DOS (Disk Operating System), were purely text-based – if you wanted to do something, you had to type in a string of commands. Recently, the Windows-style operating system was introduced, which is called a GUI (Graphical User Interface).

The GUI is a system that lets you use the PC without knowing too much about it. Programs and commands are represented as little pictures, called icons. To run a program, you move the pointer over it using the mouse, and click on it with the mouse button.

Microsoft Windows is a GUI, as is Mac OS (the operating system on Macintosh computers).

1.5.4 Data

Data is not the same as software – for example, if you wrote a letter using a word processor like Word, Word would be the software, but the letter you wrote would be called data. Anything you create or save onto your hard disk or a floppy disk is data.

1.5.5 Software Development

Software programs don't just appear on trees, or out of thin air. First of all a group of people called **systems analysts** analyse the market, figure out what software is needed, and decide what sort of things it should do.

A **designer** will then design the software, and work out how it should look and work.

After that, the **programmers** sit in dark rooms for months and actually write the thing, drinking lots of fizzy drinks and eating crisps.

Once the program is written, **testers** have to test the software and report any mistakes so that the programmers can fix them. Only then is it released to the public, to world-wide celebration and rejoicing.

1.5.6 Bugs

Nobody's perfect. Software programs are so big and complex, most of the time the people testing them can't find all the errors and problems, and they have to be released anyway. After a program has been out for a while, people notice that there are little things wrong with it here and there – these things are called *bugs* for some reason (there are "amusing" alternative words for most computer terms, you'll discover).

When the number of bugs gets too embarrassing for the software company, they release a *patch*, or *service pack*, or *bugfix*. This is a little add-on program that fixes most of the bugs that people have found.

If a program is big and complex enough, it will need several service packs as time goes by. Nearly every single software product released has bugs of some kind in it. This is why even though you have bought the latest brand new PC, and have only had it switched on for half an hour, it can still crash, or freeze for no reason.

1.5.7 Software Versions

Sometimes, software will be re-released with a different number at the end – for example, Office 2000, 2002, 2003. This means that it is a new version of the software, and will contain new features, bug fixes, and sometimes different ways of doing things. Usually it means the software is new and improved, with exciting, shiny new features.

1.5.8 Product ID Numbers

Each time a piece of software is sold, it is given a unique product ID number, often printed on a sticky label on the packet the software comes in. When the software is installed, you have to type in that number in order for it to successfully complete the installation. It's a way of protecting against piracy. On occasion you will need to find your product ID number, for example, if you are wanting technical support from the manufacturer. To do this

1. *Click on Help*

2. *Click on About Software Name (e.g. About Microsoft Word) – a box will open up with all sorts of fascinating information about the software, who wrote it and so on, and somewhere in the box will be your product ID number.*

CHAPTER 2

Using Information Technology

What You'll Do

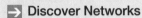 Discover Networks

 Discover the Internet and Email

2

Using Networks

2.1.1 What is a Network?

A computer network is two or more computers connected together. They could be in the same room, in the same building, or on opposite sides of the world. There are several reasons for using a network:

- If you have two PCs but only one printer, the PCs can both connect to the printer and share it. You could have a whole company full of computers but with only one printer, and everyone would be able to use it.

- As well as sharing things like printers, PCs on a network can also share files and data. Instead of making lots of copies of a file, like a company letter, one copy could be stored on a particular PC, and everyone could read it. This can also work with software – you could have one copy of a piece of software, which is shared so that other people can run it or connect to it.

- To help people work together better, users can send messages to each other through their connected computers – this is called electronic mail, or email.

2.1.2 LANs and WANs

There are two main types of network:

- **LAN (Local Area Network):** This is a small network, connecting computers spread out over a fairly small, local area – either in the same building or in a few buildings.

- **WAN (Wide Area Network):** This is a larger network, connecting computers spread out over a wide area – usually around the whole country, or around the world.

Intranets

An intranet is a website or set of websites that is stored on the server of a company network. It works in the same way as the Internet (type the address into a web browser, and so on), but as long as you are on the network, you don't need a modem or an ISP to access it. Some companies use intranets for information, ordering supplies, company diaries, or help. It is only available to people inside the company who are logged in to the network.

Extranets

An extranet is the same as an intranet, but it is also visible to people outside the company. It is usually password managed and secure, unlike a normal website which is visible to anyone.

2.1.3 Connecting Computers Together

LANs are connected by a system of cables that let the computers talk to each other. The computers must also have network cards installed in order to get them to connect to the network.

WANs use the telephone cables (the PSDN – Public Switched Data Network), as well as satellites and other clever bits and pieces. This saves companies having to lay loads of extra cable, but it means they have to use special equipment to send their information down the phone lines.

2.1.4 Clients and Servers

In a network, a server is the big, powerful PC that controls who logs in, what they can do, and where things go. A client is the PC that most people use, to log into the network. Most critical data and software is stored on the server.

2.1.5 Analogue and Digital

Computer information is digital, other information (like sound, voices, etc.) is analogue. For example, a digital watch measures the time digitally, while a wind-up watch uses analogue parts like springs, cogs, etc.

When a computer sends information down the telephone line, it has to convert it to analogue first. Once it reaches the other end, the receiving computer has to convert it back into digital information so that it can understand it.

2.1.6 Modems

A modem is a device that lets a computer convert information into analogue sounds, and back again. This is referred to as **mo**dulation and **dem**odulation.

Say you wanted to send a file down the phone line. Your modem modulates it, or converts it into analogue noise, and chucks it down the phone line. At the other end, another modem demodulates it, or converts it back into a digital file, so that the other PC can read it properly.

Modem speed, or transfer rate, is measured in bits per second – how many bits of data it can transfer in one second. Most modems have a speed of 56kbps, which is 56,000 bits per second.

2.1.7 ISDN

ISDN (Integrated Services Digital Network) is a similar way of transferring data between PCs, but is all digital. It doesn't need to convert the information to analogue and back again, so it is a lot faster, running at 128kbps, or 128,000 bits per second. The digital line doesn't have the problems with interference and quality that a normal telephone line does.

2.1.8 PSTN

PSTN (Public Switched Telephone Network) is the telephone network. It is also used for the Internet.

2.1.9 ADSL

ADSL (Asymmetric Digital Subscriber Line) is a technology which provides Internet access via existing phone lines to homes and businesses at great speed. Unlike ISDN or a dial-up modem, it costs a flat rate regardless of how much you use it and is faster. It is sometimes called "broadband".

2.1.10 Fax

A fax works in a similar way to a modem – in fact, it's like a scanner or photocopier combined with a modem. You put a piece of paper in it, the fax scans the words or pictures on the paper, and sends it down the telephone line. A fax at the other end receives the information, and prints out an exact copy of the original.

2.2 The Internet and Email

2.2.1 The Internet

The Internet consists of lots and lots of computers and networks all connected together by telephone lines and cables. People use it to share information with other users around the world. There is information available on nearly every subject imaginable – it's like a massive electronic library.

The Internet is also sometimes called the *World Wide Web*, or the *Information Superhighway*, or any one of a number of trendy words and phrases, depending on what's cool this week. However, the Internet is **not** the same as the World Wide Web – the Internet is the huge network system that connects everything together, while the World Wide Web is the method of accessing information over the Internet (using browsers like Internet Explorer or Netscape). Email, FTP, newsgroups and the Web all use the Internet to communicate.

2.2.2 Websites

The information on the Internet is stored in webpages and websites. A webpage is like a normal page of text and pictures, but in a special file format that any computer can read. A program called a browser is used to read these pages. The two main types of browser are Internet Explorer and Netscape Navigator.

A website is a collection of webpages on the same topic, or by the same person. Like references or footnotes in books, webpages can link to other sites – but if you click on the link with your mouse, it will take you directly to that page. These links are called hyperlinks.

2.2.3 What You Need

Accessing the Internet is just like accessing a normal network (LAN or WAN). You need a modem or ISDN connection, and a cable to connect to it. You also need to subscribe to an ISP (Internet Service Provider). This is a company you have to go through to get on the Internet, using a user name and password (a bit like the way you get a telephone service – you can't have a telephone line until you sign up with a telephone company). Once you have connected, you use your browser to look at the websites.

2.2.4 Searching

There are more than one billion webpages on the Internet. If you were browsing for something in particular, it could take you several hundred years to find it just by guessing. A search engine is a special webpage that lets you find what you're looking for quickly.

You type in a word or phrase, and the search engine quickly looks though all the webpages for ones that match what you're after. It then shows you a list of likely websites, which you can look through to see if they are of any use.

2.2.5 E-commerce

E-commerce (electronic commerce), basically, is doing business on the Internet. Most companies have their own websites, and a lot of them allow people to do business with them this way. For example, most airline companies have a website that lets you check flight schedules, and book tickets using your credit card details. It's all done online (on the Internet) and you don't even have to get out of your chair.

Imagine you had booked a flight to another country. You could book your hotel by contacting the hotel's webpage, you could arrange for a hired car to be waiting for you at the airport, book a meal in a local restaurant, check maps of the area for the best places to go – the opportunities are endless.

To buy something from the Internet, you will have to give the company your personal details (so that you don't run away without paying, and so they know where to send the goods), and your credit or debit card information. Just because it is the Internet, it doesn't mean that you have no rights – just like in a shop, if the item is faulty or wrong, then you are allowed to return it and get a full refund.

The good thing about buying online is that the shops are always open, 24 hours a day, 7 days a week, even when "real" shops are closed. They usually have a wider range than most physical shops, too. There is always a risk, though, that seeing a small picture of the item is not as satisfying as going into a shop and touching it – and some unscrupulous online shops might try to rip you off (just like some real shops). Make sure the website is secure before you hand over any details.

2.2.6 Email

Email can be sent over the Internet, just like in a company network. Unlike a company network, though, you can send it to anyone in the world, as long they have access to the Internet and email software.

When you want to send an email to a friend, you simply type a letter into your email software, enter your friend's email address, and send it. The software sends it off down the phone line to your ISP, they forward it to your friend's ISP, which then sends it on to your friend. The next time your friend "logs on" to the Internet and checks their email, your message will be sitting waiting for them.

2

CHAPTER 3

Computers in Everyday Life

What You'll Do

➡ Discover Computers in Everyday Life

➡ Work Safely with Computers

➡ Protect Your Work

➡ Save Your Work

➡ Protect Your PC

3.1 Home, Work and Education

3.1.1 Computers in the Home

Many people have a PC at home, for either work or entertainment. Some of the common uses for a home PC are:

- Playing games
- Doing school work
- Working from home
- Managing your finances, Internet banking, etc.
- Writing letters
- Emailing friends and relatives
- Using the Internet

3.1.2 Teleworking

Teleworking is working from home. If you have a computer at home, with the software you need, then you can do your work there. You would have no daily commute, less distractions, and could organise your own schedule. Some people thrive on teleworking, but others find it difficult to adjust to the lack of human contact, virtually nonexistent teamwork, and sense of isolation.

3.1.3 Computers in Business

Nearly every single business or office has some sort of a computer in it. Most businesses depend on them. Here are some of the ways they use them:

- **Offices:** Companies can use computers to store their records, keep track of their customers, or even help to run the business. A room full of old reports and files could be easily stored on a PC – and this would make it quicker to find something too. Computers are used to pay employees, send out letters to customers and communicate with branches in other areas. Other large-scale business uses are airline booking systems, insurance claims processing and online banking.

- **Factories:** Factories can use computers for the same tasks that an office would, and also control large machinery safely, collect customer orders, order supplies, etc.

- **Shops:** In addition to using computers in the same way that offices and factories do, shops and supermarkets use them on their checkout counters to scan in the price barcode on the things you buy. This information is shared with the warehouse, so that the stock is always kept up to date. They also use magnetic stripe readers if you pay by credit card. These check that you have enough money to pay, and then take the money from your account.

3

3.1.4 Education

It is very important to have some computer skills in today's working world. As well as storing student details, names, addresses, academic records and so on, computers can help to keep track of the class timetables. Pupils and students can connect up to other learning institutions around the world, write reports using the computers, or start newspapers. Training can be run on a computer (Computer Based Training, or CBT), and students can even learn online from home.

3.1.5 Hospitals

Hospitals use computers to help them in their day-to-day running. Patient records are stored on PCs for ease of access, appointments are booked for them, and their vital signs can be constantly monitored. Computers also run the ambulance control systems, diagnostic tools and instruments, and any specialist surgical equipment.

3.1.6 Government

Like any other large business, the government relies on computers to help it run things. Apart from the normal uses, it needs heavy computing power to keep track of the population (census), vehicle registration, bill payments, tax records, the voting register, and electronic voting.

3.2 Computers in Everyday Life

3.2.1 Computers in Everyday Life

We all recognise computers when they are a big box on a desk with a screen and keyboard. But these aren't the only computers in the world – some of them are much smaller, some of them you will never see, some of them you will use without even knowing they are there.

When you set your video to tape The Simpsons (and miss the last 10 minutes because the snooker dragged on a bit), a tiny computer chip controls the timer and the programming. When you do your laundry, a computer works out how long to spin the drum for (and how to lose one of your socks). When you take money out of a cashpoint machine, a computer checks your PIN (Personal Identification Number), works out if you have enough money and hands out the cash.

When you try and telephone most companies now, a computer controlled message gives you different options which you can access by dialling certain numbers on your telephone. Somebody has to sit and say all the words into a recorder, so that the computer can play them back in that strange, jerking way that they have. Another way of doing this is a speech synthesizer, which mimics the human voice.

3.2.2 The Information Society

Due to the many areas in which computers are being used, the world we live in now is sometimes referred to as the Information Society. Information and data are very important, and so are the machines we use to work with them – computers. Information Technology refers to computers, accessories, gadgets – anything used to work with information.

Computers are used at work, in the home, in shops, at school. They are everywhere. But you still have a choice, whether or not to use them, or how you use them. You can have a full, happy life without ever using a computer. You may want to use one every single day.

It is important to remember, though, that of all the information out there, on the Internet, in emails, stored on computers – most, if not all, of it is created by people. Just because it is on a PC or a website doesn't mean it is true, or important. Treat this information just as you would treat articles in a newspaper, things you see on television or stories you hear from real people.

Remember: a lot of people have access to the Internet, and the ability to create websites. Some of them are good people, some are bad, and this is reflected in the content of these websites. Before you blame computers and the Internet for promoting hatred, prejudice or dangerous subjects, remember that PCs only do what people tell them to do. Banning the Internet won't stop bigots from trying to spread their message around.

3.2.3 Computers or Humans?

Which is better for a job, a computer or a human being? That all depends on the job. If the job is storing millions of pieces of information, finding and sorting them quickly and doing mindless tasks 24 hours a day, then obviously a computer is better. If the job requires any creative or artistic input, then of course a real person is needed.

Computers are wonderful machines, but they can't do everything. They're not going to take your job away from you. They can't sing, dance, understand, think, or reason. You'll never find a computer police officer (apart from RoboCop, of course, who is real) or a computer author. There's no substitute for the human touch.

3.2.4 Computers and the Environment

In theory, storing documents on computers reduces how much paper we use, although the paperless office seems a long way from the reality. Try to recycle paper, and use both sides for printing wherever possible. You can also recycle printer toner cartridges and even the computers themselves. Choosing a monitor that consumes less power when it is not in use will also reduce the negative impact your computer has on the planet.

3.3 Working Safely with Computers

3.3.1 Common Sense

Computers are never going to rebel against humanity and attack you while you sleep. However, as with any objects that use electricity, or objects that you use a lot, you must use your common sense. Computers are usually safe to use, but there are some things you must look out for.

3.3.2 RSI

RSI stands for Repetitive Strain Injury. If you are typing and/or using the mouse a lot, you can strain the muscles in your hand, arm or back. Take a short break every fifteen minutes, so that your muscles can relax. Do not go longer than an hour without a break. Try to arrange your day so that you break up your computer time by doing tasks away from the screen.

A wrist rest for your keyboard can also help reduce the strain on your wrists when typing. Mouse mats are also available with a built-in wrist rest.

3.3.3 Eyes

Like your hands and arms, your eyes can get strained if you have been working on a PC for a long time without taking a break. Look away from the screen whenever you can, focus on things further away, and remember to blink – it sounds silly, but when you get heavily involved with any screen (television included) you blink a lot less. You should have adjustable controls on your screen so you can change the brightness and contrast. If you have a CRT (Cathode Ray Tube) monitor (the big, heavy ones with the glass screen), you might want to put a screen filter over it, to reduce glare. LCD (Liquid Crystal Display) monitors (the thinner, lighter ones) are also easier on the eyes.

3.3.4 Lighting

It is very important that the lighting is correct when you look at your computer screen as this can help reduce eyestrain. It's a bit like when you're watching television inside on a bright sunny day and you have to draw the curtains. Light should be soft – so fit blinds on windows and diffusers over lights.

3.3.5 Sit Properly

Your mother always used to tell you to sit up straight – it turns out she was right all along and ahead of her time. She was wrong about the brussels sprouts though. Not sitting properly can result in back problems, and shoulder pains.

- Your PC screen should be at a level where you can see it without leaning forward or backward. You should be able to adjust your screen – tilt it or swivel it in any direction.
- You should have an adjustable chair that supports your back properly.
- Think about getting a footrest.
- Your keyboard should be at a level where your arms are parallel to the floor.
- Make sure you have enough space on your desk to have your mouse and keyboard in a comfortable position.

3.3.6 Cables

There are roughly 27 million cables coming out the back of your PC. Modern technology, while making everything else smaller, has somehow increased the size and amount of the wires. It is very easy to trip over them, so make sure they are all out of the way tidily. Besides, it looks nicer.

Another thing worth mentioning: try not to plug everything into one adapter. That goes for any electrical equipment, as you can overload your fuses or start a fire. Plugging several adapters into each other is also a bad thing. Just because you can, doesn't mean that you should. Watch those 1970s public information adverts at 3am, they'll tell you the same thing. Fire bad, tree pretty.

3.4 Protecting Your Work

3.4.1 Information Security

Your data is very valuable. It may not have a cash value, but if you had spent three hours typing in a letter or big report, you wouldn't want to lose it. It is up to you to look after it.

Information Security means protecting your data and making sure it doesn't fall into the wrong hands. Every company should have an Information Security policy, which should define who handles/sees sensitive data, and how to report a breach of security. All staff members should be made aware of their responsibilities with regard to Information Security. The better protected your data is, the better protected you are.

Be careful with your computer equipment. If a laptop or PDA or mobile phone is stolen from you, the implications could be more serious than financial. The thief will have access to your address book, contact numbers, confidential files, company documents, and maybe your passwords if they are stored on your laptop.

3.4.2 Passwords and User ID's

You probably don't want people reading your documents, especially confidential information. You may want to put a password on them for security. Most software lets you password protect a document so that only you, or someone who knows the password, can read them.

- Choose a password that is easy to remember – if you forget the password, then the document is lost to you forever. Sure, it will be secure, but that's no consolation.

- Do not write the password down anywhere – passwords are supposed to be secret. If you start writing them down so you don't forget, then why bother having one at all?

- **Never** make the password your birthday, girlfriend/boyfriend/wife/brother's name, pet's name, or a football team, etc, etc. Most people's passwords can be guessed after about five goes. Choose an obscure word or number that means something to you but that nobody else will know. Better still, use a combination of letters and numbers – something that nobody will guess.

- Sometimes, for extra security or if a number of different people will be using something, you will need not only a password but a user ID as well. A user ID is the name you use to log in, which is usually your name, or a combination of your name and some numbers. The user ID is not secret, but the password is – the purpose of user ID's is so that some people can be given access to certain things, while others will be kept away from them. Access rights are a tool used to give different user ID's different access to the system – for example, managers might be able to see everything on the server, while their staff can only see things relevant to them.

3.4.3 Backups

If you came to work one day to find that the building had burned down, you would lose all of your data (and have a day off). However, if you had copied your important files onto floppy disks or some other form of storage the night before, you wouldn't lose anything. Make regular backups and keep them **away** from the office – it won't help you much if the building burns down with your backups inside. You can't insure your data – you can never get it back once it has gone.

3.4.4 Viruses

You've probably heard a lot of wild stories about viruses in the press. While they are not as ominous and disastrous as they sound, they are a very real threat to you. They are programs written by Bad People that copy themselves around sneakily and damage computers.

There are many different types of virus, some more damaging than others. Some viruses merely display a message telling of the programmer's prowess, which are full of spelling mistakes,

LOTS OF CAPITAL LETTERS and terrible grammar that it am not good. Some display a message and delete data from your hard disk. The damage levels vary from virus to virus.

Your PC can catch a virus by opening an infected email attachment (a program sent within an email message), using an infected floppy disk or getting an infected file from the Internet (not as common as the other two methods).

Your PC **cannot** get a virus by looking at webpages, using email normally, kissing girls, or sitting on infected toilet seats.

To keep your PC safe from viruses:

■ Make sure your PC has the latest virus software installed, and regularly update its data files so that it can recognise new viruses (roughly 300 new viruses appear every month).

■ Always scan floppy disks for viruses before using any information on them.

■ Be careful of opening emails from people you don't know – make sure your email software does not automatically open emails, like the Preview Pane in Outlook.

■ Never run an email attachment unless you are sure who it is from and have scanned the attachment itself for viruses.

■ Keep an emergency disk nearby just in case – your anti-virus software will create one for you. If your PC becomes infected, reboot with the emergency disk in the drive, and it will try to clean the infection for you.

If your PC gets a virus, run the anti-virus software immediately. Make sure to close any other software, as some viruses can use your email software to send the virus on to your address book contacts. Try to disconnect from the Internet first, to stop it downloading anything. When the anti-virus software scans, it should find the infected files. Ask it to "disinfect" the infected files – this means removing the virus, and restoring the files to normal. Some viruses cannot be removed in this way, though – they might be too new, or too clever. Sometimes you will just have to delete the infected files. Prevention is always the best cure.

3.4.5 Virus Hoaxes

This is a fairly recent problem, and a very annoying one: you get an email from a friend telling you about a scary new virus that has just come out. Apparently it has been reported by Microsoft or IBM or AOL or someone like that, is even worse than the last virus that came out and has no cure. The message then tells you to forward the message on to all of your friends. You later find out the whole thing was made up.

This is a type of virus in itself. It is designed to create a panic, and get everyone sending the same message to all of their friends, who then send it to all of their friends and so on and so on. It ties up your company mail PC with hundreds of emails going around and wastes everyone's time. Sometimes the email traffic is so heavy, it can crash a company network.

The email text usually goes along these lines:

WARNING: If you receive an email with the subject line *InsertSubjectHere*, do not open the file. The file contains the *InsertVirusNameHere* virus. This information was announced yesterday morning at IBM/Microsoft/*InsertCompanyNameHere*. This is a very dangerous virus, much worse than "Melissa", and there is NO remedy for it at this time. If you open/read/look at the email, it will completely delete your hard drive/do some other ridiculously frightening thing. This is a new, very malicious virus and not many people know about it. Pass this warning along to EVERYONE in your address book ASAP so that this threat may be stopped.

If you receive an email like this, do not send it to all of your friends – if you do, the hoaxer has won. Check with an online virus library, and find out if it is a hoax.

The Network Associates Virus Library:
http://vil.nai.com/vil

F Secure Hoax Warnings:
http://www.f-secure.com/virus-info/hoax

Urban Legends – Virus Hoaxes Page:
http://urbanlegends.about.com/science/urbanlegends/msubvir.htm

The last site also contains information about other email hoaxes you will receive, for example, the one about the businessman falling asleep in a hotel and waking up with his kidneys stolen, etc. These are never true, and your friends have probably received them 50 times already. If you insist on sending them on, you will lose all your friends, become a hermit and your knees will fall off.

Do not delete a file if a virus warning tells you to!

Some virus hoaxes pretend that if you have a certain file on your PC, then you are infected – this is not true! The file is usually an important one, and removing it will damage your system. Never delete files or forward virus alerts without checking the above webpages, or talking to an IT support person.

3.5 Save, Save, Save

This is the most important thing you will ever learn. **Ever**. Listen closely:

■ If you are working on a document, and your PC crashes or has a power cut, **if you haven't saved your document**, **you will lose it**.

That's it. Simple, really. But for some reason, this little fact escapes everyone. One of the most common PC support issues goes along these lines:

Person: "I was typing this letter, and the PC crashed/the plug came out, and I lost it. Can you get it back?"

PC Support Person: "Did you save the letter?"

Person: "No. Can you get it back for me?"

PC Support Person: "No."

Person: "But-"

PC Support Person: "This conversation is over."

If you haven't saved it, you haven't saved it. That's it. Repeat this to yourself 1000 times. YOU MUST SAVE YOUR WORK EVERY 10 MINUTES. Then if it all explodes, you've only lost 10 minutes' work. If you are typing a letter for 2 hours and, just before you save it, the machine dies, you have just lost all 2 hours' worth. Bye bye.

Good practice: as soon as you create the document, before you've even typed one word, save it. Find out the keyboard shortcut, find the Save icon, and every 5 or 10 minutes, click Save, hit Control + S, or whatever it is in that particular program.

Another good tip: never type a document and think "I'll just print it first, then I'll save it." This is a Very Bad Thing. Save it first, then print it. Don't tempt fate. PC's often crash when you try to print something without saving it first – there might be a good reason for this, but then again, they might just do it to annoy you.

Always save every 10 minutes. I realise I've already said that, but it's worth repeating, several times. Save – your – work. All the time. There is **nothing** more important than this.

The problem: you won't listen. I didn't. I never bothered, until one day, 7 years ago, I lost 4 hours' work due to a power cut. Since then, I do Control + S every 5 minutes, no matter what I'm doing. But you won't start doing this until you lose a large amount of work. That's just the way it is, really. Unless you start saving now, get the practice in before it's too late. Please. Not for me – for your data. And for the children. Anybody's children, it doesn't matter.

Save your work every 10 minutes!

Have I mentioned that already? I wasn't sure. Save! Save! Save! Tear this page out and tape it to your head so that you never forget. Save!

3.6 Protec-

Wait, I'm not finished talking about saving. Save! SAVE! Save your work! Every ten minutes! Okay, you can start the next section now.

3.7 Protecting Your PC

- Try not to eat or drink while using your PC – spilt drinks and dropped biscuit crumbs make your keyboard sticky and unusable, but if you spill them on your PC they can destroy it completely.

- Don't leave the PC in a place where it will get very hot or very cold.

- When you have finished using your PC, shut it down properly and wait until it shuts down completely. It will normally display a message when it is safe to switch it off, although some PCs switch themselves off when you shut them down. Don't pull the plug out or switch it off while it's still doing something. The RAM empties when the PC is switched off, and you will lose your work. Switching it off without shutting it down can damage the hard disk.

- Water and electricity don't mix. If it's plugged in, it will explode or catch fire. If it isn't plugged in, the circuits will still get damaged.

- Try to keep dust away from your PC – it clogs up the insides.

- See those air vents and holes in the case? They're there for a reason. Don't block them. Keep at least a foot between them and any walls, shelves etc.

- Don't move the PC base unit while it is switched on. The hard disk is very delicate, and moving it can cause the read/write arms to come into contact with the disk surface. This will badly damage it.

- Keep floppy disks away from the screen, speakers, and magnets – any data on them can be erased. Similarly, keep magnets away from the base unit.

- Although this should go without saying, never ever hang clothes on a PC or monitor to dry. That's not a joke, some people actually do it.

3

CHAPTER 4

Legal Issues

What You'll Do

➡ Discover Copyright and Software Legal Issues

➡ Discover the Data Protection Act

4.1 Copyright and Software

4.1.1 Copyright

The same copyright laws that apply to newspapers, books, television and film apply to data on computers or the Internet. If someone has created something – text, graphics, music, etc. – and put it on their website, you cannot take it and pass it off as your own, or even distribute it without permission from the person who made it. It remains their property. If it's a computer program you also are not allowed to change the code – even if it is an improvement. The same law applies to things offered for download – you can use them, but only within the stated conditions. You also can't put things on removable media (like floppy disks, ZIP disks, CDs) and distribute them to your friends.

4.1.2 Licensing

Software is licensed instead of sold – this means that you are paying to use it, and must agree to certain conditions (the end user license agreement most programs ask you to agree to). If a company had 200 PCs, and needed Microsoft Office on them all, it would be silly to buy 200 copies of it – they would take up a whole room. But it would be illegal to buy one copy and install it on all 200 PCs. This is where licensing comes in. There are various types of multi-user licence depending on whether you want it to cover one building or several branches or a certain number of users at one time. A company may have only one copy of the software, but have paid to use it on 200 machines.

When you install software, before you can install it, you must agree to an end user license agreement – once you click on the button that says you agree to the terms and conditions, you are legally bound to it. This usually covers things like not copying or reselling the software, but can mean other things – make sure you read them before you agree.

4.1.3 Piracy

In days of old, pirates attacked ships and stole their treasure. They usually had eyepatches, parrots, wooden legs and said "Arrrrr" a lot. For some bizarre reason, the word "pirate" is now used to refer to someone who illegally makes a copy of a piece of software. The only similarity is that theft is involved, but the word is in common use now, so it's too late to question it. Software theft/copying is piracy. Don't do it. Someone has worked long and hard to create it and if you just steal it then they lose out. Some people distribute illegally copied software over the Internet or other sources, but it's up to you to refuse it. Be responsible.

4.1.4 Freeware and Shareware

Some software is written by people who then give it away, totally free – this is called freeware. It is usually only for your personal use; if a company uses it for profit, then they will normally have to pay for it.

Shareware is similar – the program is given out free for you to try out for a month or so. If you want to keep it after that, you have to pay for it. If not, you must delete it. This relies on people's honesty; unfortunately it doesn't always work. Some software is designed to stop working after the trial period or is missing certain features; once you have paid you are given the code to unlock it, or given a complete version.

Other forms of freeware/shareware are cardware/postcardware/emailware – instead of paying, you send the programmer a card or an email saying thanks. A lesser-known version is hugware – if you like the program and want to keep it, you have to give someone a hug.

4

4.2 The Data Protection Act

4.2.1 Big Brother

Because so many businesses use computers to keep records, there are probably a lot of computers that have stored your name, address, and other details. When you apply for a mortgage or credit, companies check with your bank or a credit agency who look up your credit records. If they show you're a high risk, you get refused the loan. If not, then you are approved. Sometimes these companies have the wrong information – this can cause you to be wrongly refused credit.

Some companies sell their lists of names and addresses to marketing companies, which explains why you get loads of junk mail – offers of credit cards, "You Could Have Won Ten Million Pounds", etc. etc. The same goes for email addresses, leading to junk email – this is called spam (a reference to the Monty Python sketch where absolutely everything on the menu is served with a certain type of luncheon meat).

4.2.2 Data Protection

In the UK, the Data Protection Act 1998 is intended to safeguard the information about you.

Anyone who holds personal details about an individual on computer must register with the Data Protection Registrar, giving details of the information they hold, what it is used for, etc.

Companies who have your personal details are not allowed to use them for illegal purposes or even for a different purpose from that stated. They must be kept secure and out of the wrong hands. They must also be kept up to date and disposed of when no longer needed.

If a company has your details stored on computer, you are allowed to write to them requesting a copy of all the information about you. They must respond within 40 days, so even if they cannot give you the details immediately they have to write back and tell you this. You also have the right to correct the information if the details are incorrect or get rid of it completely.

Outside the UK, there are different data protection regulations. You should be aware of your rights, and find out what protections are in place in your particular country.

MODULE

BASIC CONCEPTS OF
INFORMATION TECHNOLOGY

1

FILE MANAGEMENT

2

WORD PROCESSING

3

SPREADSHEETS

4

DATABASES

5

PRESENTATIONS

6

INTERNET AND EMAIL

7

CHAPTER 1

The Desktop

1

What You'll Do

- → Discover the Desktop
- → Move the Taskbar
- → Use the Start Menu
- → Select and Deselect Desktop Icons
- → Move Desktop Icons
- → Arrange the Icons
- → Open a Window Using a Desktop Icon
- → Create a Shortcut on the Desktop
- → Rename and Delete Shortcuts

- → Customise Your Desktop
- → Change the Background, Colour Scheme and Screen Saver
- → Protect Your Computer with a Screen Saver
- → Change Your Pixel Resolution
- → Work with Windows
- → Minimise and Maximise Windows
- → Resize, Move and Close Windows
- → Switch Between Windows

1.1 Introduction to the Desktop

The desktop is the screen you first see when your computer has started. It can be customised to look how you want and make it easier for you to do your work.

1.1.1 The Desktop Screen

On the following page is a picture of the desktop screen. Each desktop will look a little different...

1.1.2 What is Each Part for?

The list below explains what the parts of the screen are for...

1 Icons: Pictures that represent a part of your computer, or applications or tools available on your computer. Double click on them to run programs.

2 Background: This is the main desk part, and can be customised in many different ways – you could display a picture of your pet, for example.

3 Start button/Start menu: The place that contains icons to run all your programs and tools.

4 Taskbar: The bar that shows you what applications you have open. It also provides a way of switching between open applications.

5 Quick Launch Toolbar: This is a toolbar that can be positioned anywhere but often sits somewhere on your taskbar. It provides quick access to applications on your computer.

6 System Tray: A tool that can be used to change some of your computer's settings, and also provides information (such as whether you have certain software in use, or if you are low on battery if you are using a laptop computer).

7 Clock: A normal clock that tells the time (or at least the time that your computer thinks it is).

1.1.3 Desktop Icons

The little pictures you have on your desktop are all for different things…

My Computer

1 *This lets you get at the computer's filing system. It gives you access to the different parts of your computer where information is stored (drives). You can also change your computer settings from here (using Control Panel).*

My Network Places

2 *If your PC is on a network, this contains a list of all the resources available to you, i.e. printers, folders. In older versions of Windows, this is called Network Neighborhood.*

Recycle Bin

3 *When you delete a document, it goes in here. You can then take it out if you didn't really mean to delete it.*

My Documents

4 *When you save a document, unless you instruct the machine otherwise, it will be saved in this folder.*

1.1.4 The Taskbar

At the bottom of the screen there is a grey bar that runs from left to right. When you open a window a button for that window will appear on the bar. The Start button is on the far left…

Having more than one window open…

You can work with a number of different windows at the same time. For example, you might have both Word and Internet Explorer open at the same time. To switch between the windows you have opened, just click on the button that refers to it on the Taskbar.

If you can't see the whole description on the Taskbar…

As you open more windows or programs in Windows, the buttons that represent them on the Taskbar become smaller. Just hold the mouse over the Taskbar for a second or two, and a note will pop up with a full description.

1.1.5 Moving the Taskbar

The Taskbar can be at the top, bottom, left or right of your screen. To move your Taskbar…

1 *Position the mouse pointer on an empty part of the Taskbar (where there are no buttons)*

2 *Click and hold your left mouse button and drag to the edge of the screen (left, right top or bottom)*

3 *Release the mouse button – your Taskbar will be in its new position!*

1.1.6 The Start Button

Clicking on the Start button shows the Start menu. From here you can open applications, view files, get help, find files, access your favourite websites, run programs, change your settings and shut down or restart your computer. Just about everything you might want to do!

1.1.7 Using the Start Menu

1. Click on the Start button

2. Click on the option you require (see below) – a submenu may appear

3. If necessary, click on the option you require in the submenu

4 The icons on the left of the Start menu are your most recently used programs, and will be different for every user.

Your Internet and email programs will normally be kept at the top of this section, and any other recently used files, or important programs you haven't used yet, will be stored underneath.

5 Shows you more programs that you can run.

 6 Takes you to your document files.

 7 Takes you to your picture files.

 8 Takes you to your music files.

 9 Takes you to My Computer, where you can open, copy, move or delete files.

 **10** If your PC is on a network, this contains a list of all the resources available to you, i.e. printers, folders.

 11 Where you can change your system settings, e.g. the colour of your desktop.

 **12** Where you can see what printers you have, and change their settings.

 13 This starts Help. If you are stuck, this is where you go (see page 46).

 14 Allows you to find a folder, file, programs, etc. (see page 69).

 15 From here you can start a program, or install one from a CD-ROM or disk.

16 If your computer is connected to a network, you can log off here, but keep your computer running. If you are at home and there are more than one user, you can switch users or log off.

17 Shuts down or restarts your computer.

When you click on the All Programs submenu, there are more programs to run, and these two extra options...

 New Office Document　18 *You can create a new Office document from here.*

Open Office Document　19 *You can open an existing Office document from here.*

1.2 Desktop Icons

1.2.1 Selecting Icons

Click on the icon to select it – it will turn blue

1.2.2 Deselecting Icons

Click away from the icon – it will no longer be blue

1.2.3 Moving Desktop Icons

You can rearrange your computer's desktop, just as you might rearrange your desk at work ...

1 *Position your mouse over the icon you wish to move*

2 *Click and drag to a new position*

3 *Release the mouse*

My icons won't move!

Right click anywhere over the desktop and choose Arrange Icons By. Make sure there is no tick next to Auto Arrange.

1.2.4 Arranging the Icons

You can let Windows tidy up your desktop by getting it to automatically arrange your icons...

1 *Right click anywhere over the desktop*

2 *Click on Arrange Icons By*

3 *Click on Auto Arrange*

How do I know when it's on?

When Auto Arrange is on it will have a tick before it in the menu. Click it again to switch it off!

1.2.5 Opening a Window Using a Desktop Icon

The desktop icons can be used to open a window. Just double click on the icon, and a window will open.

1.2.6 What are Desktop Shortcuts?

- You can create shortcuts that allow you to open programs, folders or documents that you use frequently. You can put a shortcut onto your desktop.

- Shortcuts always have a little curly arrow in the bottom left corner of the icon.

Cat pictures

- Shortcuts are only a link to the folder, document or program and not the actual thing.

- If you delete a shortcut, it does not delete the original object.

1.2.7 Creating a Shortcut on the Desktop

1 *Open My Computer and find the icon for the program, folder or document*

2 *Restore or resize the My Computer window so you can see the desktop as well*

3 *Hold the mouse over the icon you wish to create a shortcut to*

4 *Click and drag the icon onto the desktop using the **right** mouse button*

5 *Release the mouse – a shortcut menu will appear*

6 *Click **Create Shortcut Here***

Or

1 *Find the item that you want to create a shortcut for, using My Computer*

2 *Right click on the item – a menu will pop up*

3 *Click **Send To***

4 *Click **Desktop (create shortcut)***

1.2.8 Renaming Shortcuts

Because a shortcut just points to a document, folder or program (and is not the actual thing) you can rename the shortcut without renaming the file. So you can call it whatever you like...

1 *Position your mouse over the shortcut you wish to rename*

2 *Right click on the shortcut – a menu will pop up*

3 *Click Rename – the name of the shortcut is highlighted*

4 *Type the new name for the shortcut*

5 *Click away from the shortcut or press Return*

1.2.9 Deleting Shortcuts

You might wish to remove shortcuts that you no longer require. Deleting shortcuts does not delete the item to which the shortcut is pointing.

1 *Right click on the shortcut*

2 *Click **Delete***

3 *Click Yes to confirm it*

1.3 The Desktop Settings

1.3.1 Customising Your Desktop

Aside from creating new icons that are shortcuts to things you frequently use, you can also change...

- The colour scheme your computer uses

- The pattern or pictures (wallpaper) on your desktop background

- The images that pop up when you don't use your computer for a while (the screen saver)

1.3.2 Changing the Background

This is a picture you can have on your desktop background. It is sometimes referred to as the wallpaper or the desktop picture.

1 *Right click on a blank part of the desktop*

2 *Click Properties*

3 *Click on the Desktop tab*

4 *Click your choice in the list of backgrounds – a preview will appear above*

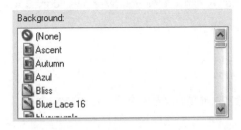

5 *Click OK*

Tile, centre or stretch?

You can have your picture repeated (tiled) over your desktop, stretched to fit or positioned as a picture in the centre of your desktop. After you choose your wallpaper from the list, click on the drop down arrow in the Position box and click on the option you require.

To use a colour for your background instead...

[1] *Right click on a blank part of the desktop*

[2] *Click Properties*

[3] *Click on the Desktop tab*

[4] *Make sure the wallpaper chosen is None*

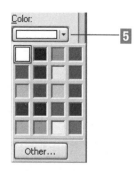

[5] *Click on the drop down arrow under Color*

[6] *Choose a colour*

[7] *Click OK*

Applying...

If you want to apply any of your changes without losing the Display Properties dialog box, click on the Apply button!

Apply

1.3.3 Changing the Colour Scheme

If you would like a different colour scheme for your windows, icons, background, etc...

[1] *Right click anywhere on the desktop*

[2] *Click Properties*

[3] *Click on the Appearance tab*

[4] *Click on the drop down arrow at the end of the Color scheme box*

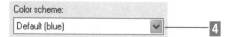

[5] *Click your choice*

[6] *Click OK*

1.3.4 Changing the Screen Saver

These pop up as full screen images or animations if your computer is left alone for a while. They save wear and tear on your screen and protect your work when you're away from the computer…

1. *Right click anywhere on the desktop*

2. *Click Properties*

3. *Click on the Screen Saver tab*

4. *Click on the drop down arrow at the end of the Screen saver box*

5. *Click on the screen saver you would like to use*

6. *Click the Preview button and don't move the mouse! Wait a few seconds and you will see a full-screen preview of the screen saver*

7. *Sit for a minute, and say "ooh" and "ahh" a lot*

8. *Move the mouse to make it go away*

9. *Change the timing if required by clicking the up and down arrows next to the number in the Wait box*

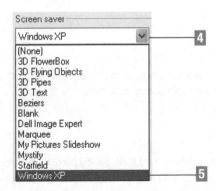

10. *Click OK*

Getting the computer screen back

To get back to your normal computer screen when a screen saver is on just press any key on the keyboard or move the mouse around. If the screen saver is protected you may need the password to stop it – see the following section.

1.3.5 Protecting Your Computer with a Screen Saver

If you do not want people to use your computer while you are away from your desk then you can specify a password that must be entered to clear the screen saver.

1. Right click anywhere on the desktop

2. Click Properties

3. Click on the Screen Saver tab

4. Select a screen saver

5. Click the box next to **On resume, password protect** so that it is ticked (if you are not on a network, this option will be **On resume, display Welcome screen**)

5———— ☑ On resume, password protect

6. Click OK

What happens when the screen saver comes on?

When the mouse is moved, the logon screen (if you are on a network) or the Welcome screen (if you are not) will be displayed. If someone else is using your computer, they will need to log in. If you have come back, you need to log in again – don't worry, all your programs and files will still be open!

Be responsible!

If someone is coming to fix your PC, don't just go off for a coffee break – the PC support person is not a mind reader, and will get very cross if they can't access your computer. Switch off the password option before leaving your desk.

1.3.6 Changing Your Pixel Resolution

Your screen is made up of lots and lots of tiny dots called pixels. The resolution is how many pixels your screen shows at one time. The more pixels it shows, the higher quality – a bit like how magazine images are clearer than newspaper images. The higher the resolution, the smaller the icons and windows. For example, say an icon is 16 pixels wide. Because there are more pixels jammed into the screen, your icon will seem smaller, because it is still only 16 pixels wide. However, it means you can fit more open windows on to your screen.

1. Right click on a blank part of your desktop background

2. Click on Properties

3. Click on the Settings tab

4. Move the slider left or right until it has the setting you want

5. Click Apply – and wait. If it's not sure about it, your computer will test the new setting, and give you 15 seconds to decide if you want to keep it. If your monitor does not

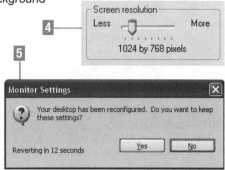

work with the new setting, you won't be able to see anything, so just wait 15 seconds, and everything will go back to normal. If it's a normal, safe setting, it will just apply it without testing it.

6 *To keep the new setting, click Yes – if it doesn't look quite right, click No, and try again, repeating steps 3 to 6 until you are happy with the way it looks*

7 *Click OK*

So what size should it be?

The standard setting these days is 1024 × 768 – 1024 pixels wide, 768 pixels high. The next most popular (for slightly smaller screens) is 800 × 600. If you have a really big monitor, you might want to go for the 1280 × 1024 setting, so that you can squeeze more windows into the screen area, but so that the text won't look terrifyingly small.

...Eh?

You need to know how to do this for the ECDL exam, but in real life, you probably shouldn't ever have to actually do it. If you are happy with how your screen looks, just leave it alone, and don't worry about it. Like most of the Basic Concepts module, this is something you'll need to know for an exam, but can happily forget all about once you've passed it. Nobody's ever going to ask you what volatile memory means in the real world, and if they do, then they're not your friend.

1.4 Working with Windows

1.4.1 What are Windows?

Every task which you perform on your computer will open in a box called a window. For instance, when you open Word, a window appears on the screen containing the software. You then work inside the window. It is possible to have many windows open at once.

1.4.2 The Elements of Windows

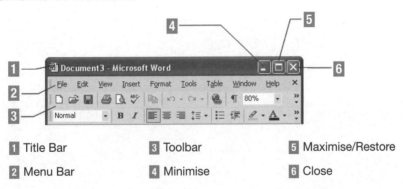

1 Title Bar   3 Toolbar   5 Maximise/Restore

2 Menu Bar   4 Minimise   6 Close

1.4.3 Minimising Windows

1 Minimising a window makes it temporarily disappear into the taskbar. Use it if you have to get a window out of the way so you can see something else. To minimise a window, click the Minimise button at the top right of the window:

2 To restore a window after it has been minimised, click the name of the window from the taskbar at the bottom of the screen:

1.4.4 Maximising/Restoring Windows

Maximise allows you to make a window fill the whole of the screen. Use it when you want to concentrate on just one window. Maximise is interchangeable with Restore. When you restore a window it is still visible, but will not fill the whole screen. You can change the restored shape to anything you want by resizing the window (see next section).

1 *Maximising a Window . . .*

Click Maximise at the top right of the window:

The window will fill the screen, and the Maximise button will change to the Restore button:

2 *Restoring a Window . . .*

Click Restore at the top right of the window:

The window will shrink, and the Restore button will change to the Maximise button:

1.4.5 Resizing Windows

1 *Ensure that the window is restored – if the window is minimised or maximised you can't resize it!*

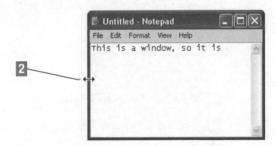

2 *Position the mouse at the edge of a window – the mouse pointer will change to a double headed arrow*

3 *Click and drag to resize the window*

1.4.6 Moving Windows

1 *Ensure that the window is restored – if the window is minimised or maximised you can't move it*

2 *Position the mouse on the blue title bar – the mouse pointer will change to a white arrow*

3 *Click and drag to move the window to a new position*

1.4.7 Closing Windows

Click the X at the top right of the window

1.4.8 Switching Between Windows

Click the window you require on the taskbar to make the window appear on the screen

CHAPTER 2

Finding Out More

What You'll Do

→ Access Help in Windows XP

→ Get Help Using the Index

→ Get Help Using the Search

→ View System Information

→ View the Date and Time

→ Set the Date and Time

→ Change the Volume

→ Change the Regional Settings

2.1 Using Help

2.1.1 Accessing Help in Windows XP

1 Click the Start button

2 Click on Help and Support

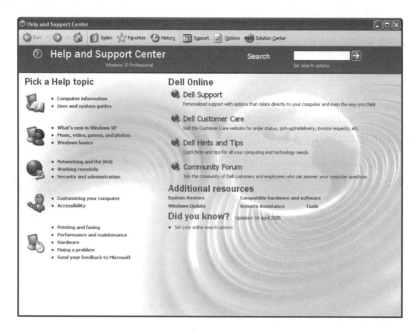

Note: this feature will only work if it has been installed when Windows XP was installed. If it doesn't work, ask your techies to help you, or telephone the support you were given when you bought your computer.

2.1.2 Help Using the Index

The Index tab allows you to find Help topics. It is organised like a book index…

[1] *Open Help (see previous page)*

[2] *Click on the Index button*

[3] *Type the first few letters of the subject you need help in*

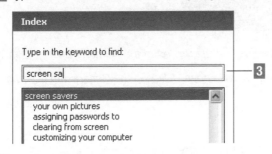

[4] *Click on the index entry you want*

[5] *Click the Display button – Help is displayed on the right*

2.1.3 Help Using the Search

Use this if you couldn't find what you wanted in the Index tab. It allows to you search for Help using a "keyword" rather than a topic…

[1] *Open Help*

[2] *Type a word or phrase into the Search box*

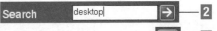

[3] *Click on the green button with the white arrow on it*

[4] *Click on a topic – help is displayed on the right*

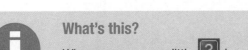

What's this?

Whenever you see a little ⟨?⟩ icon in the top right of a dialog box, you can click it, then click on part of the dialog to find out what it does (try it out and see).

2.2 System Information and Settings

2.2.1 Viewing Your System Information

If you want to find out what operating system, RAM and processor your computer has...

[1] *Click on the Start button*

[2] *Click on Control Panel*

[3] *Click on Printers and Other Hardware*

[4] *Click on the System icon at the top left of the Control Panel*

[5] *The System Properties will appear. Click on the General tab (if you are not already there)*

[A] Operating System

[B] Processor

[C] RAM (Random Access Memory)

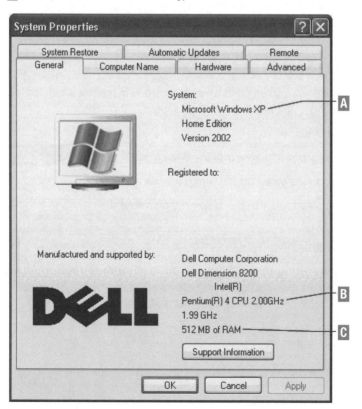

When you have finished looking…

[1] *Click OK*

[2] *Click on the X at the top right of the Control Panel window to close it*

2.2.2 How Does My Computer Know the Date and Time?

The date and time is just one of your computer's settings, and you can change it if it's wrong. You may find that your network (if you are connected to one) resets the date and time.

2.2.3 Viewing the Date and Time

[1] The time is shown on your Taskbar.

[2] To view the date…

Hover your mouse over the clock – a yellow label will pop up with the date

2.2.4 Setting the Date and Time

If the month, date, year or time is wrong…

[1] *Double click on the clock in the System Tray on your Taskbar – this will open the Date/Time Properties dialog box*

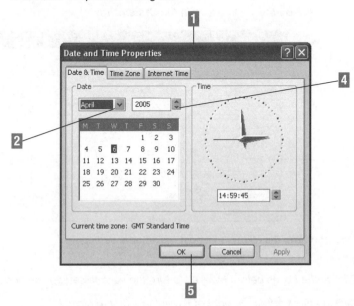

2 *Click on the drop down arrow at the end of the month*

3 *Select the correct month*

4 *Click on the up or down arrows to change the year*

or

click on the correct date from the calendar

or

double click on the hour, minutes or seconds in the Time box to select it, then click the up or down arrow to change the hour, minutes or seconds

5 *Click OK*

2.2.5 Changing the Volume

If you have speakers for your computer you may find that the volume disturbs you or those around you...

1 *Click on the Volume icon in the System Tray on your Taskbar*

2 *When the volume control appears, click and drag the slider to adjust the volume*

3 *Click in the box next to Mute to turn the sound on or off – it will appear ticked if on (ticked means the sound is Mute, or silent)*

4 *Click away from the volume control to make it disappear*

Or

1 *Double click on the Volume icon in the System Tray*

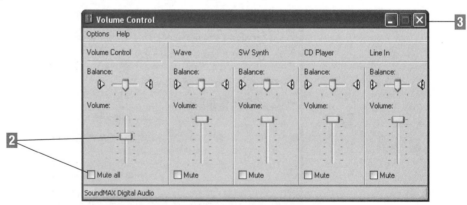

2 *Click and drag the sliders to adjust the volume settings*

or

Click in the boxes before Mute all to turn the volume settings on or off

3 *Click on the X at the top right of the Volume box to close it*

2.2.6 Changing the Regional Settings

Your regional settings affect the way that dates, numbers and times are displayed and which currency symbol is displayed in the programs you use. They are chosen by which country you are in...

1 *Click on the Start button*

2 *Click on Control Panel*

3 *Click on the Date, Time, Language, and Regional Options icon*

4 *Click on the Regional and Language Options icon*

5 *Click on the Regional Options tab, unless you are there already*

6 *Click on the drop down arrow at the end of the country*

7 *Click on the country you are in*

8 *Click OK*

9 *Click on the X to close the Control Panel window*

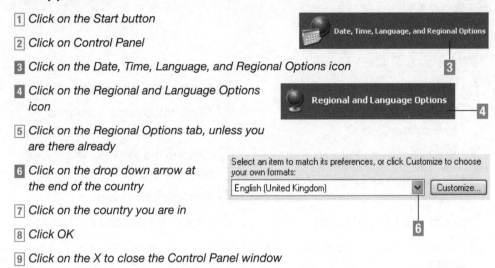

Changing the default conventions...

If you want to override any of the settings for your country, click on the Customize button and change any settings you wish.

CHAPTER 3

Working with Files and Folders

What You'll Do

→ Work with Files and Folders

→ Discover Files and Filename Extensions

→ Start Windows Explorer

→ Expand and Collapse in Windows Explorer

→ Look in a Drive or Folder

→ Open a Folder in the Right Hand Pane

→ Open My Computer

→ Open a Drive

→ Open and Close a Folder

→ Show the Standard Buttons Toolbar

→ Change the View of Your Files and Folders

→ Arrange Your Drives

→ Sort Your Files and Folders

→ View the Properties of Files and Folders

→ Change the Status of a Folder

→ Navigate Your Folders

3.1 Drives, Files and Folders

3.1.1 The Computer's Filing System

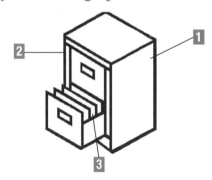

1 The computer's filing system is very much like an ordinary filing cabinet. The whole of the filing cabinet is your computer.

2 The drawers in the filing cabinet are known as **drives**. **Drives** are represented by letters of the alphabet.

3 Inside the drives are **folders** that hold your documents. Inside some of the folders may be **subfolders** to make things more organised. Inside the folders are the pieces of paper that you have written on, known as **files**. Word files are known as **documents**.

Imagine you are filing your work documents inside these drives. You may have a main folder which contains all of your work. Inside that, you may have subfolders to contain your memos, reports and letters. Inside those subfolders are the actual files that you have written on.

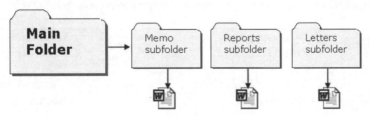

3.1.2 What Drives Do I Have?

The drives you have and the letters assigned to them can be different. The table below describes what you will find on most computers...

Letter	Drive	What do you use it for?
A:	Usually the floppy disk drive	■ Saving onto the floppy disk means that you can take the document to another machine ■ It is also useful to make copies of documents onto the floppy disk as a backup
C:	Usually the hard disk drive	■ The hard disk is your main disk drive ■ It is situated inside the box that makes up your PC ■ If you save onto the hard disk, you can only access that file from that machine, but there is much more space on the hard disk than on a floppy disk
D:	Usually the CD-ROM drive	■ You cannot save onto the CD-ROM ■ It is used for installing software from CDs
E:-Z:	Usually network drives	■ If you can see these drives you are probably connected to a network ■ A network is a group of computers connected to each other through a server. If you save onto a network drive, the information will go to the server and everyone else who is connected to the network will be able to access your document.

3.1.3 What are Files?

All the information on your computer will be stored as some type of file. There will be lots of different files on your computer. Some you have created yourself and some were already there before! For instance, if you write a letter in Microsoft Word it will be stored as a file, as a Word document file type.

3.1.4 File Icons

These are some of the file icons that you might see on your computer...

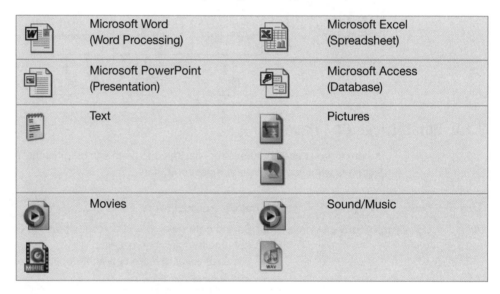

3.1.5 What are Filename Extensions?

Each different type of file (e.g. Word document, Excel spreadsheet) has three letters stuck on the end of its name. This is called the filename extension. The extension for a type of file lets Windows know what type of file it is, so it knows which icon to display and which program to open the file in.

report.doc

Underneath the icon for the file you will see the name of the file, sometimes followed by a full stop and then the filename extension. For example, the Word icon on the left has a filename of **report**, and an extension of **.doc**.

Some of the filename extensions you might see...

.doc	Microsoft Word document	.xls	Microsoft Excel spreadsheet
.ppt	Microsoft PowerPoint presentation	.txt	Plain text (e.g. Notepad file)
.mdb	Microsoft Access database	.htm	Internet Explorer webpage

3.1.6 Which Filing System?

There are two places where you can manage your files…

■ Windows Explorer (see below)

■ My Computer (see page 56)

Windows Explorer is more or less the same thing as My Computer. They both contain the same things, they are just arranged slightly differently. You'll see the differences over the next few pages. It's up to you which one you use – they're both effectively the same program, so use the one you feel more comfortable with.

3.2 Windows Explorer

3.2.1 Starting Windows Explorer

1 Click on the Start button

2 Click on All Programs

3 Click on Accessories

4 Click on Windows Explorer

3.2.2 What You See in Windows Explorer

■ The screen is divided into 2 "panes".

■ The left hand side shows the hierarchical structure of your folders on your computer.

■ The right hand side represents the contents of the selected item in the left pane.

■ If you click on a folder in the left pane, the contents of it will appear in the right pane.

3.2.3 Expanding and Collapsing

You can expand and collapse the hierarchical view of the left pane to see more or less detail.

Expanding   If you see a plus (+) by an item in the left pane then it has an additional folder within it. To display it, just click on the plus.

Collapsing   If you see a minus (–) by an object then you can hide its contents by clicking on the minus.

    ⊟ 🗀 Demos
       🗀 Fishy things
       🗀 My Fish Files
       🗀 Rubbish
       🗀 Small Fry
       🗐 Squish.zip

⊞ 🗀 Demos

Click the plus next to the folder to open it and see what's inside

Click the minus sign to "close" the folder again

3.2.4 Looking in a Drive or Folder

Click on the drive or folder in the left hand pane

The contents will be displayed in the right hand pane

3.2.5 Opening a Folder in the Right Hand Pane

Double click the folder you wish to open (in the right hand pane)

3.3   My Computer

Windows organises all of your hard drives, floppy drives, network drives, settings, plates and cutlery into an area called My Computer. Remember the idea of your computer as a big filing cabinet? Well, this is it. Let's have a look inside to see what it does.

3.3.1 Opening My Computer

My Computer

Double click the My Computer icon on the desktop

3.3.2 What You See in My Computer

The picture opposite shows the main drives and folders you might see in My Computer...

1 Hard disk drive

2 Floppy disk drive

3 CD-ROM drives

4 Control Panel

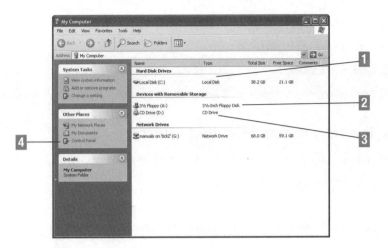

3.3.3 Opening a Drive

If you want to see what's inside a drive…

 Local Disk (C:)   *Double click on the drive icon*

Is there a disk in the floppy disk drive?

You'll need to have a disk in your computer's floppy disk drive to be able to see what's in it! Otherwise you might hear a funny whirring noise and get the following message…

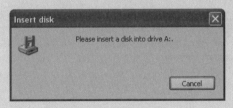

3.3.4 Opening a Folder

Double click on the folder icon to look inside

3.3.5 Closing a Folder

Each time you double click on a folder, the contents are opened in a new window. To close it, click on the X at the top right of the folder window.

3.4 Changing the View

3.4.1 Showing the Standard Buttons Toolbar

This toolbar allows you to navigate around My Computer and Windows Explorer. To switch the toolbar on and off…

1. Open My Computer or Windows Explorer

2. Click on the View menu

3. Click on Toolbars

4. Click on Standard Buttons – a tick appears next to it in the menu when it is displayed

3.4.2 Changing the View of Your Files and Folders

To change the way you see your drive, folders and files displayed....

1. Click on the View menu

or

Click on the View button – if the toolbar is displayed, see above

2. Click on the option you require (see below)

3 Thumbnails

| Cash.xls | Chiefs.ppt | Chocs.xls | Cyber.ppt |

4 Tiles

5 Icons

Cash.xls   Chiefs.ppt   Chocs.xls   Cyber.ppt

6 List

Cash.xls
Chiefs.ppt
Chocs.xls
Cyber.ppt

7 Details

Cash.xls	29 KB	Microsoft Excel Worksheet	07/02/2000 12:45
Chiefs.ppt	43 KB	Microsoft PowerPoint Presentation	04/04/2000 20:38
Chocs.xls	14 KB	Microsoft Excel Worksheet	03/02/2000 15:11
Cyber.ppt	196 KB	Microsoft PowerPoint Presentation	06/04/2000 16:46

3.4.3 Arranging Your Drives

If you are looking in My Computer you can have your drives arranged by drive letter, type, size or free space…

1. *Click on the View menu*

2. *Click on Arrange Icons By*

3. *Click on the option you require*

 Auto Arrange…

To make sure that all icons are evenly spaced you can choose Auto Arrange from the list.

3.4.4 Sorting Your Files and Folders

You can have your files and folders arranged by name, type, size or date…

1. *Click on the View menu*

2. *Click on Arrange Icons By*

3. *Click on the option you require*

 Auto Arrange…

To make sure that all icons are evenly spaced you can choose Auto Arrange from the list.

3.4.5 Viewing the Properties of a File

To find out when a file was created or last modified, its size, etc…

1. *Click on the file to select it*

2. *Click on the File menu*

3. *Click on Properties – a box will appear displaying the file's properties*

4. *Click on the General tab*

When you have finished looking…

Click OK to close the box

3.4.6 Viewing the Properties of a Folder

If you want to find out the size of a folder, when it was created and how many files and other folders it contains…

1. *Click on the folder to select it*

2. *Click on the File menu*

3. *Click on Properties – a box will appear displaying the folder's properties*

You can see how many files are in the folder, and how many subfolders it contains, and the space it takes up. When you have finished looking…

Click OK to close the box

3.4.7 Changing the Status of a File

Sometimes, you might want to make sure a file doesn't accidentally get deleted or edited, either by someone else, or by you if you're a bit tired and not watching what you're doing. You can add a small level of protection by making a file Read-only. To do this…

1 *Click on the file to select it*

2 *Click on the File menu (or right click on the file)*

3 *Click on Properties*

4 *Click on the General tab, if you are not there already*

5 *Place a tick in the Read-only box to protect the file, or remove it to put it back to its normal (read-write) state*

6 *Click OK*

When the file is Read-only, you will get a special message if you try to delete it:

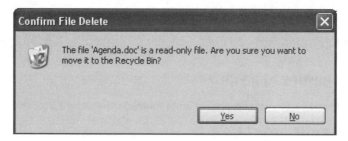

You can still say yes and delete it, but it will make you think twice. If you open the file, edit it, and try to save it, you will be forced to give it a different name – you will not be allowed to save the Read-only file over itself. It's not the most secure, ultra-safe thing in the world, but it's better than nothing. Just be careful when deleting or saving anything, really.

3.4.8 Opening a File

Double click the file to open it

3.5.1 Going Back

If you want to move back through the drives and folders you have already looked at...

 Click on the Back button

Where was I?

If you want to know what the next folder "back" is, hold the mouse pointer over the Back button for a second and a little yellow flag will pop up and tell you!

3.5.2 Going Forward

If you want to return to the drives and folders you have already looked at after going back...

 Click on the Forward button

3

What's next?

If you want to know what the next folder "forward" is, hold the mouse pointer over the Forward button for a second and a little yellow flag will pop up and tell you!

3.5.3 Going Up a Level

If you want to go up a level (e.g. if you look in a folder in the C drive and then want to go up again to see the other folders in the C drive)...

Click on the Up button

CHAPTER 4

Managing Your Files

What You'll Do

→ Create a Folder

→ Select a File or Folder

→ Rename a File or Folder

→ Move and Copy a File or Folder

→ Compress Files

→ Extract Compressed Files

→ Delete a File or Folder

→ Use the Recycle Bin

→ Empty the Recycle Bin

→ Search for a File or Folder

→ Find Files by Date or Type

→ Open a Found File

→ Use a Floppy Disk

→ Format a Floppy Disk

→ Copy a File to a Floppy Disk

4.1 | File Management

4.1.1 Creating a Folder

Once you start getting a lot of files you might want to create different folders to store them in to help you locate them quickly...

1 *Open My Computer or Windows Explorer*

2 *Open the folder or drive where you would like this folder to be stored*

3 *Click on the File menu*

4 *Click New*

5 *Click Folder – a new folder will appear*

6 *Type the name for the new folder*

7 *Press Enter to create the folder*

Subfolders...

You can have folders inside other folders. Create them in exactly the same way!

4.1.2 Selecting a File or Folder

You may need to select files or folders if you want to delete, move or copy them…

Click on a file or folder to select it – it will appear blue

4.1.3 Selecting Adjacent Files and Folders

If you want to select several files or folders that are next to each other…

1. *Select the first file or folder*

2. *Press and hold the Shift key on the keyboard*

3. *Click on the last file or folder of the group you want to select*

4. *Release the Shift key*

4.1.4 Selecting Non-Adjacent Files and Folders

If you want to select several files or folders that are not next to each other…

1. *Select the first file or folder*

2. *Press and hold the Ctrl key on the keyboard*

3. *Click on the next file or folder you want to select*

4. *Continue clicking on files until all the files or folders you want are selected*

5. *Release the Ctrl key*

4.1.5 Selecting All Files and Folders

1. *Click on the Edit menu*

2. *Click on Select All*

or

Press Ctrl + A on the keyboard

4.1.6 Deselecting Files and Folders

Click into an empty space anywhere in the window

4.1.7 Sorting Files

If you have a lot of files in a folder, it might be a bit confusing trying to have a quick look through them. To sort the folder and make some sense out of it . . .

1. *Open Windows Explorer*

2. *Go to the folder you want to inspect*

3. *Change the view to Details – see page 58 for how to do this*

4 *If the status bar is not visible at the bottom of the Windows Explorer screen, switch it on by clicking on the View menu, then clicking on Status Bar*

5 *Click on the grey bar at the top of the files to sort by name, size, type, or date modified*

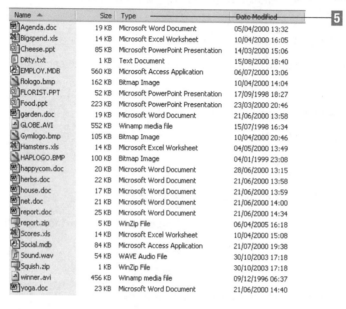

Name ▲	Size	Type	Date Modified
Agenda.doc	19 KB	Microsoft Word Document	05/04/2000 13:32
Bigspend.xls	14 KB	Microsoft Excel Worksheet	10/04/2000 16:05
Cheese.ppt	85 KB	Microsoft PowerPoint Presentation	14/03/2000 15:06
Ditty.txt	1 KB	Text Document	15/08/2000 18:40
EMPLOY.MDB	560 KB	Microsoft Access Application	06/07/2000 13:06
flologo.bmp	162 KB	Bitmap Image	10/04/2000 14:04
FLORIST.PPT	52 KB	Microsoft PowerPoint Presentation	17/09/1998 18:27
Food.ppt	223 KB	Microsoft PowerPoint Presentation	23/03/2000 20:46
garden.doc	19 KB	Microsoft Word Document	21/06/2000 13:58
GLOBE.AVI	552 KB	Winamp media file	15/07/1998 16:34
Gymlogo.bmp	105 KB	Bitmap Image	10/04/2000 20:46
Hamsters.xls	14 KB	Microsoft Excel Worksheet	04/05/2000 13:49
HAPLOGO.BMP	100 KB	Bitmap Image	04/01/1999 23:08
happycom.doc	20 KB	Microsoft Word Document	28/06/2000 13:15
herbs.doc	22 KB	Microsoft Word Document	21/06/2000 13:58
house.doc	17 KB	Microsoft Word Document	21/06/2000 13:59
net.doc	21 KB	Microsoft Word Document	21/06/2000 14:00
report.doc	25 KB	Microsoft Word Document	21/06/2000 14:34
report.zip	5 KB	WinZip File	06/04/2005 16:18
Scores.xls	14 KB	Microsoft Excel Worksheet	10/04/2000 15:08
Social.mdb	84 KB	Microsoft Access Application	21/07/2000 19:38
Sound.wav	54 KB	WAVE Audio File	30/10/2003 17:18
Squish.zip	1 KB	WinZip File	30/10/2003 17:18
winner.avi	456 KB	Winamp media file	09/12/1996 06:37
yoga.doc	23 KB	Microsoft Word Document	21/06/2000 14:40

Name	Size	Type ▲	Date Modified
flologo.bmp	162 KB	Bitmap Image	10/04/2000 14:04
Gymlogo.bmp	105 KB	Bitmap Image	10/04/2000 20:46
HAPLOGO.BMP	100 KB	Bitmap Image	04/01/1999 23:08
EMPLOY.MDB	560 KB	Microsoft Access Application	06/07/2000 13:06
Social.mdb	84 KB	Microsoft Access Application	21/07/2000 19:38
Bigspend.xls	14 KB	Microsoft Excel Worksheet	10/04/2000 16:05
Hamsters.xls	14 KB	Microsoft Excel Worksheet	04/05/2000 13:49
Scores.xls	14 KB	Microsoft Excel Worksheet	10/04/2000 15:08
Cheese.ppt	85 KB	Microsoft PowerPoint Presentation	14/03/2000 15:06
FLORIST.PPT	52 KB	Microsoft PowerPoint Presentation	17/09/1998 18:27
Food.ppt	223 KB	Microsoft PowerPoint Presentation	23/03/2000 20:46
Agenda.doc	19 KB	Microsoft Word Document	05/04/2000 13:32
garden.doc	19 KB	Microsoft Word Document	21/06/2000 13:58
happycom.doc	20 KB	Microsoft Word Document	28/06/2000 13:15
herbs.doc	22 KB	Microsoft Word Document	21/06/2000 13:58
house.doc	17 KB	Microsoft Word Document	21/06/2000 13:59
net.doc	21 KB	Microsoft Word Document	21/06/2000 14:00
report.doc	25 KB	Microsoft Word Document	21/06/2000 14:34
yoga.doc	23 KB	Microsoft Word Document	21/06/2000 14:40
Ditty.txt	1 KB	Text Document	15/08/2000 18:40
Sound.wav	54 KB	WAVE Audio File	30/10/2003 17:18
GLOBE.AVI	552 KB	Winamp media file	15/07/1998 16:34
winner.avi	456 KB	Winamp media file	09/12/1996 06:37
report.zip	5 KB	WinZip File	06/04/2005 16:18
Squish.zip	1 KB	WinZip File	30/10/2003 17:18

6 *When they are sorted, select the ones you want to count*

7 *Check the status bar to see how many files you have selected*

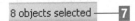

Cheese.ppt	85 KB	Microsoft PowerPoint Presentation	14/03/2000 15:06
FLORIST.PPT	52 KB	Microsoft PowerPoint Presentation	17/09/1998 18:27
Food.ppt	223 KB	Microsoft PowerPoint Presentation	23/03/2000 20:46
Agenda.doc	19 KB	Microsoft Word Document	05/04/2000 13:32
garden.doc	19 KB	Microsoft Word Document	21/06/2000 13:58
happycom.doc	20 KB	Microsoft Word Document	28/06/2000 13:15
herbs.doc	22 KB	Microsoft Word Document	21/06/2000 13:58
house.doc	17 KB	Microsoft Word Document	21/06/2000 13:59
net.doc	21 KB	Microsoft Word Document	21/06/2000 14:00
report.doc	25 KB	Microsoft Word Document	21/06/2000 14:34
yoga.doc	23 KB	Microsoft Word Document	21/06/2000 14:40
Ditty.txt	1 KB	Text Document	15/08/2000 18:40
Sound.wav	54 KB	WAVE Audio File	30/10/2003 17:18
GLOBE.AVI	552 KB	Winamp media file	15/07/1998 16:34

6

8 objects selected ———**7**

4.1.8 Renaming a File or Folder

1 *Right click the file – a menu will pop up*

2 *Click on Rename*

3 *Type a new name for the file*

4 *Press Enter*

Not including the filename extension . . .

If the filename extensions are visible in your window (see page 54) and you don't include the extension at the end when you rename a file, you may see this error message . . .

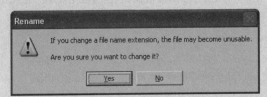

Click No and rename it again to include the existing filename extension. If you can't remember the original extension, press Escape (Esc) to go back to the original filename and start again.

4.1.9 Moving a File or Folder Using Cut and Paste

1 *Select the file(s) or folder(s) you want to move*

2 *Click on the Edit menu*

3 *Click Cut – the file(s) or folder(s) will be moved to the Windows clipboard*

4 *Open the folder where you want to place the file(s) or folder(s)*

⑤ *Click on the Edit menu*

⑥ *Click Paste – the file(s) or folder(s) will be pasted from the Windows clipboard*

4.1.10 Copying a File or Folder Using Copy and Paste

① *Select the file(s) or folder(s) you want to copy*

② *Click on the Edit menu*

③ *Click Copy – the file(s) or folder(s) will be copied to the Windows clipboard*

④ *Open the folder where you want to place the file(s) or folder(s)*

⑤ *Click on the Edit menu*

⑥ *Click Paste – the file(s) or folder(s) will be pasted from the Windows clipboard*

4.1.11 The Windows Clipboard

This is a temporary storage area in your computer where items are placed when they are cut or copied. It can only hold one selection at a time, so when you cut or copy something else this will replace the previous selection on the clipboard.

4.2 File Compression

4.2.1 What is File Compression?

If you downloaded something from the Internet, you have probably downloaded a compressed file. File compression is a way of squashing large files so that they take up less room. It's good for files which need to travel across the Internet, or for squashing files so that they will fit onto a floppy or zip disk.

4.2.2 Compressing Files

You will need a program such as WinZip or Stuffit in order to do this.

① *Open My Computer or Windows Explorer*

② *Find the file you want to compress*

③ *Right click on the file – the name of your compression software should appear in the menu*

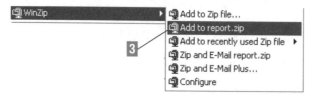

④ *Click on the name of your compression software, i.e. WinZip*

⑤ *Click on Add to (your filename) – your compressed file will be added to the folder you are currently in*

report.zip

4.2.3 Extract Compressed Files

Before you can read or edit a compressed file, you have to restore it to its original state by uncompressing it or *extracting* it.

1 *Double click on the compressed file you wish to extract*

2 *Click on the file(s) you want to extract*

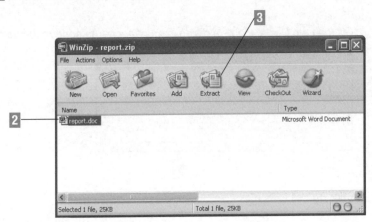

3 *Click on Extract*

4 *Click on the Folders in the Folders/drives window until you get to the folder you want to extract the file to*

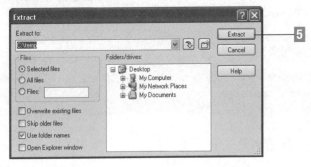

5 *Click on Extract*

4.3 Deleting and Using the Recycle Bin

4.3.1 Deleting a File

1 *Select the file you wish to delete*

2 *Press Delete on the keyboard*

or

Click on the Delete icon

3 *Click on Yes to confirm the deletion*

4.3.2 Deleting a Folder

When you delete a folder you will also delete all of its contents (any files or folders inside that folder) . . .

1 *Select the folder you wish to delete*

2 *Press Delete on the keyboard*

or

Click on the Delete icon – a dialog box will appear to confirm the deletion

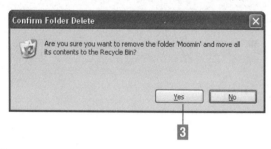

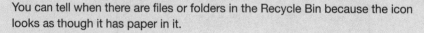

3 *Click on Yes*

4.3.3 Recycle Bin

When you delete anything from your hard disk drive (C drive or desktop) it gets sent to the Recycle Bin. This bin doesn't empty itself, so if you delete something by accident you can retrieve it from here.

Paper in the bin…

You can tell when there are files or folders in the Recycle Bin because the icon looks as though it has paper in it.

Recycle Bin

4.3.4 Opening the Recycle Bin

Double click the Recycle Bin icon on the desktop

4.3.5 Retrieving a File or Folder

1 *Double click the Recycle Bin to open it*

2 *Click on the file or folder you want to retrieve*

3 *Click on the File menu*

4 *Click on Restore – the file or folder will be returned to where it was deleted from*

4.3.6 Emptying the Recycle Bin

You may want to empty the Recycle Bin occasionally to free up some more space on your computer...

[1] *Right click on the Recycle Bin*

[2] *Click on Empty Recycle Bin*

[3] *Click on Yes, to confirm the deletion of all items in the bin*

No paper in the bin...

When the bin is empty the icon looks empty too:

Recycle Bin

Are you sure you want to empty the bin?

If you empty the Recycle Bin, you cannot get back what you deleted – ever! Make absolutely sure you want to permanently delete it. Once it's gone, it's really gone...

4.4 Searching for Files

4.4.1 Why Might I Need to Search for a File?

The Search tool is very useful if you cannot remember the exact name of a file or where you stored it. You can tell Windows everything you can remember about the file from its filename, date created, modified or accessed to the type of file and a keyword that the file contains. The more you can tell it, the quicker the search!

4.4.2 Starting a Search

[1] *Click on the Start button*

[2] *Click on Search*

[3] *Choose the type of thing you want to search for – pictures, documents, etc.*

[4] *Enter the filename (see following sections for more advanced options)*

[5] *Click Search*

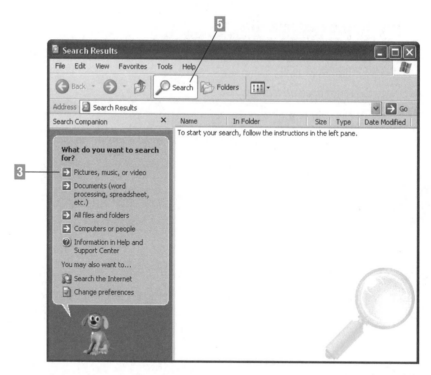

4.4.3 Searching for Files or Folders by Name

1. Click into the **All or part of the file name** box

2. Type the name (or part of the name) of the file or folder you are looking for

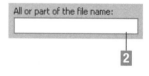

3. Click Search

Using a Wild Card

If you can only remember the first few letters of the name of a file, type those in followed by an asterisk, e.g. **letter*** (the asterisk can represent any number of letters). Find File will then pick out every file whose name begins with **letter**. It won't, however, find files that are just called **letter**!

Choosing different search types

If you already have the Search box open, and want to go back to the beginning, click the Back button until you reach the start of the Search box. This saves you having to close the Search box and start again.

4.4.4 Finding Different Types of Files

If you know the type of file it is (e.g. spreadsheet, picture) you can speed up your search. Depending on which file type you select in the first stage of the search, you will see different options:

1 Pictures, music or video

2 Documents

3 All files and folders

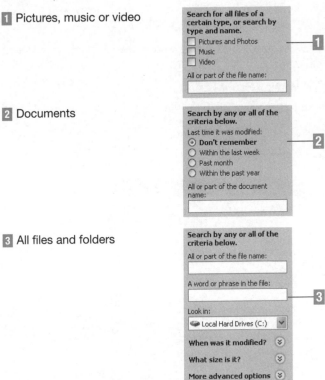

4.4.5 Finding Files Using a Keyword

You can search for files containing a particular word. For example, if you're looking for a letter about cheese, you can search for any files that contain the word cheese.

[1] Search for **All files and folders**

[2] Click into the **A word or phrase in the file** box

[3] Type the keyword which the document contains

[4] Click Search

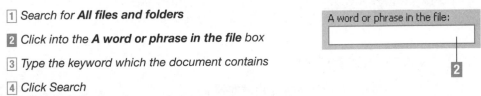

Uncommon words…

The search will be quicker if the word you are searching for is less common and doesn't appear in lots of your files. **The** would not be a good keyword!

4.4.6 Choosing Where to Look

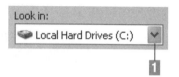

1 *Click the drop down arrow underneath Look in*

2 *Click on the drive you wish to look in*

What if I want to search through a folder?

You do not have to search through the whole drive. Just follow the steps below to search through a folder or subfolder...

From Search Dialog Box...

1 Click the drop down arrow underneath Look in

2 Click Browse... at the bottom of the list

3 Locate the folder you require

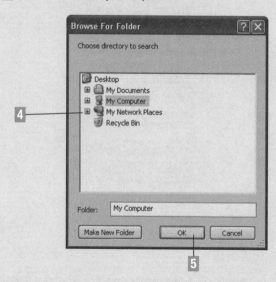

4 Double click the folders to open them, or click the plus (+) signs next to them

5 Click OK

4.4.7 Finding Files by Date

1 *Click **When was it modified?***

2 *Choose the appropriate date criteria for your search (see below)*

3 *Choose Modified, Created or Accessed from the drop down list under Specify dates*

4 *Choose the dates you require to search*

5 *Click Search*

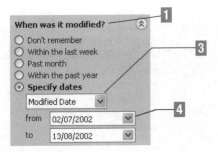

4.4.8 Finding Files by Type

If you know the type of file it is (e.g. Excel Workbook) you can use the file type to speed up your search. This tells Windows to ignore files of any other type.

1 *Start a search for All files and folders*

2 *Click on More advanced options*

3 *Click on the drop down arrow under Type of file*

4 *Click on the type of file you require*

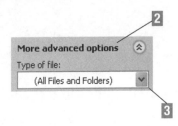

4.4.9 Finding the Files

Once you have set the criteria for the search...

Click on Search – the found files will appear in the right hand pane and the status bar will display the number of files found

4

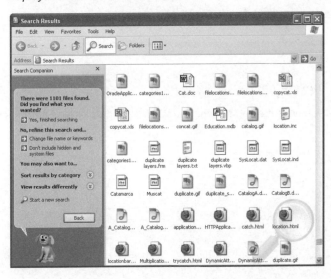

Watch the left hand window pane...

While the left pane has a moving green bar, Windows is still searching.

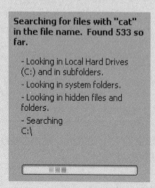

Searching for files with "cat" in the file name. Found 533 so far.

- Looking in Local Hard Drives (C:) and in subfolders.
- Looking in system folders.
- Looking in hidden files and folders.
- Searching C:\

If your file has already been found, you can stop the search by clicking on Stop on the left hand side.

Stop

4.4.10 Opening a Found File

If the file you were looking for is displayed...

Double click the file to open it

Find box stays open...

The Search box will stay open until you close it. Click the X on the title bar to close the window.

Modifying your search...

If the file you were looking for isn't found you can modify the information you have put in and try again.

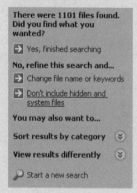

There were 1101 files found. Did you find what you wanted?

→ Yes, finished searching

No, refine this search and...

→ Change file name or keywords

→ Don't include hidden and system files

You may also want to...

Sort results by category ⌄

View results differently ⌄

🔎 Start a new search

4.4.11 Starting a New Search

When Windows has finished searching, to start a new search just click on **Start a new search**.

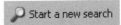

4.5 Using Floppy Disks

4.5.1 What is a Floppy Disk?

You can save your files onto floppy disks and use them in your floppy disk drive (see page 57). Although they store a lot less information than your computer, floppy disks are small and therefore portable and can be used in any PC. You can use them to…

- Make copies of your files (in case something happens to your computer) – these are called backup copies, or backups, and are a good idea if your files are valuable or would take a long time to replace (but please use CDs instead, as floppy disks are not very reliable!)

- Share files with friends and colleagues

- Copy a file from one computer to another

4.5.2 Looking at What is on a Floppy Disk

1 *Insert the floppy disk into your floppy disk drive*

2 *Open My Computer or Windows Explorer*

3 *Double click on the A drive – the files on the disk will be displayed*

3½ Floppy
(A:)

4.5.3 Formatting a Floppy Disk

Before you can use a floppy disk it must be formatted for use on your computer. Although you can buy floppy disks already formatted, it is cheaper to buy them unformatted. To format a floppy disk…

1 *Insert the floppy disk into your floppy disk drive*

2 *Open My Computer or Windows Explorer*

3 *Right click on the A drive*

4 *Click on Format*

5 *If the disk has already been formatted and you just want to wipe it clean, tick the box next to Quick Format – leave it unticked if you are not sure*

6 *Click on Start*

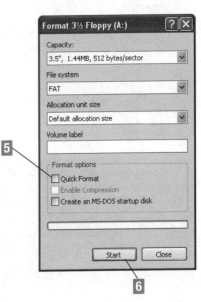

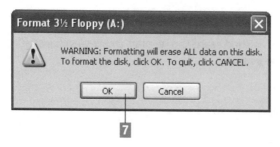

7 *Click on OK*

Formatting may take a few minutes. Check the progress bar to see how far it has got:

When the format is complete, a box displaying the results will appear:

8 *Click on OK*

9 *Click on Close*

Make sure there are no files on the disk...

Formatting a disk will overwrite any files already stored on it. If it is not a brand new floppy disk, make sure there are no files on it that you need before formatting!

Make sure there are no files open...

If there are files already on the disk and you have one of them open, you will get an error message...

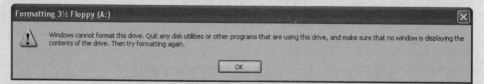

Click OK, close the file and carry on formatting if you don't require the file any more, or insert another floppy disk to format.

4.5.4 Copying a File to a Floppy Disk

If you want to make a copy of a file, for backup, to give to someone else or to transfer to another computer…

1. *Insert a disk into your floppy drive*

2. *Open My Computer or Windows Explorer*

3. *Find the file you wish to copy*

4. *Right click on the file – a menu will pop up*

5. *Click on Send To*

6. *Click on 3½ Floppy (A:) – the file will be copied to your floppy disk*

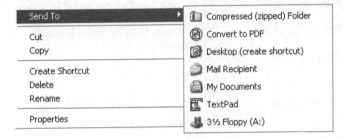

Copying more than one file…

You can copy several files to your floppy disk at once in this way by selecting the files first (see page 63).

Using Save as…

If the file you want to copy is already open, you can make a copy of it using Save as and choose to save it to the A drive (see page 105).

4

CHAPTER 5

Programs and Printing

What You'll Do

→ Start Applications

→ Use the Start Menu Programs

→ Use a Desktop Shortcut

→ Switch Between Open Windows

→ Close an Application

→ Install Software from a CD

→ Install Software Downloaded from the Internet

→ Uninstall Software

→ Use Notepad

→ Open, Create and Save a File in Notepad

→ Print from a Program

→ Change the Default Printer

→ Check the Progress of Printing

→ Cancel, Delete and Resume Printing

→ Restart a Print Job

→ Use the Print Screen Key

→ Install a Printer

→ Use a Mouse

→ Scan for Viruses

5.1 Starting Applications

5.2.1 Using the Start Menu Programs

1 *Click on the Start button*

2 *Click on All Programs*

All Programs

3 *Click on the program you want – the ▶ symbol indicates that there is more to see. Follow the direction of the arrow to get to the next menu.*

5.1.2 Using the Start Menu for a New Office Document

1 *Click on the Start button*

2 *Click on All Programs*

3 *Click on New Office Document*

④ *Click on Blank Document (to open Microsoft Word)*

or

Click on Blank Workbook (to open Microsoft Excel)

or

Click on Blank Presentation (to open Microsoft PowerPoint)

or

Click on Blank Database (to open Microsoft Access)

⑤ *Click OK*

5.1.3 Using a Desktop Shortcut

If you have a shortcut to a file or program you can open it using the shortcut. Just double click on the shortcut to open it.

5.1.4 What Programs Do I Have?

All the programs you have on your computer will be listed in All Programs on the Start menu. The following table explains what some of these applications are used for...

Program (application)	Type of application	Used for...
Microsoft Word	Word processing	Creating letters, memos, faxes, reports, etc.
Microsoft Excel	Spreadsheet	Creating graphs, managing accounts, stock control, or other mathematical or financial calculations.
Microsoft PowerPoint	Presentation	Creating presentations, slide shows, organisation charts, etc.
Microsoft Access	Database	Creating databases which hold information that can be queried or used to create reports.

5.1.5 Switching Between Open Windows

You can have several programs open at once. For every program you have open there will be a button for it on the taskbar. Whichever program is "active", the button will look as if it is pushed in on the toolbar. If you want to switch to looking at another window...

Click on the button for the window on the taskbar

5.1.6 Closing an Application

Click on the top X on the title bar

5.1.7 Closing an Application Which is Not Responding

Sometimes applications "crash", and, no matter what you press or click on, nothing happens. Closing the application safely allows the computer to check itself and correct whatever it was that upset it in the first place.

To close down an application which is not responding:

1 *Press the Ctrl, Alt and Delete keys at the same time – the Task Manager should open, but if you are on a network, you may be taken to the Windows Security dialog box. If this is the case, then click the Task Manager button*

2 *Click on the Applications tab*

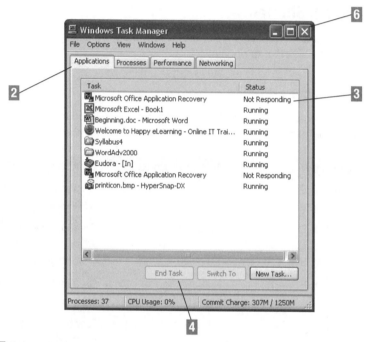

3 *Select the program which has crashed – it will usually have Not Responding next to it*

4 *Click on End Task*

5 *Click Yes*

6 *Click the X at the top right of the Task Manager to close it*

5.2 Installing Software

5.2.1 Installing Software from a CD

1 *Insert the CD ROM or floppy disk with your software on*

2 *If the CD starts itself follow the instructions on the screen*

Or, if no instructions appear on the screen

3 *Click on Start*

4 *Click on Run*

5 *Click on Browse*

6 *Click on the down arrow beside the Look In box to locate your CD drive or floppy drive*

7 *Find a file with the suffix ".exe"*

8 *Click on the file – the software should begin the installation process*

9 *Follow the instructions on the screen*

5.2.2 Installing Software Downloaded from the Internet

1 *In your Internet browser, go to the page with the link to the downloadable software*

2 *Click on the download button*

3 *Click on Save*

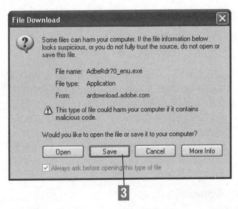

4 *Choose where you would like the program to be stored, e.g. C:\program files*

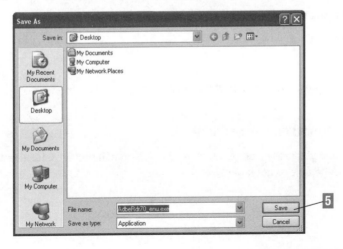

5 *Click on Save – the software will begin to download*

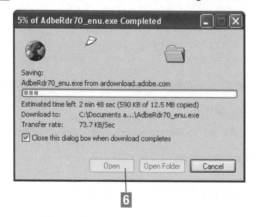

6 *When the download has completed click on Open*

7 *Follow the instructions on the screen*

Saving the file for later ...

If you want to open the file later, click Close when the download finishes. When you want to open the file, open My Computer or Windows Explorer, find the folder you saved the file in, and double click it.

5.2.3 Uninstalling Software

1 *Click on Start*

2 *Click on Control Panel*

3 *Click on Add or Remove Programs*

4 *Use the scroll bar to find the program you want to uninstall*

5 *Click on the program*

6 *Click on Change/Remove*

7 *Click Yes*

8 *Follow the instructions on the screen.*

Be careful when uninstalling!

Make sure you really want to uninstall the software! If you uninstall the wrong thing, you may not be able to get it back!

Using Software

A lot of software is opened and closed in the same way – different documents are saved and printed in the same way, too. To show you how it works, we'll be using Notepad, to keep things simple. Notepad is a text editing program.

5.3.1 Opening Notepad

1. *Click on Start*

2. *Click on All Programs*

3. *Click on Accessories*

4. *Click on Notepad*

5.3.2 Creating a New File in Notepad

When you open Notepad, a new file is automatically created. To create a new one . . .

1. *Click on the File menu*

2. *Click on New*

5.3.3 Opening a File in Notepad

1. *Click on the File menu*

2. *Click Open*

3. *If necessary, change the Look in box to the folder or drive where your document is saved – click on the drop down arrow, choose a drive, and double click on folders to open them*

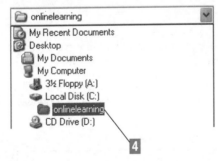

4. *Select the file you wish to open by clicking on it*

5. *Click Open*

5.3.4 Saving a File in Notepad

[1] *Click on the File menu*

[2] *Click on Save – if you have already saved the file, this will just save it again. If it is your first time saving the file, proceed to step 3*

[3] *If necessary, choose a location from the Save in box – click on the drop down arrow, choose a drive, and double click on folders to open them*

[4] *Type in a name for the file in the **File name** box*

[5] *Click Save*

5.3.5 Closing Notepad

Click on the X at the top right of the Notepad window

5.4 Printing

5.4.1 Printing from a Program

Most programs let you print in the same way.

Click on the Print icon

Or

[1] *Click on the File menu*

[2] *Click on Print*

[3] *Click OK*

5.4.2 The Default Printer

If you are connected to a network you may find that there are several printers that you could print to. This could be useful if one is broken or is often busy!

When you print from Word (or any other program) the document will be sent to the default printer. This is the printer you will see in the Print dialog box when you click on Print from the File menu.

5.4.3 Changing the Default Printer

[1] *Click on the Start button*

[2] *Click on Control Panel*

[3] *Click on Printers and Other Hardware*

4️⃣ *Click on Printers and Faxes – a window will appear showing all the printers that are available for you to print to*

5️⃣ *Right click on the printer you wish to set as default*

6️⃣ *Click on Set as Default Printer*

Which is my default printer?

The default printer has a tick at the top of the icon.

Learnfish

5.4.4 Checking the Progress of Printing

Lots of people may print to the same printer as you, and you'll find all of these files form a queue. You can have a look at the print queue to see where your file is, and how far the printer has got with printing your document:

1️⃣ *Click on the Start button*

2️⃣ *Click on Control Panel*

3️⃣ *Click on Printers and Other Hardware*

4️⃣ *Click on Printers and Faxes*

5️⃣ *Double click on the printer you require – usually the default printer (see above)*

Program used, and name of file

Status: spooling, printing, etc.

Owner of file sent to print

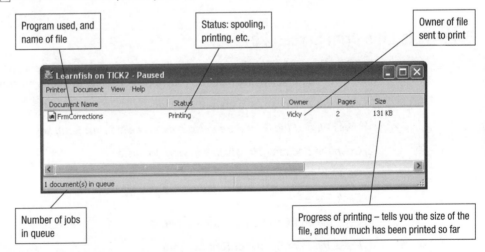

Number of jobs in queue

Progress of printing – tells you the size of the file, and how much has been printed so far

Look in the System Tray...

When you are waiting for something to print there will be a little printer icon in your System Tray. You can double click on this as a shortcut to seeing the print queue!

5.4.5 Cancelling Printing

&boxed1; *Make sure you can see the print queue your file has been sent to (see previous page)*

&boxed2; *Click on your file to select it*

&boxed3; *Click on the Document menu*

&boxed4; *Click on Cancel*

5.4.6 Pausing and Resuming Printing

&boxed1; *Make sure you can see the print queue your file has been sent to*

&boxed2; *Click on your file to select it*

&boxed3; *Click on the Document menu*

&boxed4; *Click on Pause to pause it, or Resume to continue printing*

5.4.7 Restarting a Print Job

&boxed1; *Make sure you can see the print queue your file has been sent to*

&boxed2; *Click on your file to select it*

&boxed3; *Click on the Document menu*

&boxed4; *Click on Restart*

5.4.8 Using the Print Screen key

The Print Screen key on the keyboard allows you to print an entire screen or to copy it to another document, like the pictures you've been looking at in this manual.

To copy the window that is currently active:

&boxed1; *Press Alt and the Print Screen (sometimes called Prnt Scrn) key*

&boxed2; *Open the document in which you want to paste*

&boxed3; *Click on the Edit menu*

&boxed4; *Click Paste*

To copy the entire contents of the screen:

&boxed1; *Press the Print Screen or Prnt Scrn key*

&boxed2; *Open the document in which you want to paste*

&boxed3; *Click on the Edit menu*

&boxed4; *Click Paste*

5.4.9 Installing a Printer

In order for a computer and a printer to talk to each other, your computer has to have the correct printer driver installed. This is a piece of software which tells your computer how to talk to that make and model of printer.

There are various places you might find this software:

- On a CD – if your printer is new, it will probably come with a CD with the drivers on it

- Already in Windows, or on your Windows CD

- Downloadable from the printer manufacturer's website – this is especially useful if neither of the two options above works

To install a printer which has its driver's CD:

1. *Insert the CD*

2. *Follow the instructions which appear on screen*

To install a printer if you don't have the printer CD:

1. *Click on Start*

2. *Click on Control Panel*

3. *Click on Printers and Other Hardware*

4. *Click on Printers and Faxes*

5. *Click on Add a Printer*

6. *Click on Next in the Add Printer Wizard*

7. *Click on Local Printer – if your printer is on a network and not directly connected to your PC, you must ask your technical people for help, as you may not be allowed to install a printer yourself*

8. *The wizard will search for a printer that is attached to your machine*

9. *If it finds it, it will install the software and choose the port itself – if not, Click Next, and proceed to the next step*

10. *Choose via which Port (the sockets at the back of your computer) your printer will be connected to the computer*

11. *Scroll down the Manufacturers list until you find the make of your printer – click on it*

12. *Scroll down the Model list until you find the model of your printer – click on it*

13. *Click Next*

14. *Type a name for the printer*

15. *Click Yes if you want this to be the default printer, or click No if you don't want this to be the default printer*

16. *Make sure the Yes button is selected to print a test page – this shows you that the printer is working, and the PC can talk to it properly*

17 *Click Next*

18 *Click Finish*

Ports

If you look at the back of your PC you will see a number of sockets where you can plug in your keyboard, mouse, printers, etc. These sockets are called "ports". The most common are the rectangular USB ports and the D shaped parallel ports or communication ports, which are shaped like a squareish D on its side and have 25 holes.

5.5 | Mouse Techniques

The mouse is designed to perform certain functions. This section explains some of the basic terms and the purpose of using the mouse.

5.5.1 Click

A click with the mouse will always refer to the LEFT MOUSE BUTTON. A single click is generally used to open something on the **Desktop** or in **My Computer** (i.e. a program or a document).

Or

A single click is used to select something once you are inside a program like Word or Excel.

5.5.2 Right Click

A right click is a click with the RIGHT mouse button. Right clicks are only used to bring up a pop-up menu.

5.5.3 Double Click

A double click is used to open documents inside a program like Word or Excel.

5.5.4 Click and Drag

This means click on something, hold the mouse button down, drag to another area of the screen and then release the mouse button.

5.6 | Viruses

5.6.1 Viruses

You've probably heard a lot of wild stories about viruses in the press. While they are not as ominous and disastrous as they sound, they are a very real threat to you. They are programs written by Bad People that copy themselves around sneakily and damage computers.

There are many different types of virus, some more damaging than others. Some viruses merely display a message telling of the programmer's prowess, which are full of spelling mistakes, LOTS OF CAPITAL LETTERS and terrible grammar that it am not good. Some display a message and delete data from your hard disk. The damage levels vary from virus to virus.

Your PC can catch a virus by opening an infected email attachment (a program sent within an email message), using an infected floppy disk or getting an infected file from the Internet (not as common as the other two methods).

Your PC **cannot** get a virus by looking at webpages, using email normally, kissing girls, or sitting on infected toilet seats.

To keep your PC safe from viruses:

- Make sure your PC has the latest virus software installed, and regularly update its data files so that it can recognise new viruses (roughly 300 new viruses appear every month).

- Always scan floppy disks for viruses before using any information on them.

- Be careful of opening emails from people you don't know – make sure your email software does not automatically open emails, like the Preview Pane in Outlook.

- Never run an email attachment unless you are sure who it is from and have scanned the attachment itself for viruses.

- Keep an emergency disk nearby just in case – your anti-virus software will create one for you. If your PC becomes infected, reboot with the emergency disk in the drive, and it will try to clean the infection for you.

If your PC gets a virus, run the anti-virus software immediately. Make sure to close any other software, as some viruses can use your email software to send the virus on to your address book contacts. Try to disconnect from the Internet first, to stop it downloading anything. When the anti-virus software scans, it should find the infected files. Ask it to "disinfect" the infected files – this means removing the virus, and restoring the files to normal. Some viruses cannot be removed in this way, though – they might be too new, or too clever. Sometimes you will just have to delete the infected files. Prevention is always the best cure.

5.6.2 Virus Hoaxes

This is a fairly recent problem, and a very annoying one: you get an email from a friend telling you about a scary new virus that has just come out. Apparently it has been reported by Microsoft or IBM or AOL or someone like that, is even worse than the last virus that came out and has no cure. The message then tells you to forward the message on to all of your friends. You later find out the whole thing was made up.

This is a type of virus in itself. It is designed to create a panic, and get everyone sending the same message to all of their friends, who then send it to all of their friends and so on and so on. It ties up your company mail PC with hundreds of emails going around and wastes everyone's time. Sometimes the email traffic is so heavy, it can crash a company network.

The email text usually goes along these lines:

WARNING: If you receive an email with the subject line *InsertSubjectHere*, do not open the file. The file contains the *InsertVirusNameHere* virus. This information was announced yesterday morning at *IBM/Microsoft/InsertCompanyNameHere*. This is a very dangerous virus, much worse than "Melissa", and there is NO remedy for it at this time. If you open/read/look at the email, it will completely delete your hard drive/do some other ridiculously frightening thing. This is a new, very malicious virus and not many people know about it. Pass this warning along to EVERYONE in your address book ASAP so that this threat may be stopped.

If you receive an email like this, do not send it to all of your friends – if you do, the hoaxer has won. Check with an online virus library, and find out if it is a hoax.

The Network Associates Virus Library:
http://vil.nai.com/vil

F Secure Hoax Warnings:
http://www.f-secure.com/virus-info/hoax

Urban Legends – Virus Hoaxes Page:
http://urbanlegends.about.com/science/urbanlegends/msubvir.htm

The last site also contains information about other email hoaxes you will receive, for example, the one about the businessman falling asleep in a hotel and waking up with his kidneys stolen, etc. These are never true, and your friends have probably received them 50 times already. If you insist on sending them on, you will lose all your friends, become a hermit and your knees will fall off.

Do not delete a file if a virus warning tells you to!

Some virus hoaxes pretend that if you have a certain file on your PC, then you are infected – this is not true! The file is usually an important one, and removing it will damage your system. Never delete files or forward virus alerts without checking the above webpages, or talking to an IT support person.

5.6.3 Virus Scanning

There are many different types of anti-virus software, and there isn't space to show you how to use them all here. They will usually all work in the same way – you will have to read the instructions for your particular software. Here is an example of what you would need to do if you were using Kaspersky Anti-Virus:

1 *Click on Start*

2 *Click on All Programs*

3 *Click on Kaspersky Anti-Virus*

4 *Click on Kaspersky Anti-Virus Scanner*

5 *Click on Scan*

6 *Click on Scan Now – the software will check your computer for viruses*

5.6.4 Updating Your Virus Scanner

In order to make sure you are keeping up to date with all the new viruses floating around out there, you need to regularly update your virus scanner. You need to be connected to the Internet for this to work. Again, there are too many different pieces of software to show you all of them, so here is an example of what you would need to do if you were using Kaspersky Anti-Virus:

1. *Click on Start*

2. *Click on All Programs*

3. *Click on Kaspersky Anti-Virus*

4. *Click on Kaspersky Anti-Virus Updater*

5. *In the KAV Updater wizard box click Next – the software connects to Kaspersky's database of viruses via the Internet to check for new viruses*

6. *Click Finish when it has finished updating*

5

CHAPTER 6

Switching the Computer On

What You'll Do

→ Switch the Computer On and Off

→ Use the Base Unit On/Off Switch

→ Use the Monitor On/Off Switch

→ Shut the Computer Down

6.1 Switching On and Off

6.1.1 Base Unit On/Off Switch

To switch the base unit on . . .

Press the On/Off button – a light near the button will go on

Where's the On/Off button?

Different base units will have different buttons; they might be a different shape, size or colour from the one in the picture above. However, they will all have a symbol like ⏻ or ⏽ on or close to the button.

6.1.2 Monitor On/Off Switch

To switch the monitor on . . .

Press the On/Off button – a light near the button will go on

 Where's the On/Off button?

Just like base units, the monitor on/off switches will be different shapes, sizes or colours from the one in the picture above. However, they will all have a symbol like ⏻ or ⏼ on or close to the button.

6.1.3 Switching Off

To switch the monitor off . . .

Press the On/Off button again – the light near the button will go out

 You can't use the On/Off button to switch off the base unit!

You can damage the computer and your work by just switching the computer off using the On/Off button. You must first shut down the computer as explained in the next section. Then, when it tells you it is safe to do so, you can press the On/Off button to switch it off.

6.2 Shutting Down

6.2.1 Why Can't I Use the Off Switch?

If you don't use Shut Down before you switch off the computer, you could damage it and maybe lose some of your work.

Before you switch off your computer you must first ensure that it is not still doing anything. The only way to ensure this is to use Shut Down, because you can't always see what is going on inside the computer by looking at the screen. Using this method will ensure that any settings you have changed are saved and that the computer has finished copying all the information you have saved to a safe place.

6.2.2 Shutting Down

To shut down the computer . . .

1 *Click on the Start button*

2 *Click on Shut Down*

3 *Click on the drop down arrow and choose **Shut down** by clicking on it*

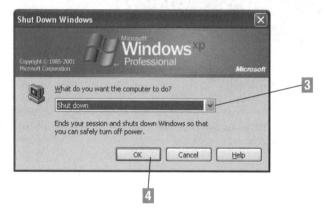

4 *Click OK*

When can I switch it off?

The computer will switch off automatically. If you are using an older version of Windows, then a message will appear on the screen telling you when it is safe to switch off the computer using the on/off button.

CHAPTER 1

Getting Started

What You'll Do

→ Get Started in Word

→ Exit Word

→ Use the Word Screen

→ Show and Hide the Task Pane

→ Enter and Delete Text

→ Save, Close and Open a Document

→ Move Around Documents

→ Use the Scroll Bars

→ Select and Deselect Text

→ Use Help

→ Correct Mistakes

→ Use Different Views

→ Display and Hide Toolbars

→ Use Print Preview

→ Print in Word

1.1 Word

Word is a word processor. You can use it to type letters, write stories, pretty much anything you could do on a normal typewriter. The great thing about a word processor is that, unlike a typewriter, you can edit your words as you go along, copy sections, rearrange bits, and do all sorts of fancy things with the text. It is also much, much quieter than a typewriter.

1.1.1 Starting Word

1 *Click on the Start button*

2 *Click on All Programs*

3 *Click on Microsoft Word*   Microsoft Word

Microsoft
Word

If you see an icon for Word in the middle of your screen, you can use that instead. Just double click on it to run Word.

How do I know if Word has opened?

You should be able to see the Word window on the screen (see the section on the Word screen, on page 99).

You should also be able to see Word as one of the tasks on the Taskbar at the bottom of the screen.

1.1.2 Exiting Word

1. *Click on the File menu*

2. *Click on Exit*

Or

Click on the X at the top right hand corner of the screen

How do I know that Word is closed?

The Word window should disappear from the screen and you should no longer be able to see it on the Taskbar.

1.2 Word Options

Word has several options which can change the way you carry out simple tasks.

1.2.1 Standard and Formatting Toolbar Sharing the Same Row

You may find that you cannot separate the Standard and Formatting toolbar – which means that you will not be able to see all the icons you need.

To turn this option on and off...

1. *Click on the Tools menu*

2. *Click Customise*

3. *Click on the Options tab*

4. *Add or remove the tick next to **Show standard and Formatting toolbars on two rows***

5. *Click Close*

The toolbars will become separated when the option is turned off...

1.2.2 Menus Showing Most Recently Used Commands First

You may find that you cannot see all the commands available on your menus, unless you pause for a short while after clicking the menu. If you can see a double headed arrow at the bottom of your menus, it means that this option is turned on.

This is designed to help you see which options you use most often, and to hide the ones you don't use that much, or don't need. In theory, this is a great idea. In practice, it is just annoying and weird, and seems to bear no relation to the options you actually use or, in fact, to anything at all. If you want to turn this option on and off...

1 *Click on the Tools menu*

2 *Click Customise*

3 *Click on the Options tab*

4 *Add or remove the tick next to **Always show full menus***

5 *Click Close*

1.3 The Word Screen

1.3.1 The Word Screen

On the next page is a picture of the Word screen in Print Layout view. The Appendix contains a description of the different icons at the top of the screen.

1 *Title Bar* Tells you the name of the document you are working on. Before you have saved your document this will be something like "Document 1".

2 *Menu Bar* Gives you access to the commands available in Word. All commands are grouped under one of the menus.

3 *Standard Toolbar* Provides a quick way of carrying out standard commands using the icons.

4 *Formatting Toolbar* Provides a quick way of changing the format, or the appearance, of your document.

5 *Ruler* Shows you the width of your page and helps you set things like margins and tabs.

6 *Scroll Bars* Helps you to move around a document – the vertical scroll bar allows you to move through a long document, whilst the horizontal scroll bar allows you to move across a wide document.

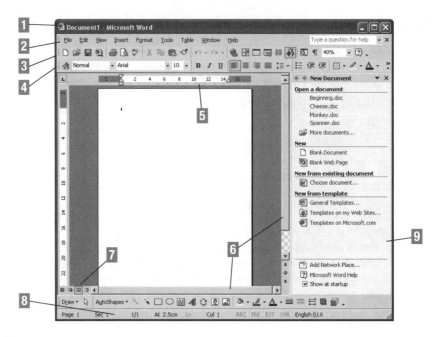

7 *Page View Icons* Changes the way you are looking at the document depending on the task that you wish to carry out.

8 *Status Bar* Tells you whereabouts your cursor is in the document and what mode Word is working in.

9 *Task Pane* This is a window that you can use for many different things, e.g. opening files, inserting pictures, formatting, mail merge, etc.

1.3.2 What is the Task Pane?

The Task Pane is a window that you can use to carry out many useful functions. It lets you open files, create files, insert clipart, search, format text, mail merge, and copy and paste objects. It normally appears when you want to create or open a new file, but you can display it manually if you need it. The Task Pane lives on the right hand side of the Word screen.

1.3.3 Showing and Hiding the Task Pane

To show or hide the Task Pane...

1 *Click on the View menu*

2 *Click on Task Pane*

If it is displayed, this will hide it. If it is hidden, then this will show it.

1.3.4 Choosing Different Task Panes

1 *Display the Task Pane if necessary*

2 *Click on the drop down arrow next to the Task Pane title*

3 *Choose the Task Pane you require by clicking on it*

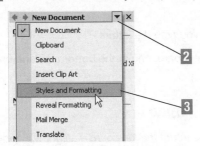

1.4 Entering and Deleting Text

1.4.1 Typing Text

- When you start Word a blank document appears ready for you to start typing

- A blinking vertical bar called the Insertion Point (or cursor) indicates where text will come out when you type

- Unlike using a typewriter, you do not have to press the carriage return when you get to the end of the line. Word will automatically wrap the text onto the next line. But if you want to finish a line and go to the next one, just press Enter or Return

- You can delete text to the left or the right of the cursor

- To type text, position your cursor where you would like to start typing and just start typing!

1.4.2 Insert or Overtype?

- Normally when you type you will be in Insert mode. This means that if your cursor is in the middle of an existing sentence and you start typing, nothing will be deleted. The text that is already there will shuffle along to make way for the new text

- If you are in Overtype mode, then any text you type will go over the top of existing text

To change modes...

Press the Insert key on the keyboard

or

REC TRK EXT **OVR**   *Double click the OVR mark on the status bar at the bottom of the screen*

1.4.3 Creating a Space

Press the Space Bar at the bottom of the keyboard – it is the long, blank key between the Alt keys.

1.4.4 Creating a New Paragraph

1. Make sure your cursor is flashing where you would like a new line

2. Press the Enter or Hard Return key (found on the right of the keyboard)

1.4.5 Creating Capital Letters

Hold down the Shift key while you type the letters

There are two Shift keys on the keyboard, one at the bottom left and one at the bottom right.

1.4.6 Capitalising All the Text You are Typing

1. Press the Caps Lock key on the left of the keyboard – a light will appear above Caps Lock on the right hand side of the keyboard

2. To turn it off, press Caps Lock again

1.4.7 Moving the Cursor Around with the Keyboard

Use the cursor keys at the bottom right of the keyboard

1. Moves the cursor left a letter

2. Moves the cursor up a line

3. Moves the cursor right a letter

4. Moves the cursor down a line

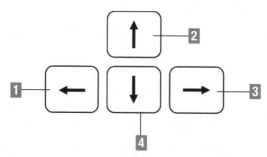

1.4.8 Adding Extra Text to What You Have Typed

1. Position your cursor where you would like to start typing

2. Start typing!

As long as you are in Insert mode (see page 101), the rest of the text will shuffle along to make way for your new text.

1.4.9 Delete and Backspace

To get rid of text, use the Delete and Backspace keys.

1. *Position your cursor next to the text you would like to get rid of*

2. *Press **Delete** (or **Del**) if the text is to the **right** of the cursor*

   or

   *Press **Backspace** if the text is to the **left** of the cursor*

1.4.10 Selecting Text to Delete

1. *Select the text to delete (see page 110)*

2. *Press Delete*

1.4.11 Displaying and Hiding Non-Printing Characters

Just because you can't see paragraph marks and spaces doesn't mean they aren't there. Displaying these non-printing characters can sometimes help when arranging text on the page, or finding out why something has gone slightly wrong. To display or hide non-printing characters...

This·is·a·poem↵
about·fish¶
I·like·fish¶
Yes·I·do¶
¶
¶

Click on the Show/Hide icon

¶

Spaces will show as dots, paragraph marks will look like the Show/Hide icon, and soft returns (see below) will look like little crooked arrows.

1.4.12 Inserting and Removing Paragraph Marks

To insert a paragraph mark, press the Return key on the keyboard – this will move your cursor to a new, blank line. This is sometimes called a hard return. To delete it, place your cursor to the left of it, and press the Delete or Del key.

1.4.13 Inserting and Removing Soft Returns

A soft return takes you to a new blank line, but keeps you in the same paragraph. If you centre the paragraph, for example, it will centre both lines. To insert a soft return, hold down the Shift key, and press Return. To delete it, place your cursor to the left of it, and press the Delete or Del key.

1.5 Saving, Closing, Opening and New

Saving a document creates a copy inside the computer that you can use again at a later date.

1.5.1 Saving a Document for the First Time

1 *Click on the File menu*

2 *Click Save*

Or just click on the Save icon

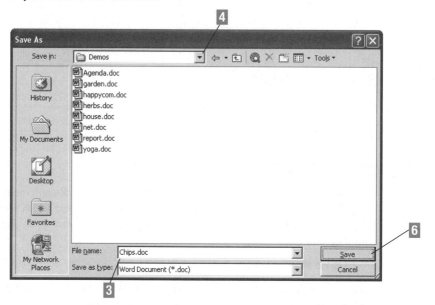

3 *Type in your filename*

- *You do not need to click into the Filename box if the name is highlighted in blue*

- *You can have up to 255 letters*

- *Ensure that your filename is relevant to the document*

4 *Click the drop down arrow in the Save in box*

5 *Click the drive/folder you wish to save into*

6 *Click on Save*

or

Press Enter

How do I know the document has been saved?

You should be able to see the filename you have given the document on the blue title bar at the top of the screen.

Word adds the extension .doc to the end of your filename...

This is to distinguish the file as a Word document.

How do I change the filename?

Click into the Filename box and the existing filename should go blue. If you press Delete while it is blue, the filename will disappear, and you can type a new one.

If you cannot get the filename to go blue, just use Delete and Backspace to get rid of the existing filename.

1.5.2 Saving a Document Again After Changes

After you have saved the document for the first time, you must continue to save any changes you make to it. Word does not save your changes automatically.

1 *Click on the File menu*

2 *Click Save*

or

Click on the Save icon – the changes will be saved

You will not be asked to enter a filename or specify the folder you wish to save in

You specified these things when you first saved the document, so Word will just save the document in the same place and with the same filename. If you want to change these things, you must use the **Save As** command from the File menu.

Save regularly!

As you are working on a document, get into the habit of clicking the Save icon every few minutes. This will update the document and protects it if your PC crashes.

1.5.3 Creating a Copy of a Document Using Save As

If you want to create a copy of your document with a different name or in a different folder, you can use Save As. Your original document will remain intact.

Save As is often used to create a copy onto a floppy disk. Floppy disks are very beneficial as a backup because they can be stored separately from your main computer. They also allow you to take your work to a different computer, if you require.

1 *Click on the File menu*

2 *Click Save As*

3 *If required, type in a name for the document next to Filename*

4 *Click on the drop down arrow next to the Save in box*

5 *Choose a location to save into*

6 *Click on Save*

or

Press Enter

Word uses the last folder you saved into…

When you first use Save As, the Save in box will show you the last folder you saved into.

If I make changes – where will they be saved?

When you use Save As and type a different filename, you are creating a copy. If you make any changes, and then click on Save, only the version you are working on will change.

1.5.4 Closing Documents

Closing a document takes it off the screen and files it away inside the computer if it is to be saved, or gets rid of it if it is not to be saved.

1 *Click on the File menu*

2 *Click Close*

or

Click on the lower X at the top right hand side of the screen – the grey and black one, not the red and white one!

The screen has gone grey and I can't use the menus or toolbars

This means that you have closed all documents, which is a bit like having an empty desk. You can't use menus and toolbars because there is no piece of paper for the commands to be carried out on. Start a new document, or open one that you have already created.

Did you remember to save?

If you have made changes to a document and forgotten to save them, Word will prompt you and ask if you would like to save when you close. If you do not want to save, just click No.

1.5.5 Opening Documents

You can only open documents which you have saved previously…

1 *Click on the File menu*

2 *Click Open*

or

Click on the Open icon

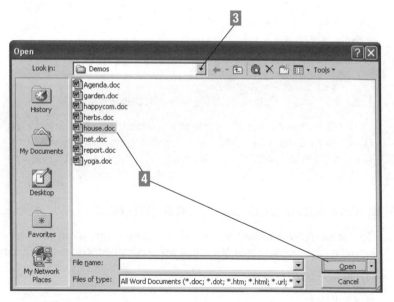

3 *If required, click the drop down arrow next to the Look in box to change the folder Word is looking in*

4 *Double click on the name of the file to be opened*

or

Click on the name of the file to be opened

Click Open

When I double click the file name, a box appears around it and a cursor starts flashing

It's very easy to just miss doing a double click and end up performing two single clicks. This signifies to Word that you want to rename the document rather than open it! Just press the Escape (Esc) key on the keyboard, or click into a white space to go back to normal.

You can open more than one file at a time

You can select and open as many files as you want in one go. To select more than one file, click the first file, then hold down Control whilst you click on the others. Then just press Enter or Return!

1.5.6 Creating New Documents

1 *Click on the File menu*

2 *Click New*

3 *Click Blank Document from the Task Pane on the right*

or

Click on the New Document icon

New

🗋 Blank Document

3

How do I know I've created a new document?

Look at the blue title bar at the top of the screen. Your filename should be something like Document 1, Document 2, etc., and you should be able to see a blank white space to start typing in the middle of the screen.

1.5.7 Creating New Documents Based on a Template

Templates give you a head-start in creating documents. When you create a new document based on a template, some of the text will already be there and you just have to fill in the rest.

[1] *Click on the File menu*

[2] *Click New*

[3] *Click General Templates in the Task Pane on the right*

New from template

📄 General Templates...

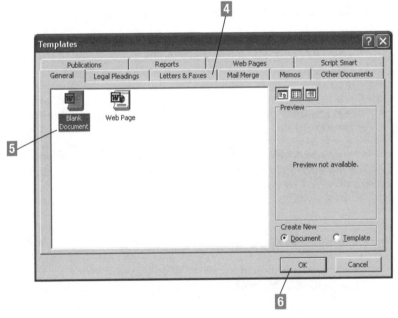

4 *Click on the tab you require, e.g. Letters & Faxes, General, etc.*

5 *Click on the template you wish to use, e.g. Blank Document*

6 *Click OK*

1.6 | Moving Around Documents

1.6.1 Where Am I?

Check the status bar at the bottom left of the screen. It tells you what page you are on, what section you are in and how many pages there are in your document. In the example shown here, you are on page 5, in section 2, and there are 12 pages in the full document.

1.6.2 Using Scroll Bars

■ Scroll bars **do not always move the cursor**. Sometimes they only change what you are **looking** at.

■ There are two scroll bars. The vertical scroll bar will move you up and down, and the horizontal scroll bar will move you left and right.

1.6.3 The Vertical Scroll Bar – Moving Up and Down

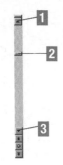

1 *Click and hold down the mouse to move up quickly through the document*
Or

Click repeatedly to move up slowly through the document

2 *Drag the box to move quickly to a certain point in the document. A yellow tip box should appear to tell you which page you are on*

3 *Click and hold down the mouse to move down quickly through the document*
Or

Click repeatedly to move down slowly through the document

1.6.4 Using the Scroll Bar to Move to a Particular Page

Click on the Next Page/Previous Page icon at the bottom of the vertical scroll bar

1 *Move to previous page*

2 *Move to next page*

1.6.5 Using the Horizontal Scroll Bar

1 *Click and hold down the mouse to move quickly to the left*
Or

Click repeatedly to move slowly to the left

2 *Click and drag the bar to move quickly to a certain point across the document*

3 *Click and hold down the mouse to move quickly to the right*

Or

Click repeatedly to move slowly to the right

Everything has disappeared!

If you scroll too far to the right, you may find that all your text disappears. When in Normal view, Word just keeps on going to the right, long past the right hand edge of the page. This means your text will go off the screen. Try scrolling back to the left.

1.6.6 Moving the Cursor Using Shortcut Keys

To go to the following places, press the keys at the same time:

1 To the top of the document | Ctrl | | Home | **1**

2 To the end of the document | Ctrl | | End | **2**

3 To the beginning of a line | Home | **3**

4 To the end of a line | End | **4**

5 Up a page | Ctrl | | Page Up | **5**

6 Down a page | Ctrl | | Page Down | **6**

7 To the previous word | Ctrl | | ← | **7**

8 To the next word | Ctrl | | → | **8**

1.7 Selecting Text

Selection is the way of letting Word know which text you want to work with. If you want to make some text bold, for example, Word doesn't know which text you mean unless you select it. You can use selection to format, move, copy or delete text.

1.7.1 To Select Text

1 *Place your mouse at the start of the text you wish to select – the mouse pointer should look like the I bar shown on the left*

2 *Click and drag over the text – the text will become white, surrounded by black,* **like this**

Smart selection

When you click and drag over text, Word uses smart selection. This means that if you start dragging from the middle of a word and carry on to other words, the beginning of the first word gets selected automatically.

My text has moved around!

If you select text and then release the mouse, it is possible to click back on the selected text and drag it to a different place. You will see a fuzzy grey line appear if this is happening. Click Undo to put it back.

1.7.2 To Deselect Text

Click once into any white space on the right hand side of your document

1.7.3 To Select a Word

Double click on the word

1.7.4 To Select a Sentence

1 *Hold down Control*

2 *Click anywhere in the sentence*

1.7.5 To Select a Line

Click to the left of the line – the cursor will change to a right-pointing white arrow when you are in the right place

1.7.6 To Select a Paragraph

Double click to the left of the paragraph – the cursor will change to a right-pointing white arrow when you are in the right place

Or

Triple click the paragraph (click three times quickly in the paragraph)

1.7.7 Selecting Multiple Words, Lines or Paragraphs

1 *Select in one of the ways described above*

2 *Do not let go of the mouse*

3 *Drag over the rest of the text you wish to select*

You can select pieces of text that are not next to each other…

If you select the first piece of text you require, then hold down Control (Ctrl) and select the next piece of text you require, both will be selected.

1.7.8 To Select the Entire Document

Press Ctrl + A

1.7.9 Selecting Text with the Keyboard

1 *Place the cursor at the start of what you wish to select*

2 *Hold down the Shift key*

3 *Use the Cursor keys to move along the text you wish to select (see page 102)*

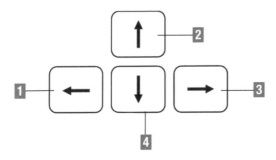

1.7.10 Deselecting with the Keyboard

Press a Cursor key again without holding down Shift

1.8 Using Help in Word

1.8.1 Getting Help

Word comes with a Help feature that lets you ask a question if you get stuck. The Office Assistant no longer exists, but this feature does more or less the same thing. You can see it in the top right hand corner of the Word screen, just under the Minimise/Restore/Close buttons.

Excel, PowerPoint, Access and Outlook all have the same features, so this section applies to them too.

1.8.2 Asking a Question

[1] *Type your question into the Help space provided on the top right of the Word screen*

[2] *Press Enter to display a list of possible topics*

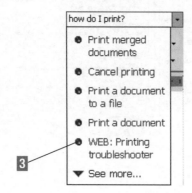

[3] *Click blue circle next to the topic you are interested in to display the answer*

1.8.3 Printing the Answer

From the Help window...

Click Print icon in Help window

1.8.4 Opening Help

[1] *Click on the Help menu*

[2] *Click on Microsoft Word Help*

Or

Press the F1 key

1.8.5 Using the Contents

[1] *Open Help (from the menu, or by pressing F1)*

[2] *Click on the Contents tab*

[3] *Double click a purple book to show the topics inside (or click the plus sign next to it)*

[4] *Click on the topic you want to display – the topic will appear on the right*

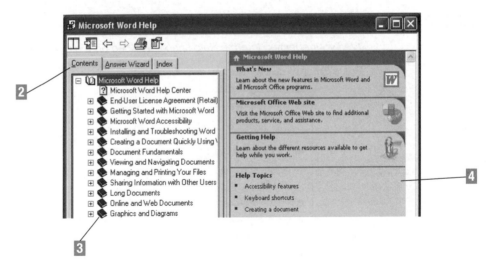

1.8.6 Using the Index

[1] *Open Help (from the menu, or by pressing F1)*

[2] *Click on the Index tab*

[3] *Type in the word you are looking for in box 1, or scroll through the keyword list*

[4] *Double click on the keyword that you need in box 2*

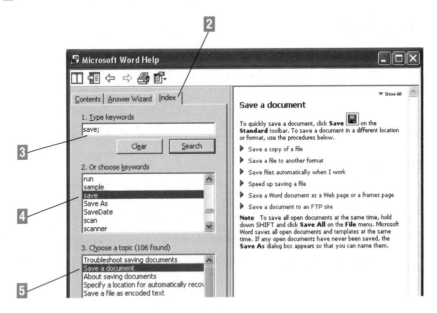

[5] *Click on a topic from the topics found in box 3*

1.8.7 Closing Help

Click on the X at the top right of the Help box

1.9 Correcting Mistakes

1.9.1 Undo and Redo

Word provides 500 levels of undo and redo. This means that not only can you undo the last thing you did, but also the one before that and the one before that and so on up to 500 actions. If you undo something that you didn't mean to, you can redo up to 500 times as well!

1.9.2 Undoing the Last Thing You Did

Click the Undo icon

or

Press Ctrl + Z

1.9.3 Redoing the Last Thing You Undid

Click the Redo icon

or

Press Ctrl + Y

1.9.4 Undoing up to 500 Actions

1 *Click on the drop down arrow next to the Undo button*

2 *Use the scroll bar to scroll to the last action you wish to undo*

3 *Click on the action – all the actions up to and including that one will be undone*

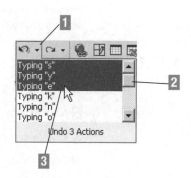

It will undo all of the actions!

You cannot pick out an isolated action from the list and just undo that. If you undo the action you did 10 steps ago, your last 9 steps will be undone as well.

1.9.5 Redoing up to 500 Things You Undid

1 *Click on the down arrow next to the Redo icon*

2 *Scroll to the last action you wish to redo*

3 *Click on the action*

1.9.6 Repeating an Action

Imagine that you have to type the same piece of text several times. Rather than typing it out again and again, you can just use the repeat command!

1. *Carry out the action you wish to repeat, e.g. typing*

2. *Click on the Edit menu*

3. *Click on Repeat Typing*

or

1. *Carry out the action you wish to repeat*

2. *Press Ctrl + Y*

What is the difference between Redo and Repeat?

Redo is used to cancel the effects of an undo. So if you make a mistake and undo your action, you can redo it again!

Repeat is for repeating your last action – it has nothing to do with the Undo command.

1.10 Views

Word provides four different ways of looking at your document depending on the task you are carrying out. Each view allows you to concentrate on a different aspect of your work.

1.10.1 Which View Am I in?

Check which of the view icons at the bottom left of the screen is pushed in

1. *Normal view*

2. *Web layout view*

3. *Outline view*

4. *Print layout view*

1.10.2 Changing the View with the Icons

Click on the icon required from the bottom left of the screen

1.10.3 Changing the View Using the Menu

1. *Click on the View menu*

2. *Click on the view you require*

1.10.4 Why Do I Use Normal View?

- It shows you the text **only**; you cannot see the margins or the way it will look on the page

- At the end of the page you will see a dotted line

- Normal view shows you hidden characters, such as page breaks (see page 152)

- You will not be able to see your headers and footers in Normal view (see page 155)

Use Normal view when you want to concentrate on typing and editing text.

1.10.5 Why Do I Use Print Layout View?

- It shows you the margins and the way it will look on the page

- At the end of a page, you will see a grey gap

- You can only see headers and footers in Print Layout view (see page 155)

- You cannot see hidden characters such as page breaks (see page 152)

This view allows you to see how your document will print while you are working on it.

1.10.6 Why Do I Use Outline View?

- It shows you the structure of a document

- You can move whole segments of text by dragging the relevant headings

- You can collapse a document, so only the main headings are visible

Use Outline view when you want to reorganise a long document.

1.10.7 The Zoom Control

The zoom control allows you to stand up close to your document, or stand back so that you can see more of it. It does not change the size that it will print out at.

To check your current zoom...

Look at the Zoom Control icon on the Standard toolbar

1.10.8 Changing the Zoom

1. *Click the drop down arrow next to Zoom Control icon*

2. *Click on the zoom level you require*

To choose your own percentage...

1. *Click inside the zoom control box*

2. *Delete the text inside using the Delete or Backspace keys*

3. *Type in a new number (you don't need to put the % symbol in)*

4. *Press Return*

Each view has its own zoom

Normal view, Print Layout view and Print Preview all have a separate zoom control.

1.11 Toolbars

You can choose which toolbars you want displayed, depending on what you are doing.

1.11.1 Displaying Toolbars

1 *Click on the View menu*

2 *Click on Toolbars*

3 *Click on the name of the toolbar you want to display*

1.11.2 Hiding Toolbars

1 *Click on the View menu*

2 *Click on Toolbars*

3 *Click on the name of the toolbar you want to hide*

Hidden or displayed?

When you go to the Toolbars submenu on the View menu, you will see a list of all the toolbars which are available in Word. Those which are currently displayed will have a tick next to them.

1.12 Print Preview

Print Preview lets you see what your document will look like when it prints out. You can check for any mistakes before you print it, saving paper, time, money and the world, probably. To see a Print Preview of your document, just click on the Print Preview icon. Or you can click on the File menu, and click Print Preview. The choice, as they say, is yours. Print Preview works the same way in all other Microsoft applications, so whenever you see this icon, you'll know what to do.

1.12.1 The Print Preview Toolbar

When you are in Print Preview you will be able to see the Print Preview toolbar at the top of the screen.

1 Print document

2 Zoom control

3 Show/hide ruler

4 Help

5 Turn magnifier on/off

6 Show one page at a time

7 Show multiple pages

8 Shrink to fit

9 Full screen view

10 Close print preview

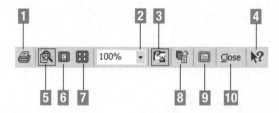

Be careful with Shrink to Fit

Shrink to Fit will shrink your document by one page, which is useful if you have a document that goes just over one page. However, it may make changes that you don't want or expect if you use it on longer documents.

1.12.2 Zooming in on Your Document

1 *Position your mouse at the point on the page where you want to zoom in – the mouse will change to a magnifying glass with a plus sign*

 2 *Click the left mouse button once*

1.12.3 Zooming out of Your Document

1 *Position your mouse over the document where you wish to zoom out – your mouse will change to a magnifying glass with a minus sign*

 2 *Click the left mouse button once*

1.12.4 Closing Print Preview

Click on Close on the Print Preview toolbar

1.13 | Printing

To print a document once, just click on the Print icon. Yes, it's that simple.

Be careful not to click the Print icon more than once!

Sometimes it can take a while for your document to reach the printer and be printed out. If you click on the Print icon again you will get two copies. Some people get impatient and think it hasn't worked, so they click a million times – then they end up with a million copies, and the forests cry.

1.13.1 Printing More Than One Copy

1 *Click on the File menu*

2 *Click on Print*

3 *Change the number of copies to the number you require – click on the up or down arrows in the box next to Number of copies, or just click inside the box and type a new number*

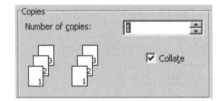

4 *Click OK*

1.13.2 What Does Collate Mean?

This box is ticked by default, but what is it? Well, if you wanted two copies of a three-page file, leave this box ticked. The printer will print pages 1 to 3, then pages 1 to 3 a second time. These copies are "collated". If you untick the box, it will print out both page 1s, then both page 2s, then both page 3s. So, if in doubt, just leave the box ticked.

1.13.3 Printing the Current Page

1 *Click on the File menu*

2 *Click on Print*

3 *Click in the circle next to Current Page*

4 *Click OK*

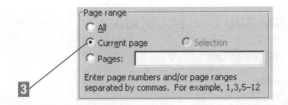

Current page means the page your cursor is on!

You must check that your cursor is on the page you wish to print out. If you have used the scroll bar to move somewhere else, what you see on the screen may not be the page the cursor is on!

1.13.4 Printing Selected Text

1. Select the text you wish to print

2. Click on the File menu

3. Click on Print

4. Click in the circle next to Selection

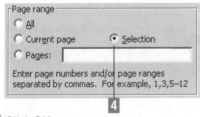

5. Click OK

1.13.5 Printing Certain Pages

1. Click on the File menu

2. Click on Print

3. Type in the pages you require into the Pages box

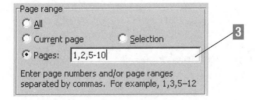

4. Click OK

Individual pages can be separated by a comma, e.g. **1,2.** If you are printing a range of pages, you can use a hyphen – for example, typing in **5–10** will print pages 5, 6, 7, 8, 9 and 10.

1.14   Changing Username and File Locations

1.14.1 Changing Your User Information

⬜1 Click on the Tools menu

⬜2 Click on Options

⬜3 Click on the User Information tab

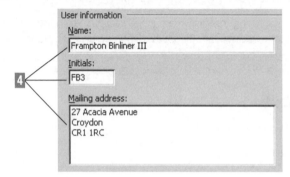

⬛4 Type your name, initials and address into the Name, Initials and Mailing address boxes

⬜5 Click OK

1.14.2 Changing Default File Locations

⬜1 Click on the Tools menu

⬜2 Click on Options

⬜3 Click on the File Locations tab

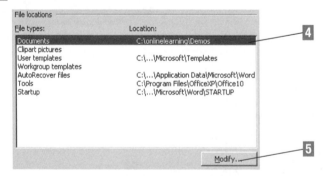

⬛4 Select the file location you wish to change

⬛5 Click on Modify

⬜6 Navigate to the correct folder

⬜7 Click OK

⬜8 Click OK

CHAPTER 2

Formatting Text

What You'll Do

→ Change the Look of Text

→ Align Text

→ Use Special Text Effects

→ Use Fields, Special Characters and Symbols

→ Use Bullets and Numbering

→ Customise Bullets

→ Customise Numbers

→ Indent Text

→ Use Borders and Shading

→ Use Format Painter

→ Change, Copy and Create Styles

→ Create and Insert Hyphens

→ Change Number Formatting

2

2.1 Changing the Look of Text

Changing the look of text is known as **formatting**. Formatting makes your documents look more professional and allows you to give emphasis to the important parts.

2.1.1 Applying Bold, Italic and Underline

1 *Select the text to change*

2 *Click on the icon you require (shown on the right)*

B *I* <u>U</u>

If you want to remove bold, italics or underline, just select the text and click the relevant icon. If you want to remove the bold, just click on the Bold icon and so on.

2.1.2 What is a Font?

A font is the style of the letters in your document. This font is Arial and has a size of 10 points.

This font is Arial, 16 points.

This font is Times New Roman, 10 points.

This font is Times New Roman, 16 points.

`This font is Courier New, 12 points.`

```
This font is Courier New,
18 points.
```

2.1.3 Which Font Am I Using?

1. *Position the cursor inside the text you wish to check*

2. *Check the Font boxes on the Formatting toolbar*

   `Arial ▾  10 ▾`

   In the picture on the right, the font face is Arial and the size is 10

2.1.4 Changing the Font Size

1. *Select the text you wish to change*

2. *Click on the drop down arrow next to the Font Size box*

3. *Click on the size you require – the bigger the number, the bigger the text*

2.1.5 Changing the Font

1. *Select the text you wish to change*

2. *Click on the down arrow next to the Font box*

3. *Click on the font you require*

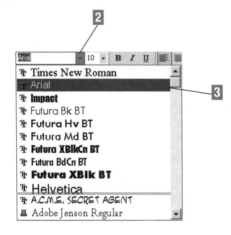

The font names are displayed in the actual font...

...so that you can see what the font looks like before you apply it. If you want to switch this off (or switch it back on if it is already off):

1. Click on the Tools menu
2. Click Customise
3. Click the Options tab
4. Add or remove a tick next to List font names in their font
5. Click Close

2.1.6 Changing Case

1. *Select the text you wish to change the case of*
2. *Click on the Format menu*
3. *Click on Change Case*
4. *Select the case you wish to apply*

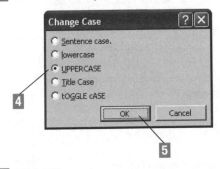

5. *Click OK*

Aligning Text

2.2.1 What is Alignment?

- Alignment decides how your text will line up on the page.

> This is left aligned for normal text
>
> This is centre aligned for headings
>
> This is right aligned for dates
>
> And this is a piece of fully justified text that has straight edges at both sides. It looks very neat and tidy, doesn't it?

- Alignment will change the whole paragraph that your cursor is in. Word thinks that paragraphs are where you have pressed Return, even if it is only a blank line.

2.2.2 Using the Icons

1. *Click into the paragraph you wish to change*

   or

   Select several paragraphs

2. *Click on the icon you require (shown below)*

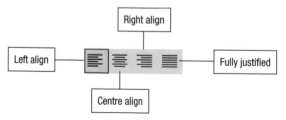

You can change the alignment at any time!

For example, if you have made a piece of text justified, you can left align it by following the instructions above again!

2.3 Special Text Effects

2.3.1 Changing the Underline

1. *Select the text you wish to change*

2. *Click on the Format menu*

3. *Click on Font*

4. *Click on the drop down arrow next to the Underline box*

5. *Click on the Underline option you require*

6. *Click OK*

Watch the Preview box...

The Preview box at the bottom will show you how your text will look, e.g.

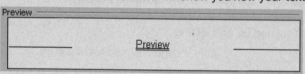

2.3.2 Changing the Text Effects

1. *Select the text you wish to change*

2. *Click on the Format menu*

③ *Click on Font*

④ *Click in the box next to the effect you require*

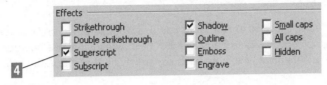

⑤ *Click OK*

When would I use special text effects?

- Use strikethrough to cross out mistakes, or show that something has been done. ~~This is strikethrough~~
- Use superscript to produce smaller characters above the normal letters, e.g. 3^3, 2^2, Trademark^{TM}
- Use subscript to produce smaller characters below the normal letters, e.g. H_2O

2.3.3 Changing Text Colour

① *Select the text you wish to apply the colour to*

② *Click on the Format menu*

③ *Click on Font*

④ *Click the drop down arrow next to the **Font color** box*

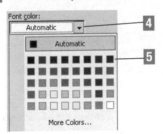

⑤ *Choose a colour by clicking on it*

⑥ *Click OK*

To remove the effect, repeat the above steps, but choose **Automatic** when you get to step 5.

Or

① *Select the text you wish to change*

② *Click the drop down arrow next to the text colour icon*

③ *Click the colour you require*

2.4 Fields, Special Characters and Symbols

2.4.1 What are Fields?

Fields are special codes in Word that you use when information changes automatically – some examples would be a Page Number field, which changes according to what page you are on, or a Date field, which changes constantly so that it always shows the correct date.

2.4.2 Inserting Fields

1 *Click on the Insert menu*

2 *Click on Field*

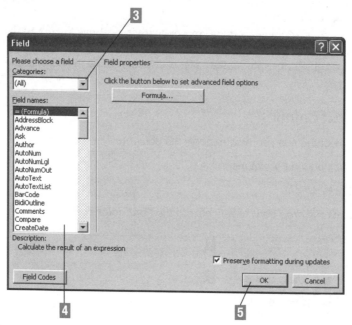

3 *Click on the Category you require from the drop down list at the top*

4 *Choose the Field name you require from the list shown*

5 *Click OK*

2.4.3 Updating Fields

To update a single field...

1 *Select the field you wish to update*

2 *Press F9*

To update all fields...

1. *Click on the Edit menu*

2. *Click on Select All*

3. *Press F9*

2.4.4 Deleting Fields

1. *Select the field you wish to delete*

2. *Press the Delete key*

2.4.5 The Two States of a Field

A field can show either the results of the field or the special codes that describe what the field does. The usual setting is to show the results.

2.4.6 Toggle Field Codes/Results

1. *Select the field*

2. *Press Shift + F9*

   or

   To toggle field codes for all fields, press Alt + F9

2.4.7 Adding Switches to Fields

Switches are optional instructions that modify the format of, or prevent changes to, the information that results from a field. To add a switch to a field, you must first delete the field and reinsert it.

1. *Delete the field you wish to add the switch to*

2. *Click on the Insert menu*

3. *Click on Field*

4. *Choose the field category and name you wish to insert*

5. *Click on Field Codes*

6. *Click on Options*

7. *Choose your field switch – a description of the switch will appear under Description*

8. *Click on Add to Field*

9. *Click OK*

10. *Click OK*

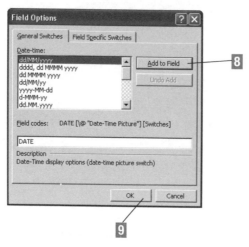

2.4.8 Inserting Symbols

Symbols can be particularly useful for foreign words and names containing accented letters that don't exist in English.

1 *Position the cursor where you require the symbol*

2 *Click on the Insert menu*

3 *Click on Symbol*

4 *Click on the Symbols tab*

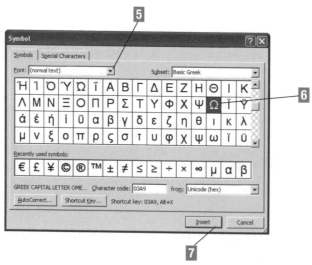

5 *Choose the font to use from the drop down list next to Font*

6 *Click on the symbol you want to insert*

7 *Click on Insert*

8 *Click on Close*

2.4.9 Creating Shortcut Keys for Symbols

1. Click on the Insert menu

2. Click on Symbol

3. Click on the Symbols tab

4. Choose the font and symbol you require a shortcut key for

5. Click on Shortcut Key

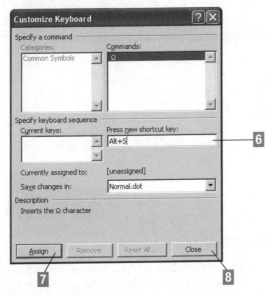

6. Press the shortcut key(s) you wish to use

7. Click on Assign

8. Click on Close

2.4.10 Inserting Special Characters

As well as providing special characters such as © or ™, this is also useful for different types of spaces between words.

1. Click on the Insert menu

2. Click on Symbol

3. Click on the Special Characters tab

4. Choose the special character you require

5. Click Insert

6. Click Close

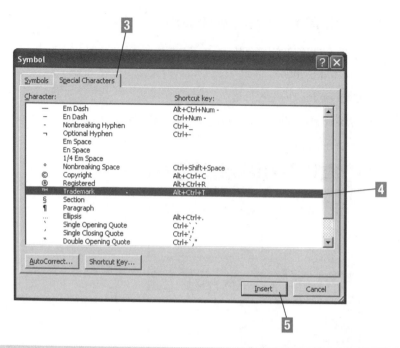

2.5 Bullets and Numbering

2.5.1 Bulleted and Numbered Lists

Bulleted and numbered lists are basically just lists. Bulleted lists have little symbols or "bullets" at the start of the lines, and numbered ones have – can you guess, boys and girls? – numbers. The entries in a list are often called "points".

- This is
- A bulleted
- List

[1] And this is

[2] A numbered

[3] List

Word will create these lists automatically for you, if you ask it nicely.

2.5.2 Creating a Simple Bulleted or Numbered List

[1] *Position your cursor where you would like to start the list*

[2] *Click the Bullets or Numbers icon*

[3] *Type your first point*

[4] *Press Return whenever you require a new number or bullet*

2.5.3 Turning Bullets or Numbers Off

Press Return twice

or

1. *Position your cursor in the paragraph where you do not require a bullet or number*
2. *Click the Bullets or Numbers icon again*

2.5.4 Applying Bullets or Numbers to Existing Text

Word will put a number or a bullet wherever there is a paragraph…

1. *Select the text to change*
2. *Click the Bullets or Numbers icon*

Adding extra points in the middle of a numbered list…

1. Place your cursor at the end of the point where you require the new point
2. Press Return – Word will automatically renumber!

2.5.5 Creating Blank Lines in the Middle of a List

Word is programmed to give you a number or a bullet wherever you press the Return key. To get a blank line, don't press Return – enter a soft return instead!

1. *Position your cursor at the end of the point before you require a blank line*
2. *Hold down Shift key and press Return at the same time to create a soft return*
3. *Press Return on its own to get the next number*

2.5.6 Removing Bullets or Numbers

1. *Select the text you wish to remove bullets or numbers from*
2. *Click the Bullets or Numbers icon*

2.6 Customising Bullets

2.6.1 Changing the Style of Bullets

1. *Select the text you want to change*
2. *Click on the Format menu*
3. *Click Bullets and Numbering*
4. *Click on the Bulleted tab if you are not there already*

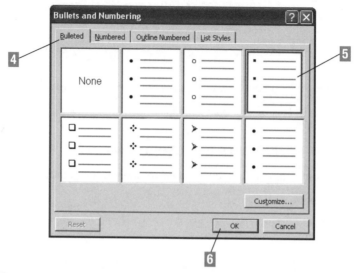

5 Click on the bullet style you require

6 Click OK

2.6.2 Getting Even More Bullet Styles

If the bullet style you require isn't listed…

1 Select the text you want to change

2 Click on the Format menu

3 Click Bullets and Numbering

4 Click on the Bulleted tab if you are not there already

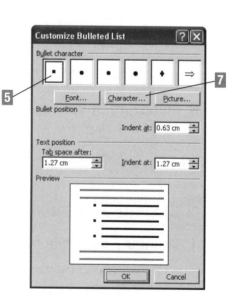

5 Click on an existing style of bullet, if you have not done so already

6 Click Customize

7 Click Character

8 Click on the drop down arrow next to Font and change the font, if required

9 Click on the bullet you require from the grid

10 Click OK

11 Click OK

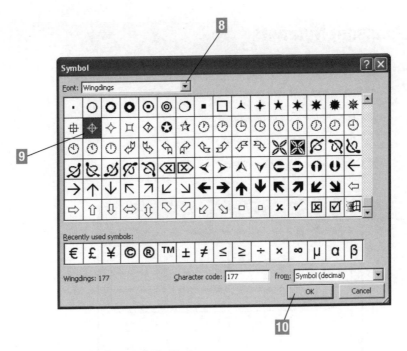

2.6.3 Changing the Indentation of Bullets

[1] Select the text you want to change

[2] Click on the Format menu

[3] Click Bullets and Numbering

[4] Click on the Bulleted tab if you are not there already

[5] Click an existing type of bullet if you have not done so already

[6] Click Customize

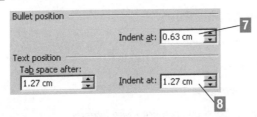

7 To increase or decrease the distance from the margin, change the number in the **Indent at** box under **Bullet position**

8 To increase or decrease the distance between the text and the bullet, change the number in the **Indent at** box under **Text position**

[9] Click OK

2.7 | Customising Numbers

2.7.1 Changing the Number Style

1. *Select the text you want to change*

2. *Click on the Format menu*

3. *Click Bullets and Numbering*

4. *Click on the Numbered tab if you are not there already*

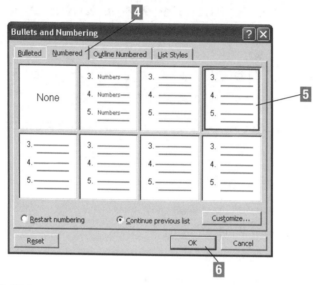

5. *Click on the number style you require*

6. *Click OK*

2.7.2 Changing the Indentation of Numbers

1. *Select the text you want to change*

2. *Click on the Format menu*

3. *Click Bullets and Numbering*

4. *Click on the Numbered tab, if you are not there already*

5. *Click a style of numbers, if you have not done so already*

6. *Click Customize*

7. *Change the number in the **Aligned at** box under **Number position** to increase the distance between the number and the margin*

8. *Change the number in the **Indent at** box under **Text position** to increase the distance between the text and the number*

9. *Click OK*

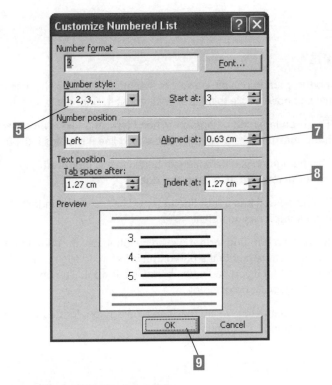

2.7.3 Continue and Restart Numbering

If your numbering does not work correctly and you find that you are getting the wrong number, you can choose to restart it again at 1 or continue a list that you were doing previously.

1. *Click the cursor into the paragraph where you would like to restart or continue numbers*

2. *Click on the Format menu*

3. *Click Bullets and Numbering*

4. *Click on the Numbered tab*

5. *Click in the circle next to* **Restart numbering**

   or

   Click in the circle next to **Continue previous list**

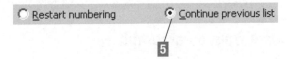

2.8 Indenting Text

2.8.1 What are Indents?

This is a normal paragraph with no sort of indentation whatsoever. It is just straightforward and normal and not a single thing is special about it. Sad, really, isn't it?

This is an indented paragraph. When I type, the text is **indented from the left hand margin**, and when I get to the next line it remains indented.

This paragraph is different again because it is **indented from the left and also from the right**.

This paragraph has a **first line indent**. The first line is indented from the left and the rest of the paragraph has no indent.

And finally here is a **hanging indent**, which we often use for numbers because the first line is normal, but the rest of the paragraph is indented slightly from the left hand side. This means that if you had a numbered list, it would line up nicely. The moral of this story? It's good to be different.

You would use indents to give emphasis to a paragraph, for quotes or for creating numbered or bulleted lists manually.

2.8.2 Indents Affect Paragraphs

Word does not see paragraphs in quite the same way as you would expect. To Word, **a paragraph is wherever you have pressed the Return key**, so even blank lines are paragraphs.

2.8.3 Indenting a Paragraph from the Left

1 *Position your cursor in the paragraph you want to change*

or

Select the paragraphs you wish to change

 2 *Click on the Increase Indent icon*

 You can indent more than once

Every time you click the Increase Indent icon, the text is indented by half an inch more.

2.8.4 Removing the Left Indent from a Paragraph

1 *Position your cursor in the paragraph you want to change*

or

Select the paragraphs you wish to change

 2 *Click on the Decrease Indent icon*

Look closely at the icons...

They look very similar, so make sure you are clicking on the right one. You might expect the Increase Indent icon to be the first one, but it isn't – it's the second one. If you click the wrong one, just click Undo, or the other indent icon.

2.8.5 Understanding the Indent Markers

On the ruler you will see several grey triangles – an upper and lower one on the left, and a lower one on the right. These represent different indents. The top triangle lines up to the first line of the paragraph you are in. The bottom triangle lines up to the rest of the paragraph which you are in, i.e. anything but the first line. If the paragraph you are in is indented from the right hand side, as well as the left, the bottom triangle will be dragged in from the right hand margin.

Indent markers will change depending on which paragraph your cursor is in

If your document has paragraphs with different indents, you must click into the paragraph you require to see the indents it contains.

2.8.6 Indent Markers in Action

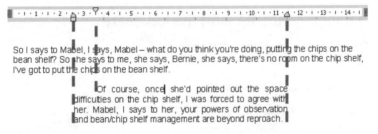

Look at the example above. The cursor is positioned in the middle paragraph, so it is the indents for that paragraph that show on the ruler.

2.8.7 Changing Indents with the Ruler

1 *Position your cursor in the paragraph to change*

or

Select the paragraphs to change

2 *Click and drag the indent marker you require:*

- Drag the top left triangle to move the first line of the paragraph

- Drag the bottom left triangle to move the rest of the paragraph

- Drag the square to move the rest of the paragraph and the first line together
- Drag the bottom right indent marker to indent the right hand side of the paragraph

Set the indents <u>after</u> the paragraphs are typed!

Otherwise the indents you set will affect everything you type afterwards and you will have to change them back again.

2.8.8 Creating a First Line Indent with the Keyboard

1. *Position your cursor at the start of the paragraph*
2. *Press the Tab key*

2.8.9 Creating a Hanging Indent with the Keyboard

1. *Position your cursor in the paragraph to change*

    or

    Select the paragraphs to change
2. *Press Ctrl + T*

2.8.10 Removing Hanging Indents with the Keyboard

1. *Position your cursor in the paragraph to change*

    or

    Select the paragraphs to change
2. *Press Ctrl + Shift + T*

2.9 Borders and Shading

Sometimes you might want to add a bit of colour to a paragraph or maybe a nice border, and there's absolutely nothing wrong with that, in this enlightened day and age. Let's have a look at how to do it.

2.9.1 Adding Shading to Paragraphs

1. *Select the text you want to change*
2. *Click on the Format menu*
3. *Click Borders and Shading*
4. *Click on the Shading tab*

5 *Click on the colour you require*

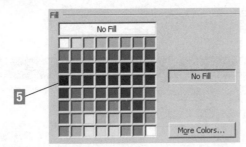

6 *Click OK*

If the colour you require is not available...

1 Click on the More Colors button

2 Click on the Standard tab

3 Click on the colour you require

4 Click OK

5 Click OK

More Colors... ──── 1

What is the shading being applied to?

Check the Apply to box:

This whole paragraph is shaded

Only this text is shaded, but not the paragraph

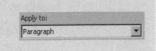
Apply to:
Paragraph

2.9.2 Removing Shading

1 *Select the text you wish to remove shading from*

2 *Click on the Format menu*

3 *Click Borders and Shading*

4 *Click on the Shading tab*

5 *Click No Fill*

6 *Click OK*

2.9.3 Applying Borders to Paragraphs

1 *Select text to apply borders to*

2 *Click on the Format menu*

3 *Click Borders and Shading*

4 *Click on the Borders tab*

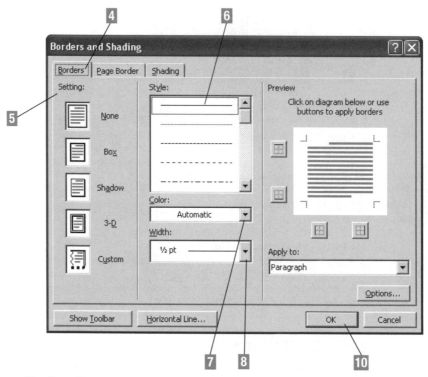

- The Box, Shadow and 3D settings give you a border all the way around your selection

- With the Custom setting, you do not have to have a border all the way around – for example, you can choose just to have a top and bottom border

- The Preview box shows you what your borders will look like

- Click on the border buttons (in and around the Preview box) to specify which borders you require

5 *Choose the setting you require from the left hand side (under Setting)*

6 *If required, choose a different style from the list underneath Style*

7 *If required, click on the down arrow underneath Color and choose a different colour for your border*

8 *If required, click on the down arrow underneath Width and change the width of your border*

9 *If you have chosen Custom settings, click the Borders buttons (in and around the Preview box) to add selected borders*

10 *Click OK*

My styles aren't working...

■ If you can't change the width of the border, you have probably chosen a style which only has one width

■ You can't apply a 3D or Shadow setting unless your border goes all the way around the selection

■ Some styles will not allow you to have a 3D or Shadow setting

2.9.4 Removing Borders

1. *Select the text you wish to remove the borders from*

2. *Click on the Format menu*

3. *Click Borders and Shading*

4. *Click on the Borders tab*

5. *In the Setting area, click on the None box*

6. *Click OK*

2.10 Format Painter

Format Painter provides a quick way of copying formatting, such as borders and shading, to other text in your document. For example, if you had a heading with lots of fancy formatting on it, you could copy those formats in one go and apply them to a different piece of text.

2.10.1 Using Format Painter Once

1. *Select some text that is already formatted*

 2. *Click on the Format Painter icon – a paintbrush appears next to your mouse*

3. *Drag your mouse over the text you wish to copy the formatting to*

2.10.2 Using Format Painter More than Once

1. *Select some text that is already formatted*

2. *Double click on the Format Painter icon – a paintbrush appears next to your mouse*

3. *Drag your mouse over the text you wish to copy the formatting to*

4. *Click on the Format Painter icon again when you have finished*

2.11 Styles

A style is a collection of formats which you can apply to your text. For example all your main headings could be in **Arial, Bold, 16 point and centred**. Taken together these formats would be your **Heading 1 Style**.

Styles are closely connected to the template you are using. Different templates will have different styles.

2.11.1 Why Use Styles?

Styles make working with Word a lot easier. Once you have mastered them you can....

- Format your documents quickly and consistently
- Change the formatting in your documents quickly and consistently
- Use the styles you create in other documents and templates
- Create a Table of Contents
- Use Outline View to work with long documents

2.11.2 Which Style is My Text in?

1 *Position your cursor in the text you wish to check*

2 *Look at the Style box on the formatting toolbar – in the example shown here, the selected text is in the Normal style*

2.11.3 The Styles and Formatting Task Pane

You can use the Styles and Formatting Task Pane to create and use styles more easily. It will show you what styles you have, which are applied, and you can rename or apply them quickly. To display the Styles and Formatting Task Pane...

1 *Click on the Format menu*

2 *Click on Styles and Formatting*

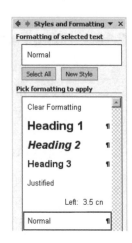

2.11.4 Applying an Existing Style

1 *Position your cursor in the paragraph you wish to change*

or

Select the text you wish to change

2 *Click on the drop down arrow next to the Style box*

3 *Click on the style you require*

Or

[1] *Select the text you wish to change*

[2] *Display the Styles and Formatting Task Pane*

[3] *Click on the style you require*

2.11.5 Changing a Style

[1] *Display the Styles and Formatting Task Pane*

[2] *Hold your mouse over the style you wish to change, and click on the drop down arrow that appears*

[3] *Click Modify*

[4] *Make any formatting changes you require*

[5] *Change the style name in the Name box if required*

[6] *Make sure **Automatically update** is selected*

[7] *Click OK*

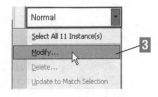

Changing styles will only affect the document you are in

If you open a new document, your new style will not be in there.

2.11.6 Creating a New Style

Type some text and format it as required

The style is created automatically by Office XP. Display the Styles and Formatting Task Pane to see your style in the list.

2.11.7 Copying Styles to the Normal Template with the Organizer

[1] *Open the document you wish to copy the style from*

[2] *Click on the Tools menu*

[3] *Click on Templates and Add-Ins*

[4] *Click on Organizer*

[5] *Click on the Styles tab if you are not there already*

[6] *Ensure that the document you wish to copy from is displayed on the left (see tip on next page)*

[7] *Ensure that the Normal template is displayed on the right (see tip on next page)*

[8] *Click on the style you wish to copy*

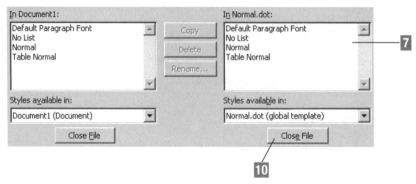

9 Click on Copy

10 Click Close File

How do I make sure the correct documents are displayed?

If the correct documents are not displayed, click on the Close File button, then the Open File button and choose the correct document.

2.12 Hyphenation

A hyphen is something that you use to join certain words together, like co-operate. If the word is near the end of a line, then Word might use it to split the word up, like this: co-operate.

2.12.1 Creating Non-Breaking Hyphens

A non-breaking hyphen does not split at the end of the line. The hyphenated words will always stay together on the same line.

1 Delete the original hyphen if necessary

2 Position your cursor where you require the non-breaking hyphen

3 Press Ctrl + Shift + Hyphen

2.12.2 Creating Optional Hyphens

Use optional hyphens when you have two words that may be split up over two lines. If you insert an optional hyphen between them, a hyphen will appear if they do get split up.

1 Delete the original hyphen if necessary

2 Position your cursor where you require the optional hyphen

3 Press Ctrl + Hyphen

2.12.3 Hyphenation and Justified Text

When you justify text sometimes it gets spread out in an attempt to keep the left and right margins in a straight line. This is particularly true if the text is in columns and contains long words. Hyphenation can be used to get rid of some of the white spaces. (See example below)

When using fully justified text particularly with long words, the text can spread out leaving unattractive white space. Using hyphenation and splitting words up over two lines can alleviate the situation.	When using fully justified text particularly with long words, the text can spread out leaving unattractive white space. Using hyphenation and splitting words up over two lines can alleviate the situation.

The options for avoiding this situation are:

- Typing in hyphens yourself
- Using automatic hyphenation
- Using manual hyphenation

2.12.4 Automatic Hyphenation

This feature inserts the hyphens automatically as you type.

1 *Click on the Tools menu*

2 *Click Language*

3 *Click Hyphenation*

4 *Put a tick in the box next to Automatically hyphenate document*

5 *If necessary, click on the Manual button to view and decide on each hyphen suggestion*

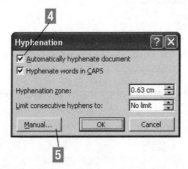

2.12.5 Manual Hyphenation

1 *Position your cursor where you require a hyphen*

2 *Click on the Tools menu*

3 *Click Language*

4 *Click Hyphenation*

5 *Click Manual – Word will suggest hyphens and you can agree or reject each suggestion*

2.12.6 Inserting a Hyphen

1 *Position your cursor where you require a hyphen*

2 *Press the Hyphen key on the keyboard – this is also the minus (–) key, and is between the* **0** *and the* **=** *keys on the top row*

2.13 Page Numbering

Page numbers are a good thing. They tell you what page you are on, and might prevent athlete's foot (though it's not likely). What page are you on now? See? If this book didn't have page numbers, you'd have been completely stumped.

2.13.1 Page Numbering with the Menu

1 *Click on the Insert menu*

2 *Click Page Numbers*

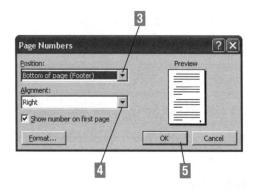

3 *Click the drop down arrow under Position and choose where you would like to put your page numbers*

4 *Click the down arrow underneath Alignment and choose the alignment for your page numbers*

5 *Click OK*

You can only see your page numbers in Print Layout view...

So don't panic if you can't see them, just check what view you're in. See page 117 for more details.

2.13.2 No Numbers on the First Page

If you have a title page on a report, you may wish to remove the numbers from the first page...

1. *Click on the Insert menu*

2. *Click Page Numbers*

3. *Click in the box next to **Show number on first page** so that it is **not** ticked*

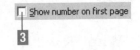

4. *Click OK*

2.13.3 Changing the Format of Page Numbers

1. *Click on the Insert menu*

2. *Click Page Numbers*

3. *Click Format*

4. *Click the drop down arrow next to the Number format box*

5. *Click on the number style you require*

6. *Click OK*

7. *Click OK*

2.13.4 Deleting Page Numbering

1. *Double click on any page number – you will be taken into the Header and Footer view*

2. *Click on top of the number – diagonal lines should appear*

3. *Click on top of the diagonal lines – black boxes should appear*

4. *Press the Delete key on the keyboard*

> **Once you have deleted one page number, all the others will be deleted as well!**

CHAPTER 3

Working with Long Documents

What You'll Do

→ Work with Long Documents

→ Move and Copy Text in Long Documents

→ Create a Page Break

→ Delete a Page Break

→ Change the Margins and Page Setup

→ Change Line Spacing

→ Use Headers and Footers

→ Use Section Breaks

→ Work with Tabs

→ Check Spelling and Grammar

→ Use the Thesaurus

→ Go to a Particular Page

→ Find and Replace Text

→ Proof Your Document

3.1 Moving and Copying Text

Sometimes you might want to move a piece of text somewhere else or copy another piece of text to save yourself from having to type it out again. Word uses the Windows Clipboard to help you do this, which is a special area where copied and cut text goes to. Let's have a look at what this means.

3.1.1 Moving Text

1 *Select the text you would like to move*

2 *Click on the Cut icon – the text is moved to the Windows Clipboard*

3 *Position the cursor in the place you would like to move the text to*

4 *Click on the Paste icon*

3.1.2 Copying Text

1 *Select the text you would like to copy*

2 *Click on the Copy icon – the text is copied to the Windows Clipboard*

⒊ *Position the cursor in the place you would like to copy the text to*

⒋ *Click on the Paste icon*

The cut or copied text remains on the clipboard...

If you click Paste more than once, whatever was last cut or copied will appear again.

3.1.3 Switching Between Documents

⒈ *Click on the Window menu to display a list of open documents*

2 *Click on the document you require*

   or

   Press Ctrl + F6 to cycle through the open documents

   or

   Click on the button for that document on the Taskbar

3

3.1.4 Copying Text Between Documents

⒈ *Open the document you are copying from*

⒉ *Open the document you are copying to – they will appear as icons on the Taskbar*

⒊ *Select the text you would like to copy*

⒋ *Click on Copy*

⒌ *Click on the document you would like to copy to on the Taskbar*

⒍ *Position the cursor where you would like to copy to*

⒎ *Click on Paste*

3.1.5 Copying or Moving More Than One Thing

Word gives you the option of putting lots of things on the clipboard, so that you can copy many separate pieces of text at once.

1 *Select the first piece of text you wish to cut or copy*

⒉ *Click Cut or Copy – the text is sent to the clipboard*

⒊ *Select the second piece of text you wish to cut or copy*

⒋ *Click Cut or Copy – the text is also sent to the clipboard*

⒌ *Click on the Edit menu*

⒍ *Click Office Clipboard – the Clipboard Task Pane will appear*

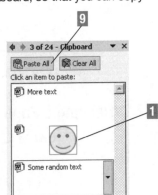

7 *Continue cutting and/or copying up to 24 times*

8 *Position the cursor where you would like to paste the text*

9 *Click on the text in the Task Pane for the text you would like to paste*

or

Click on Paste All to paste everything

Eventually the clipboard will get full up...

Once you have cut or copied 24 pieces of text, the clipboard will get full. Click on the Clear Clipboard icon to empty it.

3.1.6 Copying and Moving Objects

You can copy and move objects – pictures, drawings, charts, and so on – the same way you do with text. The Office Clipboard can be used in the same way.

3.2 Page Breaks

A page break forces Word to end the current page and start a new one. This is useful if you need to start a new page without filling up the page you are on. Sometimes people press Return lots of times to create blank lines to get onto the next page, but this is A Very Bad Thing. If you add text to the page later on, it will push all those blank lines further down, and the next page will have a big gap at the top. The document will look bad, and everyone will laugh at you.

3.2.1 Creating a Page Break

1 *Position the cursor where you would like a page break*

2 *Press Ctrl + Enter*

or

1 *Click on the Insert menu*

2 *Click Break*

3 *Click the circle next to Page Break*

4 *Click OK*

3.2.2 Deleting a Page Break

1 *Make sure you are in Normal view*

2 *Position your cursor on the page break*

3 *Press the Delete or Del key*

3.3.1 Margins

Margins are the gaps between your text and the edge of the page. There are four margins on your page: top, bottom, left and right. Word usually determines their size automatically, but you may want to change them. Here are some of the reasons why...

- If you increase the size of the margins you create more white space on the page. This makes your document more legible and also provides room for people to make notes.

- You may have a document which only has one or two lines on the last page. If you decrease the size of the margins, you create more space for text in the document, and the lines may fit back onto the previous page.

3.3.2 Changing the Margins with the Menu

1 *Click on the File menu*

2 *Click Page Setup*

3 *Change the margins as required*

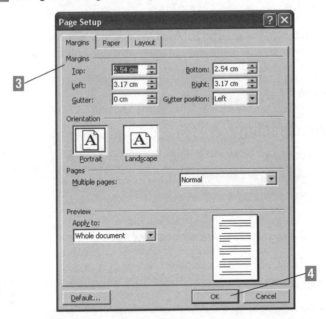

- In the box next to Top, Bottom, Left or Right, use the up or down arrows or type in the size of your new margin.

- If necessary, change the Gutter margin to make room for binding – if you are not sure about this, just ignore it.

- Tick Mirror margins if you are printing on both sides of the paper – again, if you are not sure if you need this, just leave it unticked.

- A preview of your margins is shown on the right hand side of the box.

- Under the preview, look at the box marked Apply to – you can change the margins for the whole document, just the section you are currently in or from that point forward.

4 *Click OK*

3.3.3 Changing the Paper Size

1 *Click on the File menu*

2 *Click Page Setup*

3 *Click on the Paper tab*

4 *Click on the drop down arrow underneath Paper size*

5 *Click on the paper size you require, e.g. A4*

6 *Click OK*

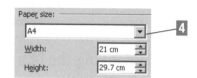

3.4 Line Spacing

Line spacing refers to the spacing between lines, funnily enough. Normally, single line spacing is fine, but sometimes you might want to space text out a bit to make it easier to read.

This is single (1) line spacing.   This is 1.5 line spacing   This is double line spacing

3.4.1 Changing the Line Spacing

1 *Position your cursor in the paragraph you wish to change*

or

Select several paragraphs

or

Press Ctrl + A to select the whole document

2 *Click on the Format menu*

3 *Click Paragraph*

4 *Click on the Line spacing drop down arrow to choose the spacing you require*

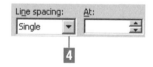

5 *Click OK*

Or

6 *Click on the drop down arrow by the Line Spacing icon and choose one of the spacing options*

3.4.2 Changing the Spacing Around Paragraphs

① *Position your cursor in the paragraph you wish to change*

or

Select several paragraphs

or

Press Ctrl + A to select the whole document

② *Click Format*

③ *Click Paragraph*

④ *Change the options as required in the Spacing section*

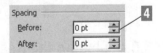

- In the Before box, use the up and down arrows or click inside the box and type the amount of space you require before the paragraph.

- In the After box, use the up and down arrows or click inside the box and type the amount of space you require after the paragraph.

⑤ *Click OK*

3.5 Headers and Footers

Headers and footers appear at the top and bottom of every page. They are usually used to display information such as page numbers, the title of the document, the date, the filename and path, the author's name, etc. If you have something that you want to appear on every page, then the header or footer is the place to put it.

3.5.1 Going into the Header and Footer Area

① *Click on the View menu*

② *Click on Header and Footer*

③ *Position your cursor in the dotted area*

④ *Start typing! What you type will appear on every page of the document*

Or, if you are getting back to Headers and Footers which you have already created…

Double click on the header or footer area on any page

When you are in the Header or Footer, the Header and Footer Toolbar will appear.

3.5.2 Using Headers and Footers

If you want to move to the middle of the header/footer, press the Tab key. Press it again to move to the right hand side. If you are on the header and want to go to the footer (or vice versa), click on the imaginatively named Switch Between Header and Footer icon, which is on the Header and Footer toolbar.

3.5.3 Inserting Items

Position your cursor where you want to insert something. If you want to insert the date or time, click on the **1 Insert Date** icon or the **2 Insert Time** icon. If you want to insert the page number, click on the **3 Insert Page Number** icon. To insert the number of pages, click on the **4 Insert Number of Pages** icon. To add the author, page number and date all in one go, place your cursor at the left of the header or footer, click on the **Insert AutoText** icon on the Header and Footer toolbar, then click on **Author, Page #, Date**.

3.5.4 Closing the Header and Footer View

Click Close on the Header and Footer toolbar

 You can only see headers and footers in Print Layout view!

3.5.5 Setting Alternate Headers and Footers

If your document is going to be printed on both sides of the page, you might want different headers and footers on the odd and even pages to make it look better.

To set alternate headers and footers....

1 *Click on the File menu*

2 *Click on Page Setup*

3 *Click on the Layout tab*

4 *Click in the **Different odd and even** box so that it is ticked*

5 *Click OK*

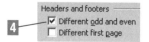

3.5.6 Adding Text into Alternate Headers and Footers

1 *Go to an odd page in your document*

2 *Click on the View menu*

3 *Click on Header and Footer – you will be taken to the Odd Page Header*

4 *Enter any text you require into the Odd Page Header*

5 Click on the Switch Between Header and Footer icon

6 Enter any text you require in the Odd Page Footer

7 Click on the Show Next icon – you will be taken to the Even Page Footer

8 Enter any text you require in the Even Page Footer

9 Click on the Switch Between Header and Footer icon

10 Enter any text you require in the Even Page Header

11 Click on Close

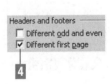

You have now set alternate headers and footers...

All odd pages will have the odd page header and footer, and all even pages will have the even page header and footer. Aren't you clever?

3.5.7 First Page Header and Footer

If you are creating a document which has a title page, you may not want to have headers and footers on the first page.

To change the first page...

1 Click on the File menu

2 Click on Page Setup

3 Click on the Layout tab

4 Tick the **Different first page** box so that it is ticked

5 Click OK

Once you have done that, it's time to change the first page...

1 Position your cursor on the first page

2 Click on the View menu

3 Click on Header and Footer – you will be taken to the First Page Header

④ *Enter or delete any text in the First Page Header*

⑤ *Click on the Switch Between Header and Footer icon*

⑥ *Enter or delete any text in the First Page Footer*

⑦ *Click on Close*

There you go – you now have a different header and footer on your first page. Show all your friends and bask in the glory of their admiration.

3.6 Section Breaks

Section breaks allow you to make the layout of a section of the document different to the rest. So a section can have different margins, orientation, page numbering and headers and footers.

You can have as many sections as you like inside a document and they can all have different layouts.

3.6.1 Page Orientation

The orientation of a page is, basically, which way up it is. Usually the pages in a Word document are in portrait orientation (standing up). However, if you are creating a poster or you wish to display a wide table, you might want to change the orientation to landscape (on its side).

A portrait page

A landscape page

3.6.2 Changing the Orientation from This Point Forward

① *Position your cursor where you wish the new orientation to start, e.g. at the top of the last page.*

② *Click on the File menu*

③ *Click on Page Setup*

④ *Click on the Margins tab*

⑤ *Click on Landscape (or Portrait, if Landscape is already selected)*

⑥ *Click on the drop down arrow under Apply to*

⑦ *Click on This point forward*

⑧ *Click OK*

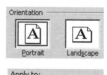

What does "This point forward" mean?

This means that everything after your cursor will be changed.

Very clever – but how does it work? Well, Word has inserted a section break before the landscape part of your document. You now have two sections to your document – one is portrait, the other is landscape.

To see the section break, switch to Normal view and scroll to the point where your pages have become landscape. You will be able to see the portrait text before the section break and the landscape text after the section break.

Portrait Portrait

==Section Break (Next Page)==

Landscape Landscape

3.6.3 Which Section Am I in?

1. *Position your cursor in the part of the document you wish to check*

2. *Check the status bar at the bottom left of the screen*

If you go to the end of the portrait section that you created above, you are in section 1. If you click into the landscape page, you will see that you have gone into section 2.

Page 2	Sec 1	2/5
Page 3	Sec 2	3/5

3.6.4 An Example of Section Breaks – a Document with Portrait and Landscape Pages

Sometimes you cannot use "This point forward", as the page you wish to make landscape is in the middle of two portrait pages. For example if you had a document with four pages and you wanted to make page 3 landscape, you would need to use section breaks, similar to the ones shown in the diagram below. The dotted lines represent the section breaks:

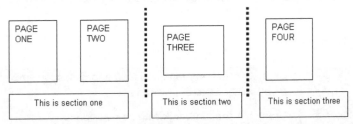

1. *Position the cursor where you would like your first section break – in the example above, it would be at the end of page 2 or the top of page 3*

2. *Click on the Insert menu*

3. Click on Break

4. Choose the type of break you require – in the example above it would be Continuous

5. Click OK

6. Position the cursor where you would like your second section break – in the example above it would be at the bottom of page 3 or the top of page 4

7. Click on the Insert menu

8. Click on Break

9. Choose the type of break you require – in the example above it would be Continuous

10. Click OK – the document now has three sections

11. Position your cursor anywhere inside the section you wish to make landscape (the middle of page 3 is safest) – don't forget, you can check which section you are in from the status bar

12. Click on the File menu

13. Click on Page Setup

14. Click on the Margins tab

15. Click on Landscape

16. Check that the Apply to box says This section

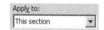

Apply to:
This section

17. Click OK – section 2 will become landscape

The principle of section breaks is always the same

1. Insert section breaks around the part of the document you wish to be different
2. Position the cursor inside the section you wish to be different
3. Make the changes you require to that section

Section breaks can only be seen in Normal view!

You must switch to Normal view if you wish to see the section breaks you have created.

3.6.5 Types of Section Break

Next Page	Creates a section break and a page break, so any text after the section break will go onto a new page
Continuous	Creates a section break with no page break
Even page	Inserts a section break and starts the next section on the next even numbered page
Odd Page	Inserts a section break and starts the next section on the next odd numbered page

3.6.6 Deleting Section Breaks

1️⃣ *Make sure you are in Normal view*

2️⃣ *Position your cursor on the section break*

▐┅┅┅┅┅┅┅┅┅┅┅┅┅┅┅┅┅┅┅┅┅┅┅┅Section Break (Next Page)┅┅┅┅┅┅┅┅┅┅┅┅┅┅┅┅

3️⃣ *Press the Delete key*

3.7 Tabs

Have you ever tried to line text up using the space bar? It may look nice and neat on the screen, but when you print, you'll find that it doesn't line up at all. Instead you should use tabs. There are invisible markers across the page called tab stops. When you press the tab key, your cursor jumps to the next available tab stop. You can then line up text to these tab stops.

You would use tabs:

■ For lining up text on the page

■ For creating neat columns of text or numbers

■ For creating forms with tab leaders (see page 163)

If you want to see tabs, have a look on the ruler – tabs are indicated by small black symbols:

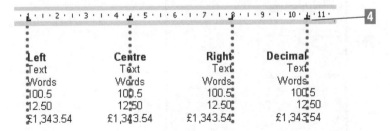

Left	Centre	Right	Decimal
Text	Text	Text	Text
Words	Words	Words	Words
100.5	100.5	100.5	100.5
12.50	12.50	12.50	12.50
£1,343.54	£1,343.54	£1,343.54	£1,343.54

3.7.1 Types of Tabs

1️⃣ **Left tab** (the start of the text will line up to the tab stop)

2️⃣ **Centre tab** (text will line up around the centre of the tab stop)

3️⃣ **Right Tab** (the end of the text will line up to the tab stop)

4️⃣ **Decimal tab** (the decimal point in figures will line up to the tab stop)

3.7.2 Lining Text up with Tabs

Press the Tab key, and the cursor will jump to the next tab stop

3.7.3 Moving Tabs with the Ruler

⌐1⌐ *Select all the paragraphs that are affected by this tab*

⌐2⌐ *Position your mouse on the tab mark at the bottom of the ruler*

⌐3⌐ *Click and drag it to the new position*

3.7.4 Removing Tabs with the Ruler

⌐1⌐ *Select all the paragraphs you wish to remove this tab from*

⌐2⌐ *Click on the tab mark at the bottom of the ruler*

⌐3⌐ *Drag down off the ruler*

3.7.5 Removing Tabs Using the Menu

⌐1⌐ *Click on the Format menu*

⌐2⌐ *Click Tabs*

3 *Click on the tab position to be deleted*

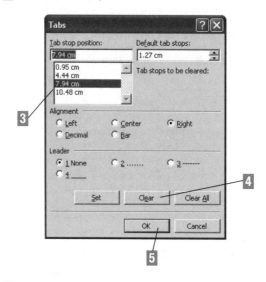

4 *Click Clear*

5 *Click OK*

3.7.6 Setting Your Own Tabs

⌐1⌐ *Click into the paragraph where you require the tab*

⌐2⌐ *Click on the Format menu*

⌐3⌐ *Click Tabs*

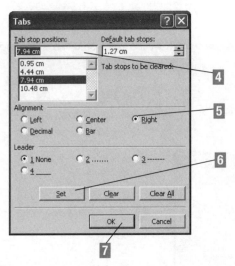

4 *Type in the position of the tab underneath **Tab stop position***:

5 *Click the circle next to the alignment you require*

6 *Click Set*

7 *Click OK*

Or

1 *Click into the paragraph where you require the tab*

2 *Click on the tab type selector on the top left of the ruler until it displays the type of tab you require (see page 161)*

3 *Position the mouse between the grey and white on the ruler where you wish the tab stop to be*

4 *Click once*

3.7.7 Tab Leaders

Tab leaders let you create complex, perfectly lined up dotted lines like this:

Name.. ....
Address... Birth date ....
.... Age..
.... Marital Status..
.... Occupation ....

There are three types of tab leaders:

Dotted ....
Dashed --
Lined _____

3.7.8 Setting Tab Leaders

⌐1¬ *Position your cursor in the paragraph where you would like a tab leader*

or

Select several paragraphs

⌐2¬ *Click on the Format menu*

⌐3¬ *Click Tabs*

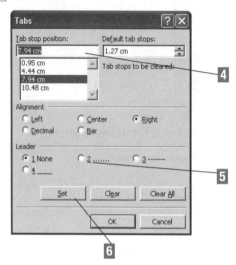

4 Type the position for the tab underneath **Tab stop position**

or

Click on an existing tab from the list on the left hand side

5 Click in the circle next to the tab leader style you require

6 Click Set

⌐7¬ *Click OK*

To use your tab leaders, type the text you require on the left hand side, and then just press the Tab key – the dots will fill in the gap up to the next tab stop.

3.7.9 What Difference Does the Tab Type Make to a Tab Leader?

```
..................................................................This is a left tab at 7cm with a leader
............This is a right tab at 7cm with a leader
.........................................This is a centre tab at 7cm with a leader
...................................................................£1.00, this is a decimal tab at 7cm with a leader
```

Nobody's perfect – even the best of us makes the odd spelling mistake now and again. Luckily, we can get Word to check the spelling of our documents for us.

1 *Click on the Spell Check icon*

- A word highlighted in red inside the white box at the top indicates a misspelling – just above this, Word says what it thinks is wrong (e.g. Not in Dictionary)

- A word or sentence highlighted in green at the top indicates a grammatical error

- In the Suggestions box, Word offers you some words to choose from that might be correct

- On the right hand side, there are buttons that let you change the spelling, ignore the word, and so on – see the next page for more on these

2 *Click on the appropriate icon on the right hand side*

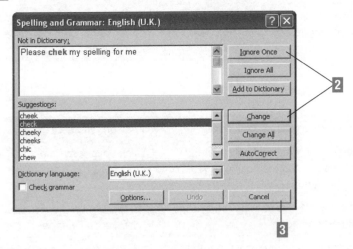

3 *Click Cancel to finish the spell check early*

or

Click OK once the spell check is complete

Word is not perfect!

Don't just casually let Word change whatever it likes – keep an eye on it, otherwise it will try to change someone's name, use American spellings, or mess up all your grammar.

3.8.1 How to Correct Your Mistakes with the Spell Check Buttons

Spelling Corrections

If the word is spelt correctly	*Click on Ignore Once*
If the word is spelt correctly and occurs several times in the document	*Click on Ignore All*
If the word is spelt correctly and is a word that you use very commonly, e.g. your name	*Click on Add to Dictionary* *This will add the word to the dictionary so that it is never seen as a misspelling again*
If the correct spelling is listed in the Suggestions box	1. *Click on the correct suggestion* 2. *Click on Change*
If the correct spelling is listed in the Suggestions box and the misspelling occurs commonly in the document	1. *Click on the correct suggestion* 2. *Click on Change All*
If the word is spelt incorrectly and the correct suggestion is not listed	1. *Click into the white box containing the text* 2. *Make the correction manually* 3. *Click on Change*

Grammar Corrections

If there is no grammatical error	*Click on Ignore Once*
If there is no grammatical error and similar sentences appear in the rest of your document	*Click on Ignore Rule*
If the correct grammar appears in the Suggestions box	1. *Highlight the correct suggestion* 2. *Click on Change*
If the grammar is incorrect, but the correct suggestion does not appear	1. *Click into the white box containing the text* 3. *Make the correction manually* 4. *Click on Change*

Quick spelling and grammar check

When you are typing the document, sometimes you will see that Word has put red or green squiggly lines under some of the words. Right click any of these words and a shortcut menu of suggested corrections will appear.

If you have the American dictionary...

Try clicking on Tools, Language, Set Language, English (UK), OK.

3.8.2 The Thesaurus

If you keep using the same word over and over, the thesaurus will help you to find other words that mean the same thing. This makes your documents look really attractive, appealing, remarkable, out of the ordinary, and fascinating. Do you see what I did there? I used the thesaurus for comic effect.

To change a word using the thesaurus:

1 *Select the word you wish to change*

2 *Click on the Tools menu*

3 *Click Language*

4 *Click Thesaurus*

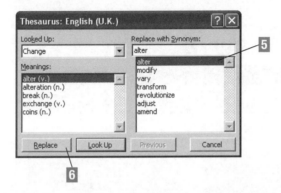

5 *Click on the word you prefer on the right hand side*

6 *Click on Replace*

3.9 Go To, Find and Replace

It's fairly easy to work out what these three tools do, but I'm going to explain them anyway. Go To lets you go to a page or section. Find lets you find text. Replace lets you replace text. It's as simple as that, really.

3.9.1 Going to a Page

1 *Press Ctrl + G to make the Go To box appear*

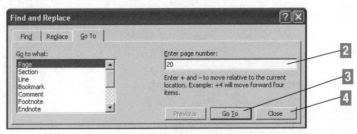

2 *Type in the page number you require in the box underneath **Enter page number***

3 *Click the Go To button – Word will move to the top of the page you typed in*

4 *Click Close*

Closing the Go To box...

The Go To box does not disappear once it has gone to the correct page. You must close it by clicking on the Close button.

3.9.2 Finding Text

1 *Click on the Edit menu*

2 *Click on Find*

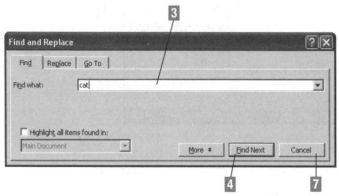

3 *Type in the word you require in the box next to **Find what***

4 *Click on the **Find Next** button – Word will highlight the first occurrence of the word in the background*

5 *Click on **Find Next** again – Word will highlight the second occurrence in the background etc.*

When Word has found all occurrences it will display the message "Word has finished searching the document"

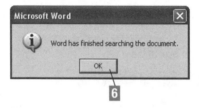

6 *Click OK*

7 *Click on Cancel to close the dialog box*

3.9.3 Replacing Text

> [1] *Click on the Edit menu*

> [2] *Click on Replace*

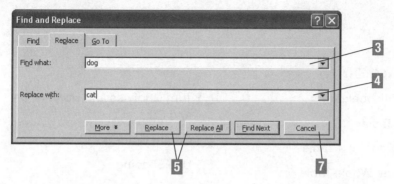

> [3] *Type the word you wish to replace in the box next to* **Find what**

> [4] *Type the word you wish to replace it with in the box next to* **Replace with**

> [5] *Click on* **Replace All** *to replace all occurrences at once*
>
> *or*
>
> *Click on* **Replace** *to replace the first occurrence*
>
> *Click on* **Replace** *again to replace the second occurrence etc.*
>
> *When Word has finished it will display a message saying that it has completed its search, and tells you how many replacements it has made*

> [6] *Click OK*

> [7] *Click Cancel to close the dialog box*

3.10 Proofing

3.10.1 Proofing Your Document

Before you print your document, or even show it to anyone, it is a good idea to check over it. Make sure it is readable, laid out correctly, and will print properly. Some things to look out for are:

- Fonts – are the fonts a reasonable size? Is one line much bigger than the next one? Are any lines too small to read easily?

- Margins – margins should be about 2.5cm (1 inch) on each side. Too much, and you won't fit much text in; too little, and it might not all get printed properly

- Spelling and grammar – make sure there are no spelling or grammar mistakes

CHAPTER 4

Tables

What You'll Do

→ Work with Tables

→ Create Tables

→ Select Parts of a Table

→ Select the Whole Table

→ Insert and Delete Rows and Columns

→ Resize Rows

→ Resize Columns

→ Move and Resize Tables

→ Turn Gridlines and Borders On and Off

→ Create Borders

→ Use Shading

→ Merge and Split Cells

→ Split a Table

→ AutoFormat a Table

→ Applying Special Formats to a Table

4.1 Creating and Editing Tables

Tables are little boxes divided up into smaller boxes, that help you to arrange text in a certain way. They look something like this:

Tables	Let	You
Line	Up	Things

4.1.1 Creating a Table with the Icon

1 *Position the cursor where you would like the table to be*

2 *Click on the Table icon, and* **hold down the mouse button** – *a set of boxes will appear just under the icon*

3 *Still holding the mouse button down, click and drag over the number of columns and rows you require*

4 *Once you have the size you require, release the mouse button*

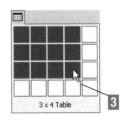

3 x 4 Table

3

4.1.2 Creating a Table with the Menu

This is useful if you require a large table…

☐1 *Position cursor where you require a table*

☐2 *Click on the Table menu*

☐3 *Click on the Insert submenu*

☐4 *Click Table*

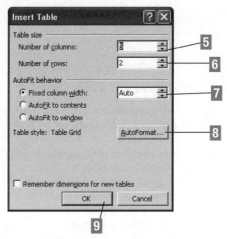

☐5 *Type in the number of columns you require (or use the up and down arrows)*

☐6 *Type in the number of rows you require (or use the up and down arrows)*

☐7 *Change the AutoFit options as required*

☐8 *If required, click AutoFormat to choose a preset format for your table*

☐9 *Click OK*

4.1.3 The Parts of a Table

A table has three parts: cells, rows and columns:

This is a cell   **This is a row**   **This is a column**

4.1.4 The Tables and Borders Toolbar

The Tables and Borders toolbar allows you to do common table tasks quickly. To display the toolbar, click on the Tables and Borders icon:  The Tables and Borders toolbar will appear on the screen with the Draw Table icon switched on, but you can click on it to switch it off if you don't need it: Click on the Tables and Borders icon again to hide the toolbar.

 Display the Tables and Borders toolbar...

It is easier to insert rows and columns using the Tables and Borders toolbar

4.1.5 Adding Text to a Table

To add text, position the cursor inside the cell you wish to add text to, and type the text.

Pressing return will increase the height of a row

You cannot use Return to get onto the next row of a table. Return will just increase the height of the row you are in.

You can move around with the keyboard using these keys:

TAB	Moves to the next cell
SHIFT + TAB	Takes you to the previous cell
↑	Up a row
↓	Down a row
←	Left a cell
→	Right a cell

If you want to move around with the mouse, just click into the cell you require. The mouse must look like the I bar just before you click.

4.2 Selecting Parts of a Table

In order to work with tables, you must know how to select the different parts. Selection will allow you to:

- Format parts of the table
- Delete parts of the table
- Add extra rows and columns

4.2.1 Selecting Cells

1 *Click at the bottom left corner of the cell – the mouse changes to a black arrow*

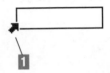

2 *Click and drag to select more cells*

Or

1 *Position the cursor at the start of the text inside the first cell*

2 *Hold down the Shift key*

3 *Press End*

4 *Press End again to select the cell to the right*

or

Press arrow keys to select adjoining cells

4.2.2 Selecting Rows

1 *Position the mouse outside the table to the left of the row – it will change to a white arrow*

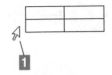

2 *Click the left mouse button*

or

Click and drag to select several rows

Or

1 *Click anywhere in the row you want to select*

2 *Click on the Table menu*

3 *Click on Select*

4 *Click Row*

4.2.3 Selecting Columns

1 *Position the mouse above the column. It will change to a black down arrow*

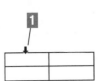

2 *Click the left mouse button*

or

Click and drag to select several columns

Or

1 *Click anywhere in the column to select*

2 *Click on the Table menu*

3 *Click on Select*

4 *Click Column*

4.2.4 Selecting the Whole Table

1. Click inside the table
2. Click on the Table menu
3. Click Select
4. Click Table

Or

1. Hold down the Alt key
2. Double click inside the table when the mouse looks like an I bar

Or

1. Hover the mouse pointer over the table
2. Click on the small box that appears over the top left of the table

4.3 Inserting and Deleting Rows and Columns

 Display the Tables and Borders toolbar before you do this…

It is easier to insert rows with the Insert icon on the Tables and Borders toolbar. This icon changes shape depending on your last action. It will look like this to start with:

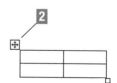

4.3.1 Inserting Rows

To insert a row at the bottom of the table…

1. Position your cursor in the last cell
2. Press the Tab key

To insert a row somewhere else in the table…

1. Position the cursor in the row above or below where you require a new one
2. Click the down arrow next to the Insert icon
3. Click Insert Rows Above

   or

   Click Insert Rows Below

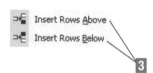

4.3.2 Inserting Several New Rows

e.g. Inserting six new rows

1. Select six rows above or below where you require six new ones

2. Click the down arrow next to the Insert icon

3. Click Insert Rows Above

   or

   Click Insert Rows Below – six new rows will be inserted

Adjust the number from six to the number of rows you require.

4.3.3 Inserting a New Column

1. Click inside the column next to where you require a new one

2. Click the down arrow next to the Insert icon

3. Click Insert Columns to the Left

   or

   Click Insert Columns to the Right

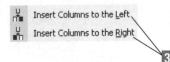

4.3.4 Inserting Several New Columns

e.g. Inserting six new columns

1. Select six columns next to where you require six new ones

2. Click the down arrow next to the Insert icon

3. Click Insert Columns to the Left

   or

   Click Insert Columns to the Right

Adjust the number from six to the number of columns you require.

4.3.5 Deleting Rows and Columns

1. Click inside the row/column to delete

   or

   Select several rows/columns to delete

2. Click on the Table menu

3. Click Delete

4. Click Rows

   or

   Click Columns

4.4 Resizing Rows

4.4.1 Changing Row Height with the Mouse

If your rows are too big or small, just resize them. Here's how:

[1] *Make sure you are in Print Layout view*

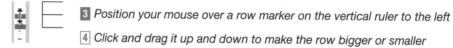 [2] *Position the mouse at the bottom border of the row you wish to resize, until the mouse pointer changes to a double headed arrow*

[3] *Click and drag to the right or left to make the row bigger or smaller*

Or

[1] *Make sure you are in Print Layout view*

[2] *Click inside the table*

[3] *Position your mouse over a row marker on the vertical ruler to the left*

[4] *Click and drag it up and down to make the row bigger or smaller*

4.4.2 Using Table Properties for Rows

[1] *Click inside the row you want to resize*

   or

   Select several rows

[2] *Click on the Table menu*

[3] *Click Table Properties*

[4] *Click on the Row tab*

[5] *Click inside the box next to Specify height*

[6] *Change the measurement to the size you require*

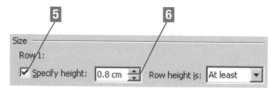

[7] *Click OK*

4.4.3 Putting Space Around Text

You can put extra space around the text in a table to make it easier to read:

[1] *Select the rows you wish to change*

[2] *Click on the Format menu*

3 *Click Paragraph*

4 *Specify a Space Before and a Space After in the appropriate boxes*

5 *Click OK*

4.4.4 Distributing Rows Evenly

After fiddling about with your rows, you might want to make them all the same height. To do this, simply select the rows you want to make even, then click on the **Distribute Rows Evenly** icon on the Tables and Borders toolbar.

4.5 Resizing Columns

4.5.1 Changing Column Widths with the Mouse

1 *Position the mouse between the border of two columns until the mouse pointer changes to a double headed arrow*

2 *Click and drag to the right or left to make the column bigger or smaller*

Or

1 *Click inside the table*

2 *Position your mouse over a column marker on the horizontal ruler at the top*

3 *Click and drag to make the column bigger or smaller*

Be careful not to select any cells!

If you have any cells selected whilst you click and drag you will only resize that cell rather than the whole column.

If you are resizing the far right hand column, you may accidentally select the end of the row marker (see image), which can lead to the same problem!

4.5.2 Using the Keyboard and the Mouse

- Holding down the **Shift** key while you drag means that only the column to the left will change its width.

- Holding down **Ctrl** and **Shift** while you drag means that the overall width of the table stays the same.

- Holding down **Alt** while you drag will show you the measurements as they change in the ruler area.

4.5.3 Using Table Properties for Columns

1. *Click inside the column you wish to change*

   or

   Select several columns that you want to change

2. *Click on the Table menu*

3. *Click Table Properties*

4. *Click on the Column tab*

5. *Tick the box next to Preferred width*

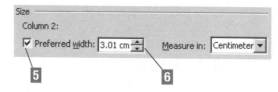

6. *Type in the width you require*

7. *Click OK*

4.5.4 Fitting Columns on the Page

1. *Click inside the table*

2. *Click on the Table menu*

3. *Click AutoFit*

4. *Choose the AutoFit option you require:*

AutoFit to Contents   Makes the columns as wide as the text they contain

AutoFit to Window   Makes the whole table as wide as the page

4.5.5 Distributing Columns Evenly

If your columns are all different sizes, you might want to make them all the same. Simply select the columns you wish to make even, then click on the **Distribute Columns Evenly** icon.

4.6 Moving and Resizing Tables

4.6.1 Moving the Table

1. *Position the mouse pointer in the middle of the table until a cross appears at the top left (a white box will also appear at the bottom right)*

2. *Move the mouse pointer towards the cross at the top left – you must not take the mouse outside the table or you will lose the cross!*

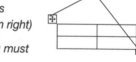

3 *Position the mouse pointer over the cross – it will change to a four headed arrow*

4 *Click and drag the table to a new position*

4.6.2 Resizing the Whole Table

1 *Position the mouse pointer in the middle of the table until a cross appears at the top left (a white box will also appear at the bottom right)*

2 *Move the mouse pointer towards the box at the bottom right – you must not take the mouse outside the table, or you will lose the box!*

3 *Position your mouse pointer over the box – it will change to a double headed arrow*

4 *Click and drag to resize the table*

4.6.3 Changing Text Wrapping Around a Table

Once you have moved or resized the whole table you can make text flow around the edge of it.

1 *Click inside the table*

2 *Click on the Table menu*

3 *Click Table Properties*

4 *Click Table tab*

5 *Click **Around** under **Text wrapping***

6 *Click OK*

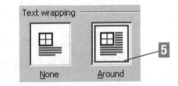

4.6.4 Putting Tables Next to Each Other

Once you have moved or resized tables, you can place them next to each other on the page.

1 *Create your first table*

2 *Resize it using the white box at the bottom right*

3 *Click your cursor underneath the table*

4 *Press Return*

5 *Create your second table*

6 *Resize it using the white box*

7 *Move one of the tables next to the other using the cross at the top right*

Make sure your tables are small enough to fit next to each other on the page!

If your tables are too big to go next to each other, Word will either refuse to place the tables where you require them, or it will put one of the tables inside the other! Word will then refuse to talk to you for a week.

4.6.5 Creating Nested Tables

You can create complicated table layouts by creating tables within tables:

1. *Create your first table*

2. *Position your cursor inside the first table where you would like to create a nested table*

3. *Create a second table to insert the new table*

4.7 Gridlines and Borders

Gridlines and Borders – an explanation

When you first create a table in Word it will have borders around it. **Borders print**. If you do not wish to print borders you can remove them, after which you will see gridlines to show you the structure of the table. **Gridlines do not print**.

4.7.1 Turning Printed Borders Off

1. *Select the whole table*

2. *Click the down arrow next to the Borders icon*

3. *Click the No Borders icon*

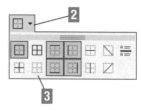

4.7.2 Turning Gridlines On and Off

If you have removed the borders, you will see gridlines in their place. These appear as light grey lines around your table. **They do not print**. To see how your table will print, you can turn the gridlines off.

1. *Click on the Table menu*

2. *Click Hide Gridlines*

To bring gridlines back…

1. *Click on the Table menu*

2. *Click Show Gridlines*

4.8 Borders

4.8.1 Creating Borders Using the Menu

1. *Select the part of the table you wish to add borders to*

2. *Click on the Format menu*

3 *Click Borders and Shading*

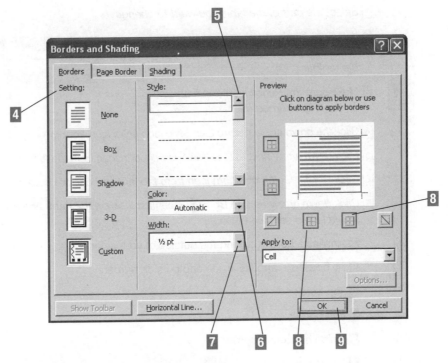

■ The **None** setting removes all borders

■ The **Box** setting gives you a border all the way around your selection

■ The **Shadow** setting lets you add a shadow to the table

■ The **3-D** setting lets you add a 3-dimensional effect

■ With the **Custom** setting, you do not have to have a border all the way around – for example, you can choose just to have a top and bottom border

■ The Preview box shows you what your borders will look like

■ Click on the border buttons (in and around the Preview box) to specify which borders you require

4 *Choose the setting you require from the left hand side (see above)*

5 *If required, click on a different style from the list*

6 *If required, click on the down arrow underneath Color and click a different colour for your border*

7 *If required, click the down arrow underneath Width and click on a different width for your border*

8 *If you have chosen the Custom setting, click the borders buttons to add selected borders (see above)*

9 *Click OK*

4.8.2 Using the Table Toolbar

[1] *Select the part of the table you want to change*

[2] *If it is not displayed already, click on the* **Tables and Borders** *icon to display the toolbar*

[2]

[3] *Make sure the Pencil icon (the first icon on the left) is turned off*

[4] *Click the down arrow next to Line Style icon (third icon from the left) and click style you prefer*

[5] *Click down arrow next to Line Width icon (fourth icon from the left) and click width you prefer*

[6] *Click Border Color icon (fifth icon from the left) and choose colour you prefer*

[7] *Click down arrow next to Borders icon (last icon on the right) and click the borders you would like to set (see below)*

A Applies a border around the outside of your selection

B All borders – applies inside and outside borders

C Top border

D Left border

E Inside horizontal border

F Inside borders

G No borders

H Bottom border

I Right border

J Inside vertical borders

K Applies diagonal borders top left to bottom right through the cells in your selection

L Applies diagonal borders top right to bottom left through the cells in your selection

M Inserts a grey decorative border wherever your cursor is

4.9 Shading

Tables, like paragraphs, can have coloured shading applied to them as well as borders. If you have a complex table, you can make it easier to read by shading parts of it.

4.9.1 Shading Using the Menu

[1] *Select the part of the table you wish to colour in*

[2] *Click on the Format menu*

3 *Click Borders and Shading*

4 *Click the Shading tab*

5 *Click on the colour you require from the grid*

> *or*

> *Click More Colors if the colour you require is not found*

> *or*

> *Click No Fill to remove the shading*

6 *Click OK*

4.9.2 Shading Using the Toolbar

1 *Select the part of the table you wish to colour in*

2 *If it's not displayed already, click the **Tables and Borders** icon to display the Tables and Borders toolbar*

3 *Make sure the Pencil icon is turned off*

4 *Click the drop down arrow next to the Shading icon*

5 *Click on the colour you require*

> *or*

> *Click More Fill Colors if the colour you require is not found*

> *or*

> *Click on No Fill to remove the shading*

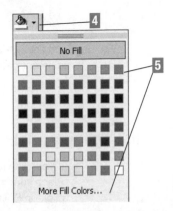

4.10 Merging and Splitting Cells

Got too many cells in your table? Merge some together. Need more cells? Split some up. Let's have a look...

4.10.1 Merging Cells Together

Look at the table below.

This is a heading, but the cell is not merged		

It would look better if the heading in the first cell was spread all across the top of the table, which means merging the cells. Just select the cells you wish to merge (in this case the top three cells), and click the Merge Cells icon on the **Tables and Borders** toolbar.

Or, once you've selected the cells, click on the Table menu and then click on Merge Cells.

This is a heading, but now the cell **is** merged		

4.10.2 Splitting Cells

You can split cells to create extra columns where needed, or split up cells which have been merged. Look at this table:

Age				Gender		Department		
16–20	21–25	26–30	31–40	Male	Female	Finance	Sales	Admin

Originally there were three cells in the bottom row. They have been split up to show the different categories. To split up a cell, select the cell(s) you want to split, and click the Split Cells icon ⊞ on the **Tables and Borders** toolbar. Type in the number of columns and/or rows you need, and click OK.

4.10.3 Splitting a Table

If you wish to create two, or more, separate tables out of one, you can split the table up. Place your cursor in the row below where you require a split, click on the Table menu, and click on Split Table.

4.11   Table AutoFormat

AutoFormat is a quick way of making your table look good. You can choose from a list of fancy table styles, and Word will do all the hard work for you.

4.11.1 AutoFormatting a Table

1 *Click inside the table you want to AutoFormat*

 2 *Click the AutoFormat icon on the Tables and Borders toolbar*
   or
   Click on the Table menu
   Click Table AutoFormat

3 *Click on the format you like in the list at the top left*

4 *Click Apply*

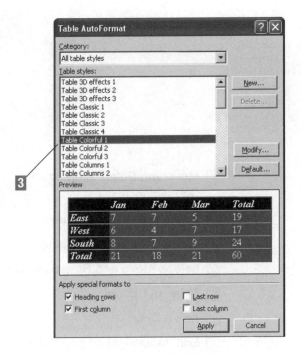

4.11.2 Applying Special Formats

These boxes indicate where AutoFormat will place distinctive formatting for the headings or totals in your table. So if your headings are in the first column, make sure that **First column** is ticked. Click inside the box next to the special format required to add or remove the tick.

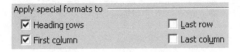

CHAPTER 5

Graphics

What You'll Do

→ Use Graphics

→ Use the Drawing Toolbar

→ Create and Select Shapes

→ Move, Resize and Delete Shapes

→ Format Shapes

→ Add 3D to Shapes

→ Add Text to Shapes

→ Draw a Text Box

→ Move and Delete Shapes Containing Text

→ Insert and Delete Pictures

→ Change the Text Wrapping

→ Select, Move and Resize Pictures

→ Delete a Picture

→ Add a Chart

→ Edit, Move, Resize and Delete a Chart

5.1 Drawing Shapes

5.1.1 The Drawing Toolbar

The Drawing toolbar is what you will use to draw shapes, create fancy pictures, draw lines, create text boxes, do 3D effects, and much more. If it is not displayed...

1 Click on the View menu

2 Click on Toolbars

3 Click on Drawing

5.1.2 Drawing Circles and Squares

1 Click on the shape you require on the Drawing toolbar

2 Release the mouse button

3 Click and drag the shape on the page – the mouse pointer will look like a cross

5.1.3 Drawing AutoShapes

1. *Click on AutoShapes on the Drawing toolbar*

2. *Click on the category you require, e.g. Stars and Banners*

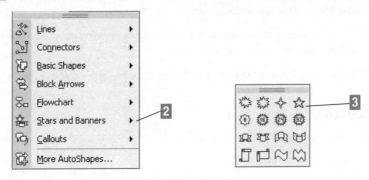

3. *Click on the shape you require*

4. *Click and drag to draw the shape on the page – the mouse will look like a cross*

5.1.4 Drawing Lines and Arrows

1. *Click on the Line or Arrow icon on the Drawing toolbar*

2. *Click and drag to draw the line or arrow on the page – the mouse will look like a cross*

5.1.5 Creating a Perfect Shape or a Straight Line

If you want to create a perfectly square shape, or a perfectly round circle, just hold down the Shift key while you are drawing the shape.

5.1.6 Selecting a Shape

Click once on the shape until white boxes (called "handles") appear around the edge. Click away from the shape to deselect it.

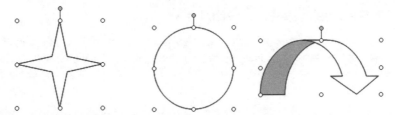

5.1.7 Selecting More Than One Shape

1. *Click on the first shape you want to select*

2. *Hold down the Shift key*

3. *Click on any other shapes you want to select – handles will appear around all selected shapes*

5.1.8 Selecting More Than One Shape with the Select Objects Icon

1. Click on the Select Objects icon on the Drawing toolbar

2. Position the mouse **underneath ALL** the shapes you wish to select and **to the left of ALL** the shapes you wish to select

3. Click and drag over the shapes as if you were drawing a big box to cover them all – a dotted line will appear around them

4. Release the mouse button – handles will appear around the selected shapes

5.1.9 Deleting Shapes

1. Select the shape you wish to delete

2. Press the Delete key

5.1.10 Moving Shapes

1. Select the shape(s) you want to move

2. Position your mouse pointer in the middle of the shapes – the mouse pointer will change to a four headed arrow

3. Click and drag the shape to a new position

5.1.11 Resizing Shapes

1. Select the shape(s) you want to resize

2. Hover the mouse pointer over a handle – the pointer will change to a double headed arrow

3. Click and drag outwards to make the shape bigger

   or

   Click and drag inwards to make the shape smaller

Which handle should I resize from?

Handles at the corner of a selected shape will allow you to resize both the height and the width at the same time. Handles in the middle will allow you to stretch or squash the shape.

5.2 Formatting Shapes

5.2.1 Changing the Fill Colour of Shapes

1. Select the shape(s) you want to change

2. Click on the down arrow next to the Fill Color icon on the Drawing toolbar

[3] *Click on the colour you require*

or

Click on More Fill Colors if the colour you require is not listed

or

Click on No Fill to remove the fill colour

 Getting a choice of colours

You **must** click the arrow next to the Fill Color icon to get a choice of colours. If you click the bucket image, the colour will change to whatever the fill colour is currently set to.

5.2.2 Formatting Lines

[1] *Select the line(s) you want to change*

 [2] *Click on the line style icon you require (shown on the left)*

- The first icon changes the thickness of lines

- The second one makes the lines dotted or dashed

- The third makes the lines into arrows

[3] *Click on the style you require*

5.2.3 Changing the Line Colour

[1] *Select the line(s) you want to change*

 [2] *Click on the down arrow next to the Line Color icon on the Drawing toolbar*

[3] *Click on the colour you require*

or

Click on More Line Colors if the colour you require is not listed

5.3 3D Shapes

Take your lines and shapes into the third dimension with the 3D tools – that sounds more exciting than it actually is, but hey, I'm doing my best here. It looks pretty cool, so who knows, you might even get a little bit excited about it. Maybe. Look at this shape – it's just one of the block arrows from the Basic Shapes AutoShapes, with a blue 3D effect. Isn't it exciting? No? Okay, suit yourself.

5.3.1 Adding 3D

1. *Select the shape(s) you want to change*

2. *Click on the 3D icon on the Drawing toolbar*

3. *Click on the 3D setting you require*

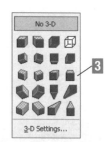

5.3.2 The 3D Toolbar

1. *Select the shape(s) you want to change*

2. *Click on the 3D icon on the Drawing toolbar*

3. *Click on **3D Settings** – the 3D toolbar will appear*

Here is what all those icons do, going from left to right:

- Adds or removes the 3D effect

- Tilt down – rotates the shape forwards

- Tilt up – rotates the shape backwards

- Tilt left – rotates the shape left

- Tilt right – rotates the shape right

- Changes the depth of the 3D effect

- Changes the direction of the 3D effect

- Changes the lighting direction and/or brightness

- Changes the surface texture

- Changes the 3D colour

5.4 Adding Text to Shapes

5.4.1 Adding Text to Shapes

To add text to a shape, simply right-click on it, click on **Add Text** from the little menu that pops up, and start typing. To format the text, just select it and format it as normal. Looks pretty fancy, doesn't it?

5.4.2 Drawing a Text Box

1. *Click on the Text Box icon on the Drawing toolbar*

2. *Click and drag over the page to create the text box, as if you were drawing a normal box*

3. *Type your text into the box*

5.4.3 Deleting Shapes that Contain Text

1. *Click inside the shape – diagonal lines will appear around the border*

2. *Click on the diagonal lines – dotted lines will replace the diagonal lines*

3. *Press the Delete key*

What is the difference between diagonal lines and dotted lines?

Diagonal lines indicate that you are working with the text inside the shape. If you press the Delete key – it only deletes the text, not the shape itself.

Dotted lines indicate that you are working with the whole shape. If you press the Delete key – the whole shape will disappear!

5.4.4 Moving Shapes that Contain Text

Once you have added text to a shape, you cannot move it by dragging from the middle. Instead you need to do this:

1. *Click inside the shape until the diagonal lines appear around the border*

2. *Click on the diagonal lines to make the dotted lines appear around the border*

3. *Position the mouse over the dotted line, NOT the handles*

4. *Click and drag the shape to a new position*

5.5 Adding Graphics

5.5.1 Inserting Pictures

1. *Position the cursor where you would like to insert the picture*

2. *Click the Clip Art icon on the Drawing toolbar*

   or

   Click on the Insert menu

   Click on the Picture submenu

   Click Clip Art – the Clip Art Task Pane will appear

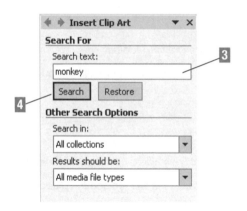

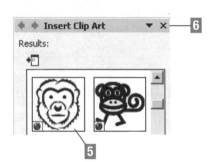

3 *Type the sort of picture you are looking for into the Search box, e.g. monkey*

4 *Click Search – some pictures will be displayed in the Task Pane*

5 *Click on the picture you require to insert it – scroll up and down using the scroll bar if necessary*

6 *Click on the X at the top right of the Clip Art Task Pane to close it*

5.5.2 Deleting Pictures

Click on the picture you want to delete, and press the Delete key.

5.5.3 Inserting Pictures from your Computer

1 *Click on the Insert menu*

2 *Click on the Picture submenu*

3 *Click on From File...*

4 *Change the **Look in** box to the folder where your picture is saved*

5 *Select the picture file you want to insert*

6 *Click Insert*

5.6 Changing the Text Wrapping

5.6.1 Clipart that is in Line with the Text

■ When you first insert a picture it is **in line** with the text. In other words, it is just like a piece of text itself.

■ If you want to move it, you move it just as you would a piece of text using cut and paste, or drag and drop.

■ An in line picture can **not** be put anywhere on the page – only where there is text.

5.6.2 Clipart that Floats Over the Text

If you want the freedom to move the picture anywhere on the page you have to change its text wrapping, so that it floats over the text.

1️⃣ *Select the picture*

2️⃣ *Click on the Format menu*

3️⃣ *Click on Picture*

4️⃣ *Click on the Layout tab*

5️⃣ *Click on a different wrapping style*

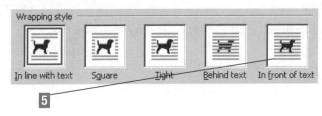

Or, if the Picture toolbar is displayed:

1️⃣ *Select the picture*

2️⃣ *Click on the Text Wrapping icon*

3️⃣ *Click on the text wrapping style you require (any except **In line with text**)*

5.7 Selecting, Moving and Resizing Pictures

5.7.1 Selecting

Select the picture as you would select anything else – click once on the picture. When a picture is selected, handles will appear around the edge (black handles for in line pictures, white handles for pictures that are floating over the text). To deselect the picture, just click away from it.

5.7.2 Moving

A picture which is in line with the text can only be moved in the same way as text. It cannot go anywhere on the page. To move it, click into the middle of the picture, then click and drag to a new location. A fuzzy grey cursor will show you where you are going. To move a picture that is floating over the top of text, click into the middle of it, and drag it to a new location. The mouse pointer should look like a four headed arrow when you are moving it.

5.7.3 Resizing

1️⃣ *Select the picture you want to resize*

2️⃣ *Position the mouse over a handle – the mouse pointer will change to a double headed arrow*

3 *Click and drag outwards to make the picture bigger*

or

Click and drag inwards to make the picture smaller

 Keeping the picture in proportion

If you drag from a corner handle then the picture will stay in proportion. If you drag from a middle handle you will stretch or squash the picture.

5.7.4 Deleting a Picture

Select the picture you want to delete, and press the Delete key.

5.8 Charts

5.8.1 Adding a Chart

1 *Place the cursor where you want the chart to appear*

2 *Click on the Insert menu*

3 *Click on Object*

4 *Click on the Create New tab*

5 *Select Microsoft Graph Chart (or Microsoft Graph 2000 Chart, depending on your installation)*

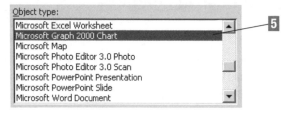

6 *Click OK*

7 *Click anywhere on the page to deselect the chart*

5.8.2 Editing a Chart

1 *Double click on the chart*

2 *Change the figures in the mini spreadsheet*

3 *Click anywhere on the page to deselect the chart*

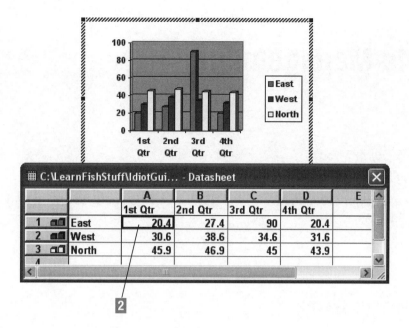

5.8.3 Moving, Resizing and Deleting a Chart

Charts are moved, resized and deleted in the same way as pictures – see the previous section on selecting, moving, resizing and deleting pictures on page 193.

CHAPTER 6

File Management

What You'll Do

→ **Manage Files**

→ **Create a Copy of a Document Using Save As**

→ **Save as a Different Format**

→ **Save a Document as a Web Page**

6.1 Advanced Saving

6.1.1 Creating a Copy of a Document Using Save As

If you need to quickly make a copy of a file you are working on, use the Save As tool. You might want to make a copy if you are testing something, and want to make sure that your original document is safe in case anything goes wrong.

1. *Click on the File menu*

2. *Click on Save As*

3. *If required, type a new name for the document*

4. *If required, change the folder to save the document into*

5. *Click on Save*

6.1.2 Saving as a Different Format

Word documents can be saved in various different formats. Which one you choose depends on what you want to do with the file:

- **RTF** (Rich text format) will allow the file to be opened in programs other than Word.

- **Web Page** (i.e. HTML, Hyper-text markup language) will allow the file to be seen on the World Wide Web (see below).

- **Word 97-2000 & 6.0/95** and **Word 6.0/95** will allow the file to be opened in previous versions of Word.

  1. *Click on the File menu*

  2. *Click Save As*

3 *Click the drop down arrow to the right of the **Save as type** box*

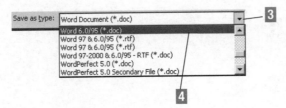

4 *Click on the file type you require*

5 *Click Save*

6.1.3 Saving a Document as a Web Page

This will save your file in HTML format, suitable for viewing on the web.

1 *Open the document you wish to save as a web page*

2 *Click on the File menu*

3 *Click on Save as Web Page*

4 *Type in the filename you require*

5 *Change the folder to save into as required*

6 *Click on Save*

6

CHAPTER 7

Mail Merge

What You'll Do

→ Use Mail Merge

→ Create a Data Document

→ Carry Out a Mail Merge

→ Use the Main Document

→ Mail Merge to Labels

7.1 Mail Merge

Mail Merge is used to send the same letter to lots of different people. Suppose you had 100 people you wanted to send your letter to – you could create the standard letter, and insert a special mail merge code for their name and address. Using a separate file containing all the names and addresses, Word can merge the letter with each name and address, printing out each one.

A Mail Merge always involves three steps...

- Creating the **Data Document** – which contains all the personal information that will change from letter to letter.

- Creating the **Main Document** – which is the letter you are sending.

- **Merging** the Data Document and the Main Document together into individual letters.

Word XP combines the second and third steps into one, using a wizard to make it easier. Once you have created the main document, you have almost finished doing the mail merge.

7.1.1 The Data Document

- The Data Document is laid out in a table.

- In the columns of the table are **fields**, or the types of information that will change from letter to letter. The **field names** are held in the first row.

- In the subsequent rows are the **records**, or the information that will show on each of the letters.

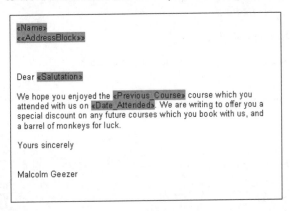

Name	Address	Salutation	Previous Course	Date Attended
Mr Frederick Bloggs	13, Cheese Lane Onion Street London	Mr Bloggs	Word Essentials	12/6/2005
Mrs Bianca Watford	27, Salt Avenue Vinegar Road London	Mrs Watford	Excel Advanced	5/2/2005
Mr Arthur Mitchell	57, Smokey Street Bacon Road London	Mr Mitchell	Access Intermediate	3/1/2005

Field names are held in first row

Records are held in subsequent rows

7.1.2 The Main Document

- The main document contains all the standard text which will not change between letters.

- At the point where information will change, a **merge field** has been inserted, to indicate to Word that it must find the required information in the data document.

> «Name»
> «AddressBlock»
>
>
> Dear «Salutation»
>
> We hope you enjoyed the «Previous_Course» course which you attended with us on «Date_Attended». We are writing to offer you a special discount on any future courses which you book with us, and a barrel of monkeys for luck.
>
> Yours sincerely
>
>
> Malcolm Geezer

7.2 Creating Your Data Document

1. *Create a new, blank document*

2. *Create a table (see page 170)*

    - The number of columns = the number of fields

    - The number of rows = the number of records + 1 (for the field names)

3. *Type the field names into the first row*

4. *Type the records into the subsequent rows*

5. *Save the data document*

6. *Close the data document*

How should the addresses be laid out?

Enter the address as it will be laid out on the letter, with hard returns after each line.

7.3 Carrying Out a Mail Merge

7.3.1 The Main Document

As part of carrying out a merge, you create a Main document. This will look exactly like a normal letter except at the points where information needs to be retrieved from the Data document, where you will see merge fields.

7.3.2 Carrying Out a Merge

[1] *Create a new, blank document*

[2] *Type all of your standard text as normal, leaving blank spaces where you normally type the name, address, etc.*

[3] *Click on the Tools menu*

[4] *Click on Letters and Mailings*

[5] *Click Mail Merge Wizard – the Mail Merge Task Pane will appear*

[6] *Select the type of merge you want to do – normally this will be **Letters***

[7] *Click Next*

[8] *Select Use the current document*

[9] *Click Next*

[10] *Click Browse*

[11] *Change the **Look in** box to the folder where your data document is saved*

[12] *Select your data document*

[13] *Click Open*

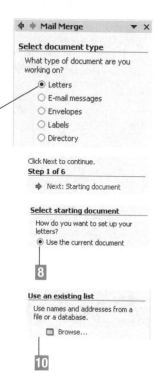

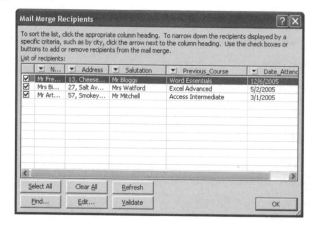

14 *Click OK*

15 *Click Next*

16 *Place the cursor where you want the address to go*

17 *Click Address Block to insert the address*

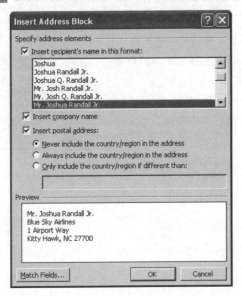

18 *Click OK*

19 *Click **More items** to insert other fields, making sure your cursor is placed where you want the fields to be inserted*

20 *Select the field you wish to insert*

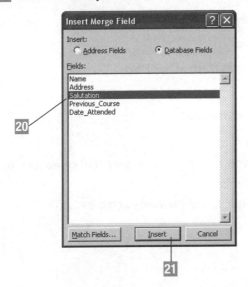

21. Click Insert

22. Click Close

23. Click Next

24. Preview your letters using the arrows – you can click Previous at any time to go back and correct mistakes

25. Click Next

26. Click Print to print the merge, or Edit individual letters to merge to a file

27. Choose the records you wish to merge

28. Click OK

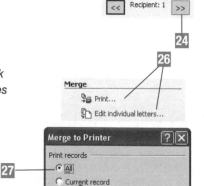

7.4 | Mail Merge to Labels

Creating a Data Document for labels

You can use the same data source for your labels as your letters, as long as it contains fields for the name and address!

7.4.1 Merging to Labels

1. Start a new, blank document

2. Click on the Tools menu

3. Click Letters and Mailings

4. Click Mail Merge Wizard

5. Select Labels from the Mail Merge Task Pane

◉ Labels

6. Click Next

7. Select **Change document layout**

◉ Change document layout

8. Click **Label options**

9. Click on the drop down arrow at the end of the **Label products** box, and click on the label type

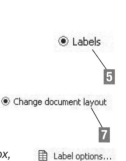

10. Click on the **Product number** of the label you require

11. Click OK

12. Click Next

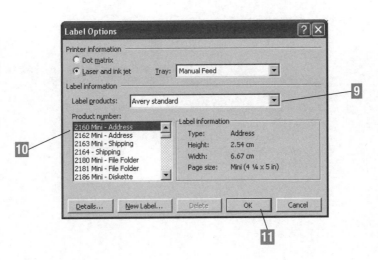

13 Select *Use an existing list*

14 Click *Browse*

15 Change the **Look in** box to the folder where your data document is saved

16 Select the data document

17 Click *Open*

18 Click *OK*

19 Click *Next*

20 Insert the fields you require (see the Carrying Out a Merge section, pages 200–202) into **the first label only**

21 Click *Next*

22 Click **Update all labels** to copy the layout to all of the labels

23 Click *Next*

24 Look through your labels to make sure they are okay, using the arrows as normal – you can click *Previous* at any stage to go back and correct mistakes

25 Click *Next*

26 Click *Print or Edit individual labels*

27 Choose the records you wish to merge

28 Click *OK*

7

MODULE

BASIC CONCEPTS OF INFORMATION TECHNOLOGY 1

FILE MANAGEMENT 2

WORD PROCESSING 3

SPREADSHEETS 4

DATABASES 5

PRESENTATIONS 6

INTERNET AND EMAIL 7

CHAPTER 1

Getting Started

What You'll Do

- → Get Started in Excel
- → Start and Close Excel
- → Open and Close Workbooks
- → Create a New Workbook
- → Save Your Workbook
- → Save Other File Types
- → Change the Zoom Control
- → Move Around a Spreadsheet

- → Hide and Show Toolbars
- → Enter Text and Numbers
- → Select Cells
- → Use the Sum Function
- → Enter Simple Formulae
- → Undo and Redo Actions
- → Correct Mistakes

1.1 What is Excel for?

Excel is a spreadsheet program. Spreadsheets are basically big tables that hold text and numbers. Calculations can then be performed on those numbers, to help you manage your accounts, work out sales figures, or calculate interest payments on loans. Excel can be used for:

- Formulae or calculations
- Storing information (as a database)
- Creating tables

1.1.1 For Formulae (Calculations)

Overleaf is a very simple domestic budget using Excel.

For more information see section 1.19.1.

	A	B	C
1	**Income**	£1,200.00	
2			
3	**Outgoings**		
4	Rent	£ 250.00	
5	Food	£ 150.00	
6	Social	£ 85.00	
7	Gas	£ 30.00	
8	Electricity	£ 30.00	
9			
10	**Total**	£ 545.00	
11			
12	**Left Over**	£ 655.00	
13			

This cell contains a formula to add up the total outgoings

This cell contains a formula which takes the total outgoings away from the income, which gives you the amount left over

1.1.2 For Storing Information (as a Database)

The diagram below shows part of a database in Excel. The columns represent the fields in the database and the rows hold the records…

	B	C	D	E	F	G
1	**Surname**	**First Name**	**Sex**	**Date of Birth**	**Department**	**Number**
2	Jekyll	Abigail	Female	23-May-60	Design	1
3	Akinlotan	Abimbola	Female	12-Mar-58	Sales	5
4	Hyde	Alexander	Male	23-May-28	Finance	3
5	Richards	Anna	Female	27-Mar-68	Sales	6
6	Dalloway	Anne	Female	15-Jun-59	Personnel	8
7	Olivelle	Anthony	Male	21-Nov-67	Technology	5

Excel has a simple database facility that allows you to:

■ Sort information into any order (e.g. by surname)

■ Extract the information you wish to see (e.g. only the females)

1.1.3 For Creating Tables

Excel can also be used very much like word processing tables, i.e. for laying information out neatly in rows and columns. Spreadsheets can then be formatted to look very impressive!

	A	B	C	D
1	**Competitor**	**Current Share**	**Share in 2 years**	
2	Largest competitor	50%	30%	
3	Second competitor	25%	20%	
4	Third competitor	15%	10%	
5				

1.1.4 Common Excel Jargon

There are a number of words used when describing Excel that you may not have come across before.

■ **Spreadsheet** – an electronic table or tables used to store data and make calculations. These tables appear as "sheets". Spreadsheet can mean either the application (e.g. Excel), or the file created by a spreadsheet application (known in Excel as a workbook).

- **Workbook** – an entire file of sheets. A workbook is the term given to a file created in Excel.

- **Worksheet** or **sheet** – these are the separate pages contained within a workbook.

- **Cell** – a single space on a spreadsheet, used to enter information.

- **Formula** – an equation used to calculate values from the data on a spreadsheet. For example, a simple formula could add the value of two cells together.

- **Column** – spreadsheets are divided into vertical columns – each represented by a letter at the top.

- **Row** – spreadsheets are also divided into rows – with each represented by a number on the left of the screen.

- **Cell reference** – each cell has its own reference, taken from the column and row it is in. So, an example of a cell reference might be B2 (B for the column it is in, 2 for the row).

1.2 Starting and Closing Excel

1.2.1 Starting Excel

1. *Click on the Start button*

2. *Click on All Programs*

3. *Click on Microsoft Excel*

Microsoft Excel

Or, if you have a shortcut…

Double click on the shortcut on the desktop

1.2.2 Closing Excel

1. *Click on the File menu*

2. *Click on Exit*

Or

☒ *Click on the X at the top right hand corner of the screen*

1.2.3 What are Workbooks?

- Excel files are known as **workbooks**

- Workbooks are made up of **sheets**, or **spreadsheets**

1.3 The Excel Screen

1.3.1 What are All the Bits Called?

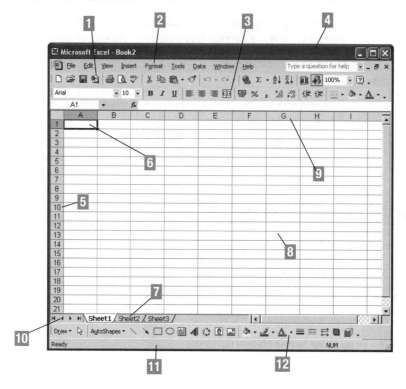

1 Standard toolbar

2 Menu bar

3 Formatting toolbar

4 Title bar

5 Row

6 The active cell

7 Sheet tabs

8 Cells

9 Column headings

10 Sheet navigation buttons

11 Status bar

12 Drawing toolbar

1.4 Task Panes

Excel makes use of the Task Pane, to help you work faster. Task panes work in the same way as all in the other Office programs. For an introduction to them, see page 100 in the Word section.

1.5 Opening and Closing Workbooks

1.5.1 Opening Your Workbook

1 *Click on the Open icon*

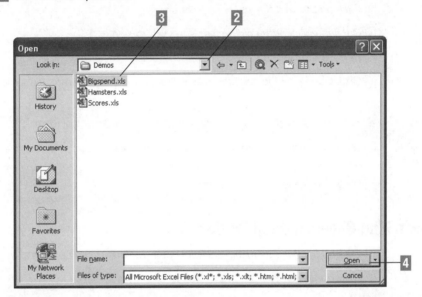

2 *Change the folder Excel is looking in if required*

3 *Click on the name of the workbook you wish to open, scrolling across if necessary*

4 *Click on Open*

Or, if you see your file in the Task Pane, you can click on it there to open it. If you don't see it, then click on More workbooks, and you will be taken to the Open Workbook box.

What are folders?

See Module 2: File Management

1.5.2 Multiple Workbooks

In Excel you can open more than one workbook at a time. If you find that you need to open another workbook, simply open it in the normal way (see previous section). You may wish to have more than one workbook open if you want to copy information from one workbook to the other.

If you know that you will want to use more than one workbook when you start, you can select all the workbooks that you will need from the Open dialog box, and then click on Open. From the Open dialog box...

1. *Click on the first file you wish to open*

2. *Hold down the Control (Ctrl) key on the keyboard*

3. *Click on the next file you wish to open*

4. *Continue clicking on all the files you wish to select*

5. *Release the Control key*

6. *Click Open – all the selected files will be opened in separate windows*

How can I switch between more than one open workbook?

1. Click on the Window menu – a list of open workbooks can be seen at the bottom of the menu

2. Click on the file you wish to switch to

1.5.3 Switching Between Open Workbooks

1. *Click on the Window menu – a list of open workbooks can be seen at the bottom of the menu*

2. *Click on the file you wish to switch to*

Or

Click on the button on the taskbar for that workbook

1.5.4 Closing Your Workbook

          *Click on the bottom X at the top right of the Excel screen – **not** the top one!*

Or

1. *Click on the File menu*

2. *Click on Close*

What happened? Excel closed completely!

You must have clicked the top X instead of the bottom one. Clicking the top one closes Excel completely, so make sure you only click the bottom X to close your workbook.

1.6 Creating a New Workbook

1.6.1 Creating a New Workbook

Click on the New icon

Or

1 Click on the File menu

2 Click on New

3 Click on General Templates in the Task Pane

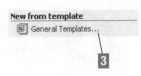

4 Ensure you are on the General tab

5 Click Workbook

6 Click OK

1.7 Saving Your Workbook

1.7.1 Saving Your Work for the First Time

1 Click on the Save icon

2 Type in a name for your workbook (up to 255 characters)

3 Change the folder to save in, if required

4 Click on Save

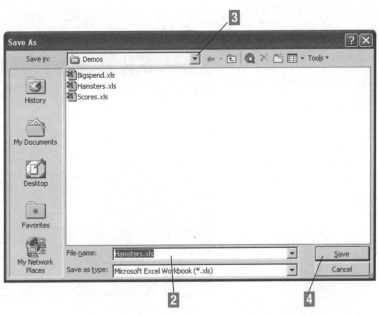

What are folders?

See Module 2: File Management

1.7.2 Saving Your Workbook After You Have Made Changes

Click on the Save icon to save your work after you have made changes. The file will be saved in the same place with the same name.

Save your work regularly!

Keep clicking on the Save icon as you are working to ensure that you do not lose your work!

1.7.3 Creating a Copy Using Save As

Using Save As will allow you to make a copy of your workbook with a different name and/or in a different location.

1 *Click on the File menu*

2 *Click on Save As*

3 *Type in a new file name for the workbook if required*

4 *Change the folder if required*

5 *Click Save*

1.7.4 Changing the Default Folder

1 *Click on the Tools menu*

2 *Click on Options*

3 *Click on the General tab*

4 *Click inside the box next to **Default file location***

5 *Type in the drive and folder you wish to save to, e.g. C:\work*

6 *Click OK*

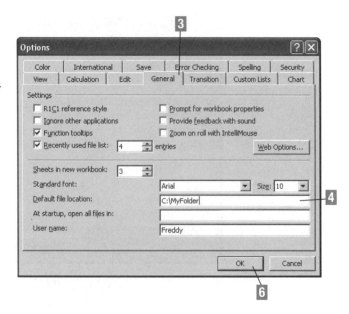

1.7.5 Changing the Default User Name

This is the name that will be saved as the author of the spreadsheet when you save a file. To change this name . . .

[1] *Click on the Tools menu*

[2] *Click on Options*

[3] *Click on the General tab*

[4] *Click inside the box next to **User name***

[5] *Type in the new user name*

[6] *Click OK*

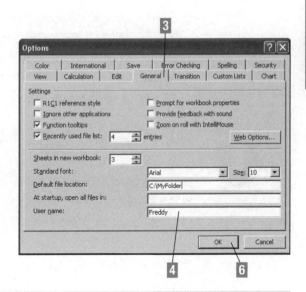

1.8 Saving Other File Types

1.8.1 Other File Types

To save a spreadsheet as an older version of Excel, or even in a different format entirely . . .

[1] *Click on the File menu*

[2] *Click on Save As*

[3] *Click on the drop down arrow at the end of the Save as type box*

[4] *Click the version of Excel you require (e.g. Microsoft Excel 5.0/95 Workbook, Text, Template, etc.)*

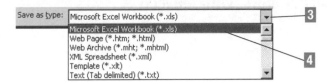

[5] *Click Save*

1.8.2 Saving a Spreadsheet as a Webpage

Saving a spreadsheet as a webpage allows you to put it onto the World Wide Web.

[1] *Open the spreadsheet you wish to save as a webpage*

[2] *If required, select the range of cells you wish to save*

[3] *Click on the File menu*

④ *Click on Save as Web Page*

⑤ *Use the arrow on the right of the Save in box to select a location to save to*

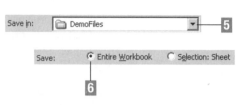

⑥ *Click in the circle before Entire Workbook*

or

Click in the circle before Selection: Sheet

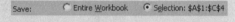

What if I only want a part of my worksheet as a webpage?

Make sure you select the range of cells required in step 2. There will be a Selection option instead of the Sheet option in the Save as dialog box.

Click into the circle before Selection.

⑦ *Click in the File name box*

⑧ *Type in a file name*

⑨ *Click on Save*

1.9 Changing the Zoom Control

1.9.1 What is the Zoom Control?

This allows you to zoom out from your spreadsheet, so you can see more of it, or zoom in closer, so you can see fine details. It does not change the size of the spreadsheet when it prints out.

1.9.2 Changing the Zoom Control with the Icon

① *Click on the drop down arrow next to the the Zoom icon*

② *Click on the zoom level you require (the higher the percentage, the closer you get!)*

1.9.3 Changing the Zoom Control with the Menu

① *Click on the View menu*

② *Click on Zoom*

③ *Click in the circle next to the zoom you require*

or

Type in your required zoom into the Custom box

④ *Click OK*

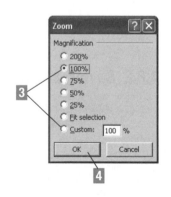

1.10 Moving Around a Spreadsheet

1.10.1 Moving Around with the Scroll Bars

There are two scroll bars around the spreadsheet, horizontal and vertical.

To move up and down, use the vertical scroll bar to the right of the spreadsheet:

- Click on the up arrow repeatedly to move up slowly
- Click and hold the mouse button down on the up arrow to move up quickly
- Click and drag the grey box to move quickly up or down
- Click on the down arrow repeatedly to move down slowly
- Click and hold the mouse button down on the down arrow to move down quickly

To move left or right, use the horizontal scroll bar:

- Click on the left arrow repeatedly to move slowly to the left
- Click and hold the mouse button down on the left arrow to move left quickly
- Click and drag the grey box to move quickly left or right
- Click on the right arrow repeatedly to move slowly to the right
- Click and hold the mouse button down on the right arrow to move right quickly

1.10.2 Moving Around with the Keyboard

Press this on the keyboard...	You will move...
Up arrow key	Up one cell
Down arrow key	Down one cell
Left arrow key	Left a cell
Right arrow key	Right a cell
Ctrl + right arrow key	To the furthest right column of the current spreadsheet
Ctrl + left arrow key	To the furthest left column of the current spreadsheet
Ctrl + up arrow key	To the top row of the sheet
Ctrl + down arrow key	To the bottom row of the sheet
Home	To column A
Ctrl, Home	To cell A1
Ctrl, End	To the bottom right cell of the current spreadsheet
Page Up	The active cell up one screen
Page Down	The active cell down one screen

1.10.3 Moving Around with the Mouse

 To move, your mouse pointer must look like a big white cross!

1. *Position the mouse over the middle of the cell you wish to move to*
2. *Click when your mouse looks like the big white cross*

1.11 Toolbars

1.11.1 Hiding and Showing Toolbars

1. *Click on the View menu*
2. *Click on the Toolbars submenu*

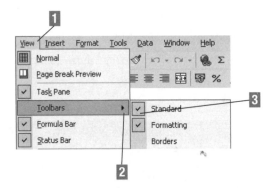

3. *Click on the toolbar you wish to show or hide – the toolbar is ticked when on*

1.12 Entering Text and Numbers

1.12.1 What Happens When I Enter Text and Numbers?

- When you enter text or numbers into a cell, the state of the cell changes.
- When you have finished typing you must confirm that you have finished by pressing Enter or clicking on the green tick

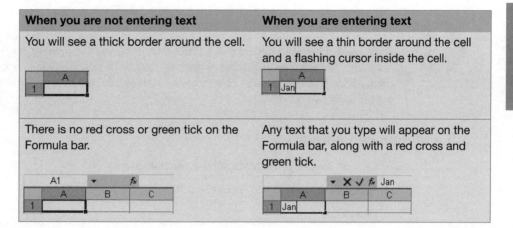

When you are not entering text	When you are entering text
You will see a thick border around the cell.	You will see a thin border around the cell and a flashing cursor inside the cell.
There is no red cross or green tick on the Formula bar.	Any text that you type will appear on the Formula bar, along with a red cross and green tick.

1.12.2 Entering Text

1 *Click on the cell you want to enter text into*

2 *Type the text you require*

3 *Press Enter*

or

Click on the green tick – the text will appear on the left hand side of the cell

1.12.3 Entering Numbers

1 *Click on the cell you want to enter a number into*

2 *Type the number you require*

3 *Press Enter*

or

Click on the green tick – the number will appear on the right hand side of the cell

1.12.4 Entering Dates

1 *Click on the cell you want to enter a date into*

2 *Type the date you require with forward slashes in it, e.g. 1/1/2000*

3 *Press Enter*

or

Click on the green tick – the date will appear on the right hand side of the cell

Always enter dates with forward slashes

If you enter dates with dots, e.g. 1.1.2000, then Excel will see them as text rather than numbers. You will then be unable to perform calculations on the date. Performing calculations on dates is very common when you wish to calculate how many days there are between two dates.

1.12.5 Entering Percentages

1️⃣ *Click on the cell you want to enter a percentage into*

2️⃣ *Type the percentage you require, e.g. 10%*

3️⃣ *Press Enter*

or

Click on the green tick – the percentage will appear on the right of the cell

1.12.6 What is the Difference Between Enter and the Green Tick?

- If you press Enter, you move down one cell after you have pressed it.

- If you click on the green tick, you remain in the same cell after you have clicked it.

1.12.7 Why Do Numbers Go on the Right?

When Excel puts data on the right it confirms that calculations can be performed on the data you have entered. Any data that appears on the left cannot be used in a calculation.

1.12.8 What if I Make a Mistake?

If you make a mistake, and you have not yet confirmed the entry…

 Click on the red cross on the Formula bar

1.13 Selecting Cells

To select, your mouse must look like a big white cross!

1.13.1 Why Select Cells?

If you want to work with just a part of your spreadsheet, you must select the part you wish to work with. The list below shows some of the situations in which you may need to select.

- When you are formatting part of the spreadsheet, e.g. making it bold, italic, changing the size

- When you are copying or moving part of the spreadsheet

- When you are adding or deleting rows and columns

- When you are choosing the cells you wish to use in a calculation, or formula

- When you are printing part of your spreadsheet

1.13.2 Selecting a Range of Cells

1 *Position the mouse over the middle of the cell, at the top left hand corner of the area you wish to select*

2 *Make sure your mouse looks like a big white cross*

3 *Click and drag the mouse pointer over the cells you require*

What do cells look like when they are selected?

All the cells, apart from the first one you selected, will go black. The first cell remains white (this indicates the active cell of the selection).

5	Female	27-Mar-68	Sales
6	Female	15-Jun-59	Personnel
7	Male	21-Nov-67	Technology
8	Female	02-Apr-74	Manufacture

1.13.3 Selecting Columns

Click on the grey column letter you require (see below)

| A | B | C | D | E | F |

Or

Click and drag over the column letters to select several columns

1.13.4 Selecting Rows

| 1 |
| 2 |
| 3 |
| 4 |
| 5 |

Click on the grey row number you require

Or

Click and drag over the row numbers to select several rows

1.13.5 Selecting the Whole Spreadsheet

| | A |
| 1 | |

Click on the grey square at the top left of the spreadsheet

1.13.6 Selecting Cells Which are Not Next to Each Other

1 *Select the first range of cells you require*

2 *Hold down Control (Ctrl) on the keyboard*

3 *Select the second range of cells you require*

4 *Release the mouse*

5 *Release Control*

1.13.7 Deselecting Cells

Click onto a cell outside the selection

Or if you have selected the whole spreadsheet…

Click into the middle of the sheet

1.14   Adding Numbers Up with AutoSum

1.14.1 What is AutoSum?

AutoSum is a quick and easy way of adding up a list of figures.

1.14.2 Using AutoSum

1 *Click on the cell where you would like to put the answer*

 2 *Click on the AutoSum icon – moving lines will appear around the figures you are adding up*

3 *The formula will appear in the cell*

4 *Press Enter or click on the green tick*

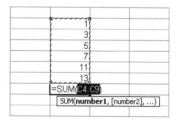

What does the Sum formula mean?

When you use AutoSum, you will see a formula similar to the one shown below in the cell.

=SUM(A1:A6)

SUM means that Excel is going to add numbers up. The cell references in brackets show the range of cells which will be included in the addition. The last cell reference (A6 in the example above) should always be a blank cell (see next page).

Always include a blank cell between the figures and the answer

This ensures that if you need to add any more figures to the list you are adding up, the answer will update to include the new information. If you do not leave a blank line, you may end up with an incorrect answer.

1.14.3 What If AutoSum Has Put Moving Lines Around the Wrong Figures?

1 *Ensure that you can still see the moving lines around the wrong figures*

(if you can't, click on the cell and click on the AutoSum icon again!)

2 *Click and drag over the correct figures, remembering to include the blank cell*

3 *Press Enter or click on the green tick*

1.14.4 What is a Circular Reference?

A circular reference occurs when the cell which contains the formula is used in the formula. Excel can't give you the answer because the answer is part of the calculation. This can happen when you correct AutoSum after it has put moving lines around the wrong figures, if you have selected the formula cell by mistake. You will see this error message after you confirm the formula.

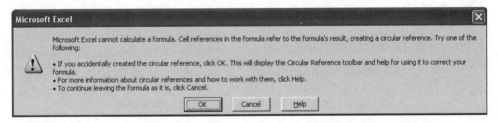

The diagram below shows an example of a spreadsheet with a circular reference...

A7	▼	*fx* =SUM(A1:A7)	
	A	**B**	**C**	**D**
1	1			
2	3			
3	5			
4	7			
5	11			
6	13			
7	0			
8				

To correct a circular reference...

1 *Click on the cell which contains the formula*

2 *Press the Delete key*

3 *Enter the formula again, without including any reference to the cell which the formula is in!*

1.15 Typing the Sum Function to Add Numbers Up

1.15.1 The Sum Function

Typing the Sum function gives you exactly the same result as using the AutoSum icon. It just means that you type in the formula yourself, rather than getting AutoSum to do it for you. This can save you having to correct AutoSum when it guesses at the wrong cells. Here's how:

1 *Select the cell you want to put the answer into*

2 *Type* **=SUM**

3 *Type an open bracket, like this (*

4 *Type in the first cell reference from the list you want to add up*

5 *Type a colon, like this :*

6 *Type the last cell reference from the list you want to add up (this should be a blank cell)*

7 *Type a closed bracket, like this)*

8 *Press Enter or click on the green tick*

So if you wanted to add up the cells from cell A2 to D6, you would type in **=SUM(A2:D6)**

1.16 Entering Simple Formulae

1.16.1 Formula/Formulae?

Formula is the term used for a calculation in a spreadsheet. The word **formulae** just means more than one formula. One formula, two formulae, three formulae, etc. You can say formulas if you like, but the correct word is formulae.

1.16.2 Types of Calculation

There are four main types of calculation:

▪ Addition	For adding numbers together, e.g. finding totals.
▪ Subtraction	For finding the difference between two numbers, e.g. subtracting expenses from income.
▪ Multiplication	For multiplying two numbers together. This is commonly used in spreadsheets to find VAT and other percentages – if you see the word **of**, then you need a percentage multiplication: e.g. 20% **of** £100 is 20% multiplied by £100 $3/4$ **of** 200 is $3/4$ multiplied by 200.
▪ Division	Used when you wish to divide an amount by another number. For example, finding the amount per month for a loan would involve dividing the total amount of the loan by the number of months you need to repay it.

Addition is usually carried out by using AutoSum or typing the Sum function. If you need to do another sort of calculation, you will have to create a formula as detailed below.

1.16.3 Creating a Formula

1. *Click on the cell where you require the answer*

2. *Type the = sign*

3. *Type the first cell reference you require*

   or

   Click on the first cell you require – flashing lines will appear around the cell, and the cell reference will be inserted

4. *Type in the mathematical symbol you require (see below)*

5. *Type the next cell reference you require – flashing lines will appear around the cell, and the cell reference will be inserted*

   or

   Click on the next cell you require

6. *Press Enter*

   or

   Click on the green tick to confirm the formula – the answer will appear in the cell, and the formula will appear on the Formula bar

Always use cell references in formulae – and never numbers!

Although formulae will still work if you use numbers instead of cell references, it is never advisable. Using cell references means that if the number contained in the cell should change, the formula will update to show the correct answer. So your spreadsheet is always correct!

1.16.4 Mathematical Symbols

Press **+**	To perform an addition
Press **–**	To perform a subtraction
Press *****	To perform a multiplication
Press **/**	To perform a division

Use the number keypad!

The easiest way of typing the mathematical symbols is to use the keys around the number pad on the right hand side of the keyboard. If they don't work, press the Num Lock key – the Num Lock light must be on to use these numbers.

1.16.5 Precedence of Calculation

Calculations are not simply done from left to right, as you might expect. Below is the order in which all calculations are performed:

Priority	Symbol	Explanation
1	( )	Anything in brackets is done before anything outside the brackets is even considered.
2	^	Raises a number in order of magnitude: raises it to the power of something else, e.g. 2^4 is the same as $2 * 2 * 2 * 2$
3	* /	Multiply and divide are on the same level. Whichever is the furthest left in the formula is done first.
4	+ –	Plus and minus are on the same level. Whichever is the furthest left is done first.

The acronym for this is **BODMAS** :

Brackets **O**rder **D**ivide **M**ultiply **A**dd **S**ubtract

1.17　Undo and Redo – A Licence to Make Mistakes

Undo allows you to cancel up to 16 of your previous actions if you have made a mistake. If you then decide that you hadn't really made a mistake after all, you can redo up to 16 things you have undone. But if you keep going backwards and forwards, you might go a bit mad.

1.17.1 Undoing Your Last Action

Click on the Undo button

Or

Press Control (Ctrl) + Z on the keyboard

Or

1 *Click on the Edit menu*

2 *Click on Undo*

1.17.2 Redoing Your Last Undo

Click on the Redo button

Or

Press Control (Ctrl) + Y on the keyboard

Or

1 Click on the Edit menu

2 Click on Redo

1.17.3 Undoing up to 16 Actions

You can't select one action to undo

When you undo more than one action, you cannot pick out just one from the previous 16 actions and undo that alone. In other words, if the action you want to undo was 5 actions ago, you must undo ALL 5 of your last actions.

1 Click on the down arrow next to the Undo icon

2 Locate the action(s) you want to undo, scrolling down if necessary

3 Click on the action you wish to undo from the list

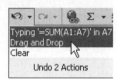

1.17.4 Redoing up to 16 Actions

1 Click on the down arrow next to the Redo icon

2 Locate the action(s) you wish to redo from the list, scrolling down if necessary

3 Click on the last action you want to redo

1.18 Correcting Mistakes

1.18.1 Deleting the Contents of a Cell

1 Click on the cell you wish to delete

2 Press the Delete key

Or

1 Click on the cell you wish to delete

2 Click on the Edit menu

3 Click Clear

4 Click Contents

1.18.2 Replacing the Contents of a Cell

1 Click on the cell you wish to replace

2 Type in the new text – the original contents will disappear

1.18.3 Editing the Contents of a Cell

There are three ways of editing the contents of a cell . . .

[1] *Double click on the cell you wish to edit – a cursor will appear inside the cell*

[2] *Enter or amend the text*

[3] *Press Enter or click on the green tick*

Or

[1] *Click on the cell you wish to edit*

[2] *Press F2 on the keyboard – a cursor will appear inside the cell*

[3] *Enter or amend the text*

[4] *Press Enter or click on the green tick*

Or

[1] *Click on the cell you wish to edit – the formula bar will show the contents of the cell*

[2] *Click on the text on the Formula bar*

[3] *Enter or amend the text*

[4] *Press Enter or click on the green tick*

1.19 Formulae

1.19.1 What is a Formula?

Formula is the term used for a calculation in a spreadsheet. The diagrams below show an example formula being entered.

To work out the surplus, we need to do a calculation by taking away the expenditure from the income. You can see this being entered on the left hand side. On the right hand side, you can see what happens after the formula has been entered.

1.19.2 How is the Formula Made Up?

- Formulae always start with an equals (=) sign – that's how Excel knows it's a formula

- Cell references are used in the calculation instead of numbers. This means that if the number inside the cell changes, the answer to the formula will update!

- A mathematical symbol is used to denote the type of calculation.

Here is the formula from the example above which found us the surplus (or money left over).

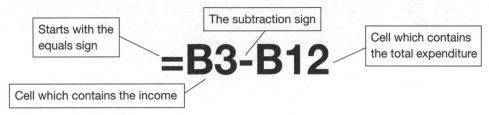

Starts with the equals sign

The subtraction sign

Cell which contains the total expenditure

=B3-B12

Cell which contains the income

1.20 Error Messages

1.20.1 What Do the Error Messages Mean?

When something goes wrong with a formula, Excel produces messages that attempt to describe what the problem is:

#DIV/0!	You have attempted to divide by zero – make sure all the cells being used in the formula have numbers in them.
#N/A!	Part of your formula is using a cell that does not have information in it, or the information is not yet available.
#NAME?	There is some text in the formula that does not mean anything to Excel. There may be a range name in the formula that Excel does not recognise.
#NULL!	Two areas do not intersect. You may have forgotten to include a comma between two ranges of cells.
#NUM!	You have used text instead of numbers whilst performing a function, or the result of the formula is too big or too small to be shown by Excel.
#REF!	One of the cells being used in the formula does not exist. It may have been deleted after you created the formula.
#VALUE!	A cell containing text has been used in the formula.

You may also see error messages about circular references (see page 223).

1.20.2 Correcting Formulae

1 *Select the cell containing the formula*

2 *Click on the formula on the Formula bar*

3 *Amend the formula as required*

4 *Press Enter*

or

Click on the green tick

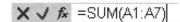

Amending the formula

You can delete the parts of the formula you do not want with the Delete or Backspace keys on the keyboard. If you want to enter new cell references, you can either type them in, or click on the cells you require.

CHAPTER 2

Editing a Worksheet

What You'll Do

→ Edit a Worksheet

→ Move and Copy Text with Drag and Drop

→ Cut, Copy and Paste Data

→ Use Autofill to Copy Text and Formulae

→ Use Find and Replace

→ Check Spelling

→ Use Symbols and Special Characters

→ Sort by More than One Column

→ Insert, Delete, Move and Copy Sheets

→ Move Through the Book

2

2.1 Drag and Drop

ⓘ To use drag and drop, your mouse pointer must look like a white arrow with four smaller arrows at the tip

2.1.1 Moving Text with Drag and Drop

1 *Select the cells you wish to move*

2 *Position your mouse at the edge of the selection – the mouse pointer will change to a white arrow*

3 *Click and drag to the new postion – a fuzzy grey line will show you where you are going*

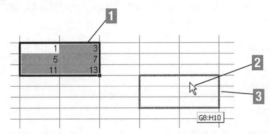

4 *Release the mouse when you are in the correct place*

2.1.2 Copying Text with Drag and Drop

[1] *Select the cells you wish to copy*

[2] *Position your mouse at the edge of the selection – mouse will change to a white arrow*

[3] *Hold down Control (Ctrl) on the keyboard – a plus sign will appear next to the white arrow*

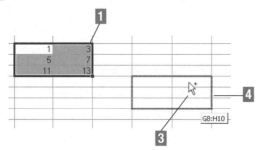

[4] *Click and drag to the new position – a fuzzy grey line will show you where you are going*

[5] *Release the mouse button when you are in the correct place*

[6] *Release Control*

2.2 Cut, Copy and Paste

The Clipboard

When you copy or cut anything it is temporarily stored on an area called the clipboard until you need it again. The clipboard can only hold one item at a time, and when you copy or cut a new item it will overwrite what was previously there.

2.2.1 Moving Data

[1] *Select the cells you wish to move*

[2] *Click on the Cut icon – the selection will have flashing lights around it, and will be moved to the Windows clipboard*

[3] *Select the cell you wish to move to – this cell will become the top left hand corner of the cells you cut*

[4] *Click on the Paste icon*

2.2.2 Copying Data

[1] *Select the cells you wish to copy*

[2] *Click on the Copy icon – the selection will have flashing lights around it, and will be moved to the Windows clipboard*

3 *Select the cell you wish to copy to – this cell will become the top left hand corner of the cells you copied*

4 *Click on the Paste icon*

You can copy more than one item using the Office Clipboard!

See the section called Copying or Moving More Than One Thing on page 151.

2.3 Using AutoFill to Copy Text and Formulae

Your mouse must look like the small black cross to use AutoFill!

2.3.1 What is AutoFill?

AutoFill is a quick way of entering standard information onto your spreadsheet such as the months or days of the week. You can also use it to copy text or formulae very quickly.

2.3.2 Using AutoFill

1 *Click on the cell(s) you wish to copy*

2 *Position the mouse pointer over the small square at the bottom right hand corner of the active cell – your mouse pointer will change to a small black cross*

3 *Click and drag over the cells you wish to copy to – a fuzzy grey line will appear around the cells, and labels will appear to show you what is being copied*

4 *Normally, this is all you have to do – but if the results are not what you expect, click on the Smart Tag (an Office XP feature) that appears at the bottom right of the cells, and choose Fill Series*

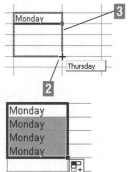

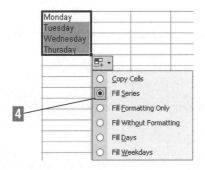

2.3.3 Special Lists

Certain text works well with AutoFill, such as months, days or dates. Have a look at the examples below, which were all created using AutoFill:

January		Qtr 1		01/05/2005
February		Qtr 2		02/05/2005
March		Qtr 3		03/05/2005
April		Qtr 4		04/05/2005
May				05/05/2005
June				06/05/2005
Monday	Tuesday	Wednesday	Thursday	Friday

2.3.4 Starting the Sequence Off for AutoFill

Sometimes you may want to start off a sequence of numbers or dates for AutoFill, e.g. when you want to enter a list of dates that go from week to week, rather than day to day. To achieve this, you must first start the sequence off for AutoFill.

1. *Type in the first date or number you require*

2. *Type the second date or number you require in the next cell*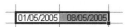

3. *Select both of the cells*

4. *AutoFill as normal*

01/05/2005	08/05/2005	15/05/2005	22/05/2005	29/05/2005	05/06/2005

2.4 Find and Replace

2.4.1 Using Find

1. *Select the cells you wish to search, or click in any cell to search the entire sheet*

2. *Click on the Edit menu*

3. *Click on Find*

4. *Type the text or number you are searching for into the white box*

5. *Click Find Next*

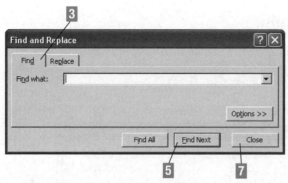

⑥ *Keep clicking Find Next until you have found what you are looking for*

⑦ *Click Close*

2.4.2 Find and Replace

① *Select the cells you wish to search, or click in any cell to search the entire sheet*

② *Click on the Edit menu*

③ *Click on Replace*

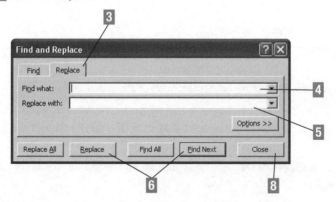

④ *Type what you are searching for into the **Find what** box*

⑤ *Type what you want to replace it with into the **Replace with** box*

⑥ *Click Find Next and Replace to replace individual occurrences*

⑦ *Keep clicking Find Next until you have found what you are looking for*
  or
  Click Replace All to replace all occurrences

⑧ *Click Close*

2.5 Checking the Spelling

2.5.1 Checking the Spelling

1 Click on the Tools menu

2 Click Spelling

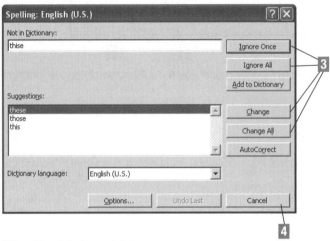

3 When Excel finds a mistake:

Click **Ignore Once** to leave it alone

or

Click **Ignore All** to leave all occurrences of this word alone

or

Choose a suggested replacement, and click **Change** to correct the spelling

or

Choose a suggested replacement, and click **Change All** to correct all the spellings

4 Keep checking the spellings, or click **Cancel** to finish

2.6 Symbols and Special Characters

For years, Excel could not insert symbols or special characters – you had to copy them over from Word, and it caused mayhem. From XP onwards, you can now insert symbols in Excel, and life will never be the same again.

2.6.1 Inserting Symbols

1 Select the cell where you want to put the symbol

2 Click on the Insert menu

3 *Click on Symbol*

4 *Click on the Symbols tab to insert a symbol (shape), or the Special Characters tab to insert a special character (like the paragraph symbol ¶, etc.)*

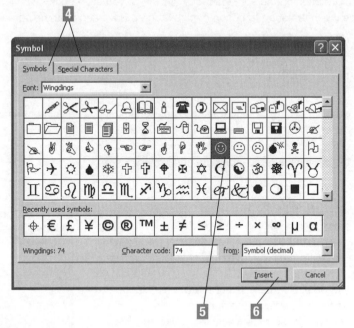

5 *Select the symbol you want to insert*

6 *Click Insert*

7 *Click Close*

2.7 Sorting

Sorting is usually used to sort a database by one or more of its **fields**, e.g. name, date, cost etc.

1 *Click into any cell in the column you wish to sort (**do not** select the whole column)*

2 *Click on the Sort Ascending icon*

   or

3 *Click on the Sort Descending icon*

Why can't I select the whole column?

If you select a column before you sort, only the data in that column moves. The rest of the information on the spreadsheet stays still. If you are working with a database this can cause the information to become mismatched. Have a look at the spreadsheet below…

	A	B	C	D	E
1	Payroll Number	Title	Surname	First Name	Sex
2	5	Mr	Olivelle	Anthony	Male
3	23	Miss	Duck	Caroline	Female
4	19	Mr	Dodgson	Charles	Male
5	26	Miss	Richards	Anna	Female

You want to sort this spreadsheet by order of sex. If you select column E before you sort (which contains the sex), look at what happens…

	A	B	C	D	E
1	Payroll Number	Title	Surname	First Name	Sex
2	5	Mr	Olivelle	Anthony	Female
3	23	Miss	Duck	Caroline	Female
4	19	Mr	Dodgson	Charles	Male
5	26	Miss	Richards	Anna	Male

The information in column E gets sorted, but everything else stays in the same place – so Anthony Olivelle in row 2 is apparently female, and Anna Richards in row 5 is apparently male!

If you do accidentally select the whole column, you will see the message on the right.

If you want to sort the whole list, make sure to select **Expand the selection**, and then click **Sort**.

What is the difference between ascending and descending?

If you are sorting this…	Ascending means…	Descending means…
Text	A to Z	Z to A
Numbers	Lowest to highest	Highest to lowest
Dates	Earliest to latest	Latest to earliest

2.7.1 Sorting by More Than One Column

Sometimes you may wish to sort by more than one bit of information. This tends to happen when you have a certain field which people can be *grouped* by, e.g. Department, Gender, etc., and you want to sort them within their groups. The spreadsheet below has been sorted by Department initially, and then within this, people have been sorted by their surname.

	A	B
1	**Department**	**Surname**
2	Design	Jekyll
3	Design	Jospin
4	Design	Pullen
5	Design	Robinson
6	Design	Sierra de la Guerra
7	Finance	Corwall
8	Finance	Hyde
9	Finance	Minniver
10	Finance	Ross
11	Manufacture	Al Said
12	Manufacture	Duck
13	Manufacture	Hull
14	Manufacture	Scot
15	Manufacture	Sutherland
16	Manufacture	Zhivago
17	Personnel	Brown
18	Personnel	Dalloway
19	Personnel	Day
20	Personnel	Huntington
21	Personnel	Lazarus
22	Personnel	Mulley
23	Personnel	Plod

1. Click into any cell within the database you wish to sort

2. Click on the Data menu

3. Click Sort – the text in the spreadsheet will become highlighted

4. Click the down arrow underneath **Sort by**

5. Click on the field you wish to sort

6. Click next to Ascending or Descending for the first field

7. Click on the down arrow underneath **Then by**

8. Click on the next field you wish to sort

9. Click next to Ascending or Descending for the second field

10. Enter sort information for a third field if required

11. Click in the circle next to **Header row** if the fieldnames are held in the top row

12. Click OK

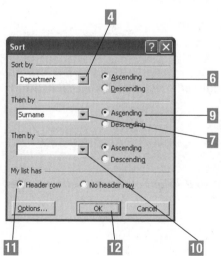

2.8 Inserting, Deleting, Moving and Copying Sheets

Excel files are called **workbooks**. Just like any book they contain several sheets, or pages. To begin with you will only have three, but you can have up to 255 sheets, or delete the ones that you don't need.

2.8.1 Why Have More Than One Sheet?

Imagine that you have to store information about your organisation's budget over five years. If you try and put all this information onto one sheet it will become impossible to navigate and find things easily.

If, however, you set up similar sheets for each year, or even for each month, then it becomes a lot easier to find the information you are looking for.

2.8.2 Selecting Sheets

   Click on the sheet tab you require – it will become white

2.8.3 Moving Through the Book

1 *Click on the Sheet Navigation buttons*

Going from left to right:

- Go to the first sheet in the workbook

- Go one sheet to the left

- Go one sheet to the right

- Go to the last sheet in the workbook

2 *Click on the sheet tab you require*

2.8.4 Inserting Sheets

1 *Click on the sheet **to the right of** where you want the new sheet to appear*

2 *Click on the Insert menu*

3 *Click Worksheet*

Or

1 *Right click on the sheet tab **to the right of** where you want the new sheet to appear – a menu will appear*

2 *Click Insert*

3 *Click Worksheet*

4 *Click OK*

2.8.5 Renaming Sheets

1 *Double click on top of the name on the sheet tab – it will go black*

2 *Type in the new name*

3 *Press Enter*

Or

[1] *Right click on the sheet tab – a menu will appear*

[2] *Click Rename – it will go black*

[3] *Type the new name*

[4] *Press Enter*

2.8.6 Deleting Sheets

[1] *Click on the sheet tab you require*

[2] *Click on the Edit menu*

[3] *Click Delete Sheet*

[4] *Click OK*

Or

[1] *Right click on the sheet tab – a menu will appear*

[2] *Click Delete*

[3] *Click OK*

2.8.7 Copying Sheets

[1] *Click on the sheet tab you wish to copy*

[2] *Click on the Edit menu*

[3] *Click Move or Copy Sheet*

[4] *Click in the box next to **Create a copy** so that it is ticked*

[5] *Click on the sheet that you wish to place the copied sheet before*

or

*Click **(move to end)***

[6] *Click OK*

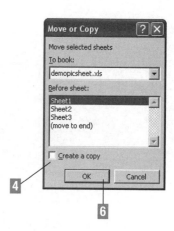

Or

[1] *Click on the sheet tab you wish to copy*

[2] *Hold down the Control (Ctrl) key on the keyboard*

[3] *Click and drag the sheet to its new position*

2.8.8 Moving Sheets

1. *Click on the sheet tab you wish to move*

2. *Click on the Edit menu*

3. *Click Move or Copy Sheet*

4. *Ensure that the* **Create a copy** *box is* **not** *ticked*

5. *Click on the sheet you wish to move the sheet before*

   or

   Click on **(move to end)**

6. *Click OK*

Or

Click and drag the sheet tab you require to its new location

CHAPTER 3

Functions and Cell References

What You'll Do

→ Use Functions and Cell References

→ Create Absolute Cell References

→ Create Mixed Cell References

→ Use Functions

→ Find the Average

→ Use the IF Function

→ Use the Minimum Function

→ Use the Maximum Function

3

3.1 Using Absolute Cell References

3.1.1 What are Absolute Cell References?

- Formulae usually use **relative cell references**. When you AutoFill a relative cell reference it adjusts as you move down or across (see the section on AutoFilling on page 233). This is, on the whole, what you need in order for your spreadsheet to make sense.

- Occasionally, however, you will want one of the cell references to stay the same when it is AutoFilled. A cell reference that does not adjust when it is AutoFilled is an **absolute cell reference**.

The spreadsheet below shows an absolute cell reference in action. Everyone's salary is due to increase by 10%. The first formula, to find Bloggs' new salary, has been created. We multiply his current salary (cell C4) by 10% (cell B1).

	D4	▼	*fx* =C4*B1		
	A	B	C	D	E
1	**Salary Rise**	**10%**			
2					
3		*Name*	*Old Salary*	*Increase*	
4		Bloggs	£67,895.00	£6,789.50	
5		Richards	£15,678.00		
6		Dalloway	£26,748.00		
7		Olivelle	£20,000.00		
8		Duck	£12,500.00		
9					

However, everyone's salary is being increased by 10%. If we AutoFill the formula as it is, then the cell reference B1 will be adjusted to B2, then B3 etc., and we'll end up with some funny answers…

	A	B	C	D	E
1	Salary Rise	10%			
2					
3		Name	Old Salary	Increase	
4		Bloggs	£67,895.00	=C4*B1	
5		Richards	£15,678.00	=C5*B2	
6		Dalloway	£26,748.00	=C6*B3	
7		Olivelle	£20,000.00	=C7*B4	
8		Duck	£12,500.00	=C8*B5	
9					

	A	B	C	D	E
1	Salary Rise	10%			
2					
3		Name	Old Salary	Increase	
4		Bloggs	£67,895.00	£6,789.50	
5		Richards	£15,678.00	£ -	
6		Dalloway	£26,748.00	#VALUE!	
7		Olivelle	£20,000.00	#VALUE!	
8		Duck	£12,500.00	#VALUE!	
9					

AutoFill has adjusted the reference to the 10% in cell B1

The answers don't make sense, because Excel has changed the B1 reference

We actually need cell B1 to remain constant or **absolute** as it is AutoFilled down. In other words, we need to tell Excel that this is an **absolute cell reference**! The diagrams below show what happens when you make B1 absolute.

	A	B	C	D	E
1	Salary Rise	10%			
2					
3		Name	Old Salary	Increase	
4		Bloggs	£67,895.00	=C4*B1	
5		Richards	£15,678.00	=C5*B1	
6		Dalloway	£26,748.00	=C6*B1	
7		Olivelle	£20,000.00	=C7*B1	
8		Duck	£12,500.00	=C8*B1	
9					

	A	B	C	D	E
1	Salary Rise	10%			
2					
3		Name	Old Salary	Increase	
4		Bloggs	£67,895.00	£6,789.50	
5		Richards	£15,678.00	£1,567.80	
6		Dalloway	£26,748.00	£2,674.80	
7		Olivelle	£20,000.00	£2,000.00	
8		Duck	£12,500.00	£1,250.00	
9					

B1 stays the same all the way down

Now the answers make sense!

3.1.2 Creating Absolute Cell References

1. *Click on the cell where you require the answer*

2. *Enter the formula as normal*

3. *Position the cursor next to the cell reference which you need to make absolute*

4. *Press F4 on the keyboard – dollar signs will appear around the cell reference*

5. *Press Enter or click on the green tick*

6. *AutoFill the formula as normal*

Existing formulae can be changed to have absolute cell references

Just edit the contents of the cell (see page 228), and follow the instructions from step 3 above!

Not sure whether you need an absolute cell reference?

Absolute cell references are only needed when you want to AutoFill formulae. If you aren't sure, just AutoFill your formula and see if it works. If you find that you are getting strange answers, you may very well need an absolute cell reference.

3.2 Mixed Cell References

3.2.1 What are Mixed Cell References?

- Relative cell references are used when you want a cell reference to adjust when you AutoFill it across or down.

- Absolute cell references are used when you want a cell reference to stay exactly the same when you AutoFill it across or down.

- **Mixed cell references** are used when you want the column letter or the row number of the cell reference to remain the same when you AutoFill it across or down.

The worksheet below shows mixed cell references in action. There is a list of newspapers on the left hand side with the price shown in Sterling. You need to find the price in the other currencies listed. The exchange rate of the currencies is shown in row 1. We have already found the cost of Animal Weekly in Francs. We multiply the price in Sterling (Cell B4) by the exchange rate for Francs (Cell C1). Cell C4 contains the cost of Animal Weekly in Francs:

C4	▾	ƒx =B4*C1			
	A	B	C	D	E	F
1	*Exchange Rate*		*10.1*	*3.4*	*25*	*2.5*
2						
3		Sterling	Francs	Marks	Pesetas	Dollars
4	Animal Weekly	£ 0.90	£ 9.09			
5	Kitten News	£ 1.10				
6	Bear Daily	£ 0.50				
7	Puppy Chronicle	£ 0.75				
8	Monkey Times	£ 0.85				

We need to AutoFill this across, to get the price of Animal Weekly in Marks, Pesetas and Dollars. However, we also need to AutoFill it down to get the price of the other newspapers in Francs. We could use absolute cell references to copy it in one direction, but this would take ages. Instead you can use mixed cell references.

Think about what will happen if you AutoFill the formula across. The column letters are going to be adjusted, which is fine for the exchange rate, but it means that you will move away from the price in Sterling – look at the results below (the formulae are shown in row 4, just to show you what happens – it will not normally look like this):

Exchange Rate		*10.1*	*3.4*	*25*	*2.5*
	Sterling	Francs	Marks	Pesetas	Dollars
Animal Weekly	£ 0.90	£ 9.09	£ 30.91	£ 772.65	£1,931.63
	Formulae:	B4*C1	C4*D1	D4*E1	E4*F1

The first cell reference moves away from B4 (the price in Sterling), which means that you get a very silly answer for Dollars. The formula to find Dollars is currently the price of Animal Weekly in Pesetas multiplied by the exchange rate for Dollars. So Excel is telling you that Animal Weekly costs 1931.63 dollars! The second cell reference adjusts as necessary, moving to the different exchange rates, which is what we want. But, if you make the price in Sterling absolute, you can't AutoFill it down, as the cost of Animal Weekly will always be used.

Think about what will happen if you AutoFill the same formula down. The row numbers are going to be adjusted which is fine for the cost of the newspapers, but a disaster for the exchange rates! Look at what happens (again, the formulae are displayed next to the results, just to show you how it works):

Exchange Rate			10.1	
		Sterling	Francs	Formulae:
Animal Weekly		£ 0.90	£ 9.09	B4*C1
Kitten News		£ 1.10	£ -	B5*C2
Bear Daily		£ 0.50	#VALUE!	B6*C3
Puppy Chronicle		£ 0.75	£ 6.82	B7*C4
Monkey Times		£ 0.85	£ -	B8*C5

The first cell reference adjusts as necessary, moving to the different newspaper costs, which is fine. The second cell reference, however, moves down from the exchange rate for Francs, so your answers are useless. There is nothing in cell C2 which is why you are getting 0 in the second formula, and there is text in cell C3 which is why you are getting #VALUE!

You could make the exchange rate for Francs absolute, and copy it down, but then you wouldn't be able to copy the formula across as you would always be using the exchange rate for Francs.

In fact, in order to AutoFill this formula both across and down, you only need to fix half of the cell references: the row that the exchange rates are in, and the column that the prices in Sterling are in. Have a look at the results below – the first image shows you the formulae after AutoFilling, and the second shows you the actual results:

	A	B	C	D	E	F
1	Exchange Rate		10.1	3.4	25	2.5
2						
3		Sterling	Francs	Marks	Pesetas	Dollars
4	Animal Weekly	0.9	=$B4*C$1	=$B4*D$1	=$B4*E$1	=$B4*F$1
5	Kitten News	1.1	=$B5*C$1	=$B5*D$1	=$B5*E$1	=$B5*F$1
6	Bear Daily	0.5	=$B6*C$1	=$B6*D$1	=$B6*E$1	=$B6*F$1
7	Puppy Chronicle	0.75	=$B7*C$1	=$B7*D$1	=$B7*E$1	=$B7*F$1
8	Monkey Times	0.85	=$B8*C$1	=$B8*D$1	=$B8*E$1	=$B8*F$1

	A	B	C	D	E	F
1	Exchange Rate		10.1	3.4	25	2.5
2						
3		Sterling	Francs	Marks	Pesetas	Dollars
4	Animal Weekly	£ 0.90	£ 9.09	£ 3.06	£ 22.50	£ 2.25
5	Kitten News	£ 1.10	£ 11.11	£ 3.74	£ 27.50	£ 2.75
6	Bear Daily	£ 0.50	£ 5.05	£ 1.70	£ 12.50	£ 1.25
7	Puppy Chronicle	£ 0.75	£ 7.58	£ 2.55	£ 18.75	£ 1.88
8	Monkey Times	£ 0.85	£ 8.59	£ 2.89	£ 21.25	£ 2.13

Column B is fixed, so that you never leave the Sterling column. Row 1 is fixed so that you never move down from the exchange rates row.

3.2.2 Creating Mixed Cell References

1 Click on the cell where you require the answer

2 Enter the formula as normal

3 Position the cursor to the left of the column letter or row number which is to remain the same

=$B4*C$1

4 *Type a dollar sign*

5 *Press Enter or click on the green tick*

6 *AutoFill the formula across as normal*

7 *Select all of the formulae you have AutoFilled*

8 *AutoFill all the formulae down while they are selected*

Existing formulae can be changed to have mixed cell references

Just edit the contents of the cell and follow the instructions from step 3 above!

Not sure whether you need mixed cell references?

Mixed cell references are only needed when you want to AutoFill a formula both across and down. If you aren't sure, just AutoFill your formula both across and down and see if it works. If you find that you are getting strange answers, you may very well need a mixed cell reference.

Another clue may be that you have created a lot of formulae with absolute cell references on your worksheet, which you are then AutoFilling in one direction. You may be able to achieve the same effect a lot quicker with mixed cell references.

3.3 Finding the Average

3.3.1 What are Functions?

Some calculations can become a bit long-winded if you try to create them with straightforward formulae, such as finding the average of a group of numbers. Functions let you quickly perform complex calculations, like finding the average of a group of cells.

3.3.2 Finding the Average

1 *Select the cell where you want to put the answer*

2 *Type =*

3 *Type **AVERAGE***

4 *Type an open bracket, like this (*

5 *Type the first cell reference you require*

6 *Type a colon, like this :*

7 *Type the last cell reference you require – this should be a blank cell*

8̲ *Type a closed bracket, like this)*

9̲ *Press Enter, or click on the green tick*

e.g. **=AVERAGE(A1:A6)**

3.3.3 Using the Count Function

This function counts the amount of cells that contain numbers.

1̲ *Select the cell where you require the answer*

2̲ *Type* **=**

3̲ *Type* **COUNT**

4̲ *Type an open bracket, like this (*

5̲ *Type the first cell reference you require*

6̲ *Type a colon, like this :*

7̲ *Type the last cell reference you require*

8̲ *Type a closed bracket, like this)*

9̲ *Press Enter, or click on the green tick*

e.g. **=COUNT(A1:A6)**

3.3.4 The IF Function

This function returns one value should a condition you specify prove to be true, and another if the condition should prove to be false. For instance, imagine you are preparing a budget sheet. You could use the IF function to tell Excel this . . .

IF the total expenditure is over a certain level, then enter 'Over Budget' into the cell. But IF total expenditure is not over a certain level, then enter 'Within Budget' into the cell.

The true condition should be entered before the false condition. So a formula including the IF function will take this format . . .

=IF(logical test, "value if true", "value if false")

e.g. **=IF(B10>450, "Over Budget", "Within Budget")**

The above formula will have the results seen on the next page, depending on the value of cell B10:

	B11	▼	fx	=IF(B10>450,"Over Budget","Within Budget")	
	A	B	C	D	E
1	*Expenses*				
2					
3					
4	*Rent*	200			
5	*Food*	150			
6	*Social*	100			
7	*Bills*	35			
8	*Monkeys*	10			
9					
10	*Total*	495			
11	*Within Budget?*	Over Budget			
12					

	B11	▼	fx	=IF(B10>450,"Over Budget","Within Budget")	
	A	B	C	D	E
1	*Expenses*				
2					
3					
4	*Rent*	200			
5	*Food*	150			
6	*Social*	100			
7	*Bills*	35			
8	*Monkeys*	10			
9					
10	*Total*	395			
11	*Within Budget?*	Within Budget			
12					

3.3.5 Using the IF Function

1 *Select the cell where you require the answer*

2 *Type =IF*

3 *Type an open bracket*

4 *Type the condition for the function*

5 *Type a comma*

6 *Inside quotation marks, type the data to be entered into the cell if the condition is true*

7 *Type a comma*

8 *Inside quotation marks, type the data to be entered into the cell if the condition is false*

9 *Type a closed bracket*

10 *Press Enter, or click on the green tick*

3.3.6 Using the Minimum Function

This function finds the smallest number from a range of values.

1 *Select the cell where you require the answer*

2 *Type =MIN*

3 *Type an open bracket*

4 *Type the first cell reference you require*

5 *Type a colon*

6 *Type the last cell reference you require*

7 *Tye a closed bracket*

8 *Press Enter, or click on the green tick*

e.g. **=MIN(A1:A6)**

3.3.7 Using the Maximum Function

This function finds the largest number from a range of values.

1 *Select the cell where you require the answer*

2 *Type* **=MAX**

3 *Type an open bracket*

4 *Type the first cell reference you require*

5 *Type a colon*

6 *Type the last cell reference you require*

7 *Type a closed bracket*

8 *Press Enter, or click on the green tick*

e.g. **=MAX(A1:A6)**

CHAPTER 4

Printing Workbooks

What You'll Do

→ Print Workbooks

→ Get a Print Preview

→ Print from Print Preview

→ Print a Workbook

→ Print Selections

→ Print More Than One Copy

→ Change the Page Setup

→ Change the Margins

→ Change the Orientation

→ Print Gridlines and Row/Column Headings

→ Change the Paper Size

→ Use Help in Excel

→ Create Headers and Footers

4

4.1 | Print Preview and Printing a Worksheet

4.1.1 Why Check Your Spreadsheet?

The spreadsheet you work with on screen will look very different when you print it out. Before you distribute the spreadsheet you have created, you need to make sure it fits on the page properly, and that the calculations you've used are correct. You can examine the spreadsheet more closely by changing the view you are using.

4.1.2 What is Print Preview?

There are two views in Excel:

- **Normal View**: used for the majority of the time you are working with Excel.

- **Print Preview**: used to show you how the spreadsheet will print out.

Print Preview is especially important in Excel, as Normal View does not give you a clear indication of where your pages begin or end, or whether there is page numbering etc.

4.1.3 Getting a Print Preview

 Click on Print Preview icon – a new toolbar will appear

Or

1 *Click on the File menu*

2 *Click Print Preview – a new toolbar will appear*

4.1.4 Moving Between Pages in Print Preview

 You can see how many pages will print out at the bottom left of the screen.

 Click on Next or Previous to move through the pages

Or

Use the scroll bar on the right of the screen

4.1.5 Using the Zoom in Print Preview

1 *Position the mouse pointer over the page – it will change to a magnifying glass*

2 *Click once with the left mouse button – if you are zoomed out, you will zoom in, and if you are zoomed in, you will zoom out*

Or

`Zoom` *Click on Zoom*

4.1.6 Printing from Print Preview

`Print...` **1** *Click on the Print button*

2 *Click OK*

4.1.7 Closing Print Preview

`Close` *Click on the Close button*

4.1.8 Printing a Worksheet

 Click on the Print icon

Be patient with your printer!

Sometimes it can take a while for your spreadsheet to print out, and it is tempting to click the Print icon again. If you do, you will get two copies!

4.2 Printing Ranges and More Than One Copy

4.2.1 Printing Selections

[1] *Select the cells you wish to print*

[2] *Click on the File menu*

[3] *Click Print*

[4] *Click in the circle next to **Selection** underneath **Print what***

[5] *Click OK*

4.2.2 Printing More Than One Copy

[1] *Click on the File menu*

[2] *Click Print*

[3] *Change the number of copies to the number you require*

- Use the up and down arrows to change the number of copies, or click into the box and type in the number of copies you require.

- Tick Collate if you require the copies to come out in the order page 1,2,3, page 1,2,3, etc.

- Do not tick Collate if you require the copies to come out in the order page 1, page 1, page 2, page 2, etc.

[4] *Click OK*

4.2.3 Printing the Entire Workbook

[1] *Click on the File menu*

[2] *Click Print*

[3] *Click in the circle next to **Entire Workbook** underneath **Print what***

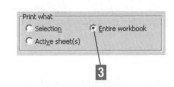

[4] *Click OK*

4.3 Changing the Page Setup

4.3.1 Opening the Page Setup

There are two ways of getting into Page Setup – through Print Preview, or from the Normal View. Going to Page Setup from Print Preview means that you can see how your changes have affected the spreadsheet. If you go from Normal View, you will not be able to see the changes.

From Print Preview . . .

Setup...   *Click on the Setup button*

From Normal view

   1 *Click on the File menu*

   2 *Click Page Setup*

4.3.2 Changing the Margins

If you need to make a bit of extra room on your page, you might want to make the margins a bit smaller:

1 *Bring up the Page Setup dialog box*

2 *Click on the Margins tab*

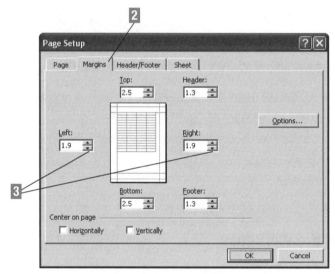

3 *Type the margins you require into the boxes*

or

Use the up and down arrows next to the margin sizes

4.3.3 Changing the Margins from Print Preview

Margins   1 *Click on the Margins button*

   2 *Position your mouse pointer over the margin you wish to resize – the pointer will change to a cross arrow (the dotted lines represent the margins)*

   3 *Click and drag the lines to change the margins*

Members

Title	Surname	First Name	Sex	Date of Birth	Department	Number
Dr	Jekyll	Abigail	Female	23-May-60	Design	1
Ms	Akinlotan	Abimbola	Female	12-Mar-58	Sales	5
Mr	Hyde	Alexander	Male	23-May-28	Finance	3
Mrs	Richards	Anna	Female	27-Mar-68	Sales	6
Mrs	Dalloway	Anne	Female	15-Jun-59	Personnel	8
Mr	Olivelle	Anthony	Male	21-Nov-67	Technology	5
Miss	Duck	Caroline	Female	02-Apr-74	Manufacture	3
Mr	Dodgson	Charles	Male	06-Sep-54	Sales	1
Miss	Mulley	Claire	Female	28-Jul-77	Personnel	5
Mrs	Windsor	Elizabeth	Female	19-Jul-34	Sales	3
Ms	Lazarus	Emma	Female	01-Apr-78	Personnel	6
Miss	Ross	Hannah Elizabeth	Female	19-Sep-75	Finance	8
Mr	Jospin	Jacques	Male	06-Sep-61	Design	5
Mr	Scot	James	Male	06-Sep-61	Manufacture	3
Mrs	Minniver	Jane	Female	12-Mar-57	Finance	1
Miss	Pullen	Jane Elizabeth	Female	12-Apr-78	Design	5
Mrs	Robinson	Jean	Female	23-Dec-62	Design	3
Miss	Huntington	Joanna	Female	23-Apr-72	Personnel	6
Mr	Sutherland	John	Male	06-Sep-61	Manufacture	8
Ms	Hill	Lilias	Female	23-Sep-56	Technology	5
Miss	Day	Lorraine	Female	12-Dec-77	Personnel	3
Ms	Sierra de la Guerra	Maria Consuelo	Female	17-Sep-60	Design	1
Mr	Sharfiz	Muhammed	Male	18-Jun-48	Technology	5
Mr	Al Said	Mummar	Male	30-Jul-59	Manufacture	3
Miss	Cortes	Nicky	Female	04-May-69	Sales	6
Dr	Jekyll	Abigail	Female	23-May-60	Design	1
Ms	Akinlotan	Abimbola	Female	12-Mar-58	Sales	5
Mr	Hyde	Alexander	Male	23-May-28	Finance	3
Mrs	Richards	Anna	Female	27-Mar-68	Sales	6
Mrs	Dalloway	Anne	Female	15-Jun-59	Personnel	8
Mr	Olivelle	Anthony	Male	21-Nov-67	Technology	5
Miss	Duck	Caroline	Female	02-Apr-74	Manufacture	3
Mr	Dodgson	Charles	Male	06-Sep-54	Sales	1
Miss	Mulley	Claire	Female	28-Jul-77	Personnel	5
Mrs	Windsor	Elizabeth	Female	19-Jul-34	Sales	3
Ms	Lazarus	Emma	Female	01-Apr-78	Personnel	6
Miss	Ross	Hannah Elizabeth	Female	19-Sep-75	Finance	8
Mr	Jospin	Jacques	Male	06-Sep-61	Design	5
Mr	Scot	James	Male	06-Sep-61	Manufacture	3
Mrs	Minniver	Jane	Female	12-Mar-57	Finance	1
Miss	Pullen	Jane Elizabeth	Female	12-Apr-78	Design	5
Mrs	Robinson	Jean	Female	23-Dec-62	Design	3
Miss	Huntington	Joanna	Female	23-Apr-72	Personnel	6
Mr	Sutherland	John	Male	06-Sep-61	Manufacture	8
Ms	Hill	Lilias	Female	23-Sep-56	Technology	5
Miss	Day	Lorraine	Female	12-Dec-77	Personnel	3
Ms	Sierra de la Guerra	Maria Consuelo	Female	17-Sep-60	Design	1
Mr	Sharfiz	Muhammed	Male	18-Jun-48	Technology	5
Mr	Al Said	Mummar	Male	30-Jul-59	Manufacture	3
Miss	Cortes	Nicky	Female	04-May-69	Sales	6
Ms	Corvall	Susan	Female	23-Oct-46	Finance	1
Miss	Williams	Tessa	Female	12-Jun-76	Technology	5
Mr	Plod	Vaclav	Male	24-Aug-65	Personnel	3
Ms	Hull	Victoria	Female	12-Mar-74	Manufacture	6
Mr	Tibbs	Virgil	Male	01-Aug-62	Technology	8

Page 1

4.3.4 Changing the Orientation

1 *Bring up the Page Setup dialog box (see page 254)*

2 *Click on the Page tab*

3 *Click in the circle next to Portrait or Landscape*

4 *Click OK*

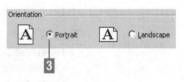

4.3.5 Scaling the Size of a Spreadsheet

If your spreadsheet is too big to fit on the page, or it is too small to read, you can scale it up or down in size.

1️⃣ *Bring up the Page Setup dialog box*

2️⃣ *Click on the Page tab*

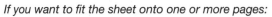

3️⃣ *Increase or decrease the percentage next to* **Adjust to**

or

If you want to fit the sheet onto one or more pages:

Click on **Fit to**

Enter the number of pages you would like to adjust it to

4️⃣ *Click OK*

4.3.6 Printing the Gridlines and Row/Column Headings

When you print a spreadsheet, the little gridlines that divide each cell will not print, unless you tell Excel to do so. Similarly, the row and column headings (A, B, C, and 1, 2, 3, etc.) will not print either, unless you tell them to. To change the print settings for these:

1️⃣ *Bring up the Page Setup dialog box*

2️⃣ *Click on the Sheet tab*

3️⃣ *If required, click in the box next to* **Gridlines** *so that it is ticked*

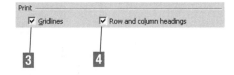

4️⃣ *If required, click in the box next to* **Row and column headings** *so that it is ticked*

5️⃣ *Click OK*

4.3.7 Printing the Title Row or Column

If you have a list with headings at the top (Name, Address, and so on), you might want to repeat these at the top of every page, to make the printout easier to read. The same thing could apply if your headings run down the first column. To make these headings print:

1️⃣ *Bring up the Page Setup dialog box*

2️⃣ *Click on the Sheet tab*

3️⃣ *Click on the red arrow next to* **Rows to repeat at top** *(for a normal header row), or* **Columns to repeat at left** *(for headings in the first column)*

4️⃣ *Select the row(s) or column(s) you want to repeat, by clicking on the grey row or column header*

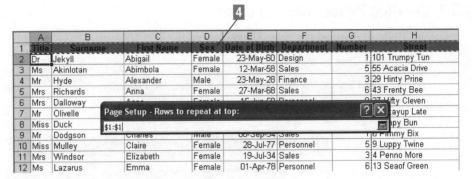

	A	B	C	D	E	F	G	H
1	Title	Surname	First Name	Sex	Date of Birth	Department	Number	Street
2	Dr	Jekyll	Abigail	Female	23-May-60	Design	1	101 Trumpy Tun
3	Ms	Akinlotan	Abimbola	Female	12-Mar-58	Sales	5	55 Acacia Drive
4	Mr	Hyde	Alexander	Male	23-May-28	Finance	3	29 Hinty Prine
5	Mrs	Richards	Anna	Female	27-Mar-68	Sales	6	43 Frenty Bee
6	Mrs	Dalloway		Female				Hifty Cleven
7	Mr	Olivelle						ayup Late
8	Miss	Duck						ppy Bun
9	Mr	Dodgson	Charles	Male	06-Sep-34	Sales		Fimhy Bix
10	Miss	Mulley	Claire	Female	28-Jul-77	Personnel	5	9 Luppy Twine
11	Mrs	Windsor	Elizabeth	Female	19-Jul-34	Sales	3	4 Penno More
12	Ms	Lazarus	Emma	Female	01-Apr-78	Personnel	6	13 Seaof Green

5 *Click on the red arrow at the right of the small Page Setup box*

6 *Click OK*

Now, when you print, the row(s) or column(s) you selected will be repeated on each page. To reverse the process, follow the above steps, but delete the contents of the **Rows to repeat at top** or the **Columns to repeat at left** box.

4.3.8 Changing the Paper Size

1 *Bring up the Page Setup dialog box*

2 *Click on the Page tab*

3 *Choose the paper size you require from the drop down list next to* **Paper size**

4 *Click OK*

4.4 Using Help in Excel

Excel comes with a Help feature which works in exactly the same way as the help in Word – see the Help section in the Word chapters on page 46 for more details.

4.5 Creating Headers and Footers

4.5.1 What are Headers and Footers?

■ Headers and footers contain information which appears at the top and bottom of every page of your spreadsheet when it is printed.

■ They usually include things like the date, the name of the file, your organisation name, page numbers etc.

■ You can only see headers and footers in Print Preview.

4.5.2 Creating Headers and Footers

[1] *Bring up the Page Setup dialog box*

[2] *Click on the Header/Footer tab*

[3] *Click on the drop down arrow underneath* **Header**

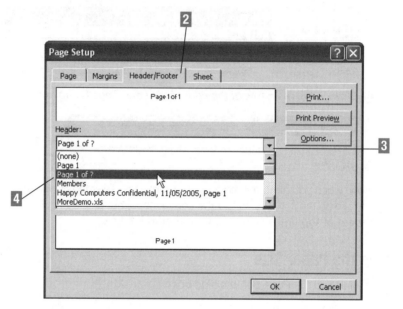

[4] *Click on the header you require*

[5] *Click on the drop down arrow underneath* **Footer**

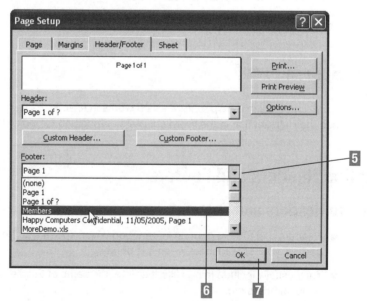

6 *Click on the footer you require*

7 *Click OK*

4.5.3 Removing Headers and Footers

1 *Bring up the Page Setup dialog box*

2 *Click on the Header/Footer tab*

3 *Click on the drop down arrow underneath **Header** or underneath **Footer***

4 *Scroll to the top of the list*

5 *Click **(none)***

6 *Click OK*

4.5.4 Creating Custom Headers and Footers

If you want a bit more flexibility, you will need to customise your headers and footers.

1 *Bring up the Page Setup dialog box*

2 *Click on the Header/Footer tab*

3 *Click Custom Header*

   or

   Click Custom Footer

4 *Click into the section you require*

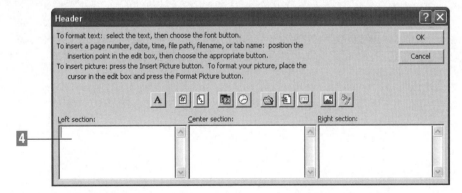

5 *Enter the text you require*

   or

   Click on one of the icons shown to enter text (see next page)

6 *Click OK*

7 *Click OK*

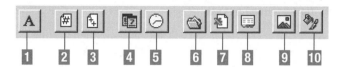

Going from left to right, here is what the icons mean:

1 Changes the font

2 Inserts the page number

3 Inserts the number of pages

4 Inserts the date

5 Inserts the time

6 Inserts the file name and path

7 Inserts the file name

8 Inserts the sheet name

9 Inserts a picture

10 Formats the picture

What do the codes mean?

When you enter information from the toolbar, such as the date, you will see a code rather than the actual information, e.g. **&[Pages]** for number of pages, and **&[Tab]** for the name of the sheet.

When you look at your spreadsheet in Print Preview, or print it out, however, the real information will appear.

CHAPTER 5

Formatting Worksheets

What You'll Do

→ Format Worksheets

→ Insert and Delete Rows and Columns

→ Resize Rows and Columns

→ Change the Font and Font Size

→ Change the Number Format

→ Use the Format Painter

→ Rotate and Wrap Text

→ Change the Alignment

→ Apply Borders

→ Remove Borders

→ Add Colours to Cells

→ Freeze Rows and Columns

5.1 Inserting and Deleting Rows and Columns

5.1.1 Inserting a Row

1 *Select the row (or a cell in the row)* ***below*** *where you want a new one*

2 *Click on the Insert menu*

3 *Click Rows – a new row will be inserted above the selection*

Or

1 *Select the row* ***below*** *where you want a new one*

2 *Press* ***Control*** *(Ctrl) and + on the keyboard*

If you select row 5 --

	A	B
1	Fishcakes	5
2	Monkeysuits	10
3	Stoat polishers	15
4	Cheese wobblers	20
5	Egg spanners	25
6	Chicken dancers	30
7		

-- a new row is inserted above row 5.

	A	B
1	Fishcakes	5
2	Monkeysuits	10
3	Stoat polishers	15
4	Cheese wobblers	20
5		
6	Egg spanners	25
7	Chicken dancers	30

5.1.2 Inserting a Column

1️⃣ Select the column (or a cell in the column) to the **right** of where you want a new one

2️⃣ Click on the Insert menu

3️⃣ Click Columns – a new column will be inserted to the left of the selection

Or

1️⃣ Select the column to the **right** of where you want a new one

2️⃣ Press **Control** (Ctrl) and **+** on the keyboard

If you select column B --

-- a new column is inserted to the left of column B.

	A	B	C
1	Fishcakes	5	
2	Monkeysuits	10	
3	Stoat polishers	15	
4	Cheese wobblers	20	
5	Egg spanners	25	
6	Chicken dancers	30	

	A	B	C
1	Fishcakes		5
2	Monkeysuits		10
3	Stoat polishers		15
4	Cheese wobblers		20
5	Egg spanners		25
6	Chicken dancers		30

5.1.3 Inserting Several Rows and Columns

If you want to insert several rows or columns, you can do them all at once. Let's look at how you would insert six rows:

1️⃣ Select six rows **below** where you want the six new ones

2️⃣ Click on the Insert menu

3️⃣ Click Rows – six new rows will be inserted above the selection

Or

1️⃣ Select six rows **below** where you want the six new ones

2️⃣ Press **Control** (Ctrl) and **+** on the keyboard

Inserting columns works the same way – select six columns to the right of where you want the new ones, click on the Insert menu, and click Column (or select the columns and use **Ctrl +**) .

5.1.4 Deleting Rows and Columns

1️⃣ Select the row(s) or column(s) you wish to delete

2️⃣ Click on the Edit menu

3️⃣ Click Delete

Or

1️⃣ Select the row(s) or column(s) you wish to delete

2️⃣ Press **Control** (Ctrl) and **–** on the keyboard

Pressing Delete on the keyboard doesn't work!

This will only delete any text that the row or column contains, rather than the row or column itself.

5.2 Resizing Rows and Columns

To resize columns or rows...

Your mouse must look like the cross arrow. You can only see this if you position your mouse on the grey line between column letters or row numbers.

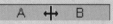

5.2.1 Resizing Rows and Columns

1 *Position your mouse on the grey line to the right of the column letter you wish to resize*

or

Position your mouse on the grey line below the row number you wish to resize

2 *Click and drag to the size you require*

If you make a column too narrow for the text it contains...

You will see hash signs (#) inside the cells. If you make the column a bit wider, you'll be able to read the text clearly again.

5.2.2 Using AutoFit

AutoFit will make a column or row just big enough for the information it contains.

1 *Position your mouse on the grey line to the right of the column letter you wish to resize*

or

Position your mouse on the grey line below the row number you wish to resize

2 *Double click*

5.2.3 Resizing Several Rows or Columns at Once

1 *Select the rows or columns you wish to resize*

2 *Place your mouse on the grey line at the right hand edge of the selected columns*

or

Place your mouse on the grey line underneath the selected rows

3 *Click and drag to the required size – all columns and rows will become that size*

5

5.2.4 Resizing All the Columns and Rows

1 *Select the whole of the spreadsheet (see page 221)*

2 *Resize column A to the desired size*

and/or

Resize row 1 to the desired size

3 *Click in the middle of the spreadsheet to deselect*

5.3 Changing the Font and Font Size

5.3.1 What is Formatting?

Formatting is changing the appearance of your spreadsheet, either to give emphasis to important parts, or to make it easier to read.

Common types of formatting are: **bold**, *italic*, underline, font (or typeface), size, borders and shading.

5.3.2 Applying Bold

1 *Select the cell(s) you wish to make bold*

B   2 *Click on the Bold icon – the Bold icon will look "pushed in"*

5.3.3 Applying Italic

1 *Select the cell(s) you wish to make italic*

I   2 *Click on the Italic icon – the Italic icon will look "pushed in"*

5.3.4 Applying Underline

1 *Select the cell(s) you wish to underline*

<u>U</u>   2 *Click on the Underline icon – the Underline icon will look "pushed in"*

5.3.5 Removing Bold, Italic or Underline

1 *Select the cell(s) you wish to remove bold, italic or underline from*

2 *Click on the Bold, Italic or Underline icon to remove it*

5.3.6 Changing the Font Size

1 *Select the cell(s) you wish to change*

2 *Click on the drop down arrow in the Font Size box*

3 *Click on the size you require – you may need to scroll through the sizes*

Or

☐1 *Select the cell(s) you wish to change*

☐2 *Click inside the Font Size box – the font size number will go blue*

☐3 *Type in the size you require*

☐4 *Press Enter*

5.3.7 Changing the Font

☐1 *Select the cell(s) you wish to change*

☐2 *Click on the drop down arrow next to the Font box*

☐3 *Click on the Font you require – you may need to scroll through the fonts*

Or

☐1 *Select the cell(s) you wish to change*

☐2 *Click inside the Font box – the Font name will go blue*

☐3 *Type in the name of the font you require*

☐4 *Press Enter*

5.3.8 Changing the Font Colour

☐1 *Select the cell(s) you wish to change*

☐2 *Click on the drop down arrow next to the Font Colour icon*

☐3 *Click on the colour you require*

☐4 *Deselect the cells – the colour may look strange until you deselect*

5.4 Changing the Number Format

5.4.1 What are Number Formats?

When you enter numbers they are usually unformatted. They may, however, represent money or a percentage. In order to make them look like what they represent, you can apply a number format to them. Common number formats include:

- Currency

- Percentage

- Commas

- Dates

- Displaying Negative Numbers in Red

5.4.2 Applying Number Formats

$\boxed{1}$ *Select the cell(s) you wish to change*

$\boxed{2}$ *Click on the number format you require (see below)*

Going from left to right, here is what each icon means:

1 Currency

2 Percentage

3 Commas

4 Increase decimal places

5 Decrease decimal places

5.4.3 Changing Number Formats with the Menu

Changing number formats with the menu gives you a much greater choice of formats.

$\boxed{1}$ *Select the cell(s) you wish to change*

$\boxed{2}$ *Click on the Format menu*

$\boxed{3}$ *Click Cells*

4 *Click on the Number tab*

5 *Click on the category you require from the left hand side*

6 *Click on the style you require on the right – each category has different options*
   e.g. date

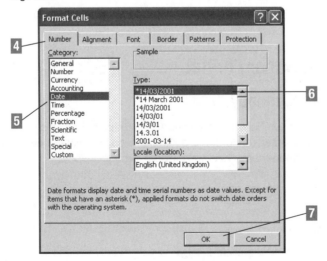

7 *Click OK*

5.4.4 Removing Number Formats

⒈ *Select the cell(s) you wish to remove number formats from*

⒉ *Click on the Edit menu*

⒊ *Click on the Clear submenu*

⒋ *Click Formats*

5.5 Using the Format Painter

5.5.1 The Format Painter

Once you have formatted a cell, you can easily duplicate the formatting using the Format Painter. This saves you from having to go through the whole process of setting up formatting for the new selection of cells.

⒈ *Select the cell(s) with the formatting you wish to copy*

⒉ *Click the Format Painter icon on the toolbar*

⒊ *Select the cell(s) you wish to copy the formatting to – the cells will be formatted like the first one*

5.6 Rotating and Wrapping Text

Text can be displayed in a number of different ways inside cells. You can rotate it, or choose if a long sentence stays on one line, or wraps around to keep the cell the same width.

5.6.1 Rotating Text

⒈ *Select the cell(s) you wish to rotate*

⒉ *Click on the Format menu*

⒊ *Click Cells*

⒋ *Click on the Alignment tab*

⒌ *Change the rotation using the Orientation section:*

- Click on the vertical text in the first white box to make the text vertical

- Click and drag the line in the second white box to change the angle of the text

- Use the up or down arrows next to the Degrees box to change the angle, or type in the angle you want

⒍ *Click OK – your text will now be rotated at your chosen angle*

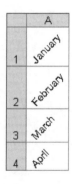

5.6.2 Wrapping Text

1. *Select the cell(s) you want to change*

2. *Click on the Format menu*

3. *Click Cells*

4. *Click the Alignment tab*

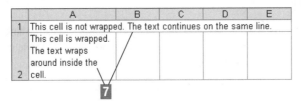

5. *Click inside the **Wrap text** box under **Text control** so that it is ticked*

6. *Click OK*

7. *In the example the text in cell A1 is not wrapped, while the text in cell A2 is wrapped:*

	A	B	C	D	E
1	This cell is not wrapped. The text continues on the same line.				
2	This cell is wrapped. The text wraps around inside the cell.				

5.7 Changing the Alignment

5.7.1 What is Alignment?

Alignment refers to the position of data inside the cell. There are three main types in Excel:

1. **Left** (usually for text)

2. **Right** (usually for numbers)

3. **Centre** (usually for headings)

5.7.2 Changing the Alignment

1. *Select the cell(s) you wish to change*

2. *Click on the alignment icon you require*

5.7.3 Merge and Centre

Centre align will only centre text inside a column. Sometimes, however, you may require a heading to be centred in the middle of several cells.

1. *Select the cell containing the text, and the cells you wish to put it in the middle of*

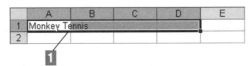

	A	B	C	D	E
1	Monkey Tennis				
2					

2 *Click on the Merge and Centre icon*

3 *The cells have been merged together, and the heading is now centred:*

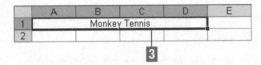

	A	B	C	D	E
1			Monkey Tennis		
2					

3

5.7.4 Removing Merge and Centre

1 *Select the cell that has been merged*

2 *Click on the Merge and Centre icon again*

5.7.5 Vertical Alignment

If you have tall rows, you may wish to change the vertical alignment (top, centre, bottom, justify) rather than the horizontal (left, centre, right). Look at these cells:

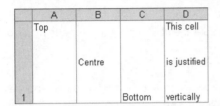

	A	B	C	D
	Top			This cell
		Centre		is justified
1			Bottom	vertically

They have been aligned vertically. Cell A1 has the text at the top, B1 has it in the centre, and C1 has it at the bottom. Cell D1 is vertically justified, which means that the text is spaced out so that it touches the top and bottom of the cell.

1 *Select the cell(s) you want to change*

2 *Click on the Format menu*

3 *Click Cells*

4 *Click on the Alignment tab*

5 *Click on the drop down arrow under the **Vertical** box*

6 *Click on the alignment you require*

7 *Click OK*

5

5.8 Applying Borders

5.8.1 What are Borders?

The lines that you can see around the cells in your spreadsheet don't necessarily print out. They are known as **gridlines**. If you want lines to print out, or you need to add decorative lines to your spreadsheet, then you can use **borders** to format it.

5.8.2 Applying Borders with the Icon

[1] *Select the cell(s) you wish to apply a border to*

[2] *Click on the arrow next to the Borders icon*

[3] *Click on the border style you require*

[4] *Deselect the cells – you can't see the border if the cells are still selected!*

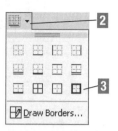

Careful which cells you select!

Sometimes you have think carefully about which cells to select. Imagine that you want to add a double line above the selection of cells shown below.

10	Loan	£ 100.00	
11			
12	*Total*	£ 535.00	
13			
14	*Surplus*	£1,465.00	
15			

There is no option for adding a double line above, only one for adding a double line below:

However, if you select the cells in row 11 above the total, you can apply a double line below those. This has the same effect as applying a double line to the top of the cells containing the total.

10	Loan	£ 100.00	
11			
12	*Total*	£ 535.00	
13			
14	*Surplus*	£1,465.00	
15			

5.8.3 Applying Borders with the Menu

[1] *Select the cell(s) you wish to apply a border to*

[2] *Click on the Format menu*

[3] *Click Cells*

[4] *Click on the Border tab*

[5] *Click on the line style you require from the right hand side*

[6] *Click on the drop down arrow underneath Colour and click on a different colour if required*

[7] *Click on the Border icons to set the borders you require*

[8] *Click OK*

5.8.4 Removing Borders

1. Select the cells you wish to remove the borders from
2. Click on the arrow next to the Borders icon
3. Click on the blank border style

5.9 Adding Colours to Cells

5.9.1 Changing the Background Colour

You can add colours to cells, rows and columns to make spreadsheets easier to read. Don't go overboard though – too many colours will make into a fascinating, but unreadable, mess . . .

1. Select the cell(s) you wish to change
2. Click on the Format menu
3. Click Cells
4. Click the Patterns tab
5. Click on the colour you wish to use – or click **No Color** to remove the colours
6. Click OK

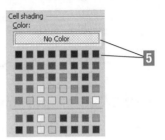

5.10 Freezing Rows and Columns

5.10.1 Why Freeze Rows and Columns?

Freezing rows or columns lets you keep titles visible on the screen at all times. For example, in the spreadsheet below, row 1 remains on screen, even though we have scrolled far down into the spreadsheet:

	A	B	C	D
1	Jan	Feb	Mar	Apr
74	5	7	5	3
75	4	5	4	5
76	7	3	7	6
77	5	5	5	5
78	3	6	3	4
79	5	5	5	2

This is useful if you have a large spreadsheet, which you have to scroll through to see all the details. No matter which area you are working on, you will always be able to see the titles for the sheet.

5.10.2 Freezing Rows

1. *Select the row below where the split should appear*
2. *Click on the Window menu*
3. *Click Freeze Panes*

5.10.3 Freezing Columns

1. *Select the column to the right of where the split should appear*
2. *Click on the Window menu*
3. *Click Freeze Panes*

5.10.4 Freezing Rows and Columns

1. *Click the cell below and to the right of where the split should appear*
2. *Click on the Window menu*
3. *Click Freeze Panes*

5.10.5 Unfreezing Rows and/or Columns

1. *Click on the Window menu*
2. *Click Unfreeze Panes*

CHAPTER 6

Charts

What You'll Do

- ➡ Create Charts
- ➡ Move, Resize and Delete Charts
- ➡ Format Charts
- ➡ Change the Colours in a Chart
- ➡ Resize and Move Parts in a Chart
- ➡ Use the Chart Toolbar
- ➡ Show/Hide Legend
- ➡ Show/Hide Data Table
- ➡ Change Chart Options
- ➡ Print Charts

6.1 Creating Charts

Creating a chart makes it easier to compare and contrast the figures in a spreadsheet. Charts are also sometimes called graphs.

6.1.1 Which Chart Should I Use?

Area chart

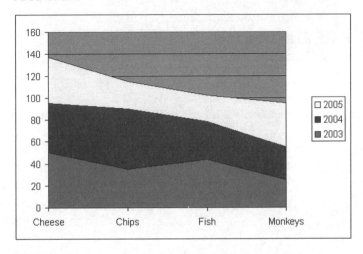

Use this when you want to emphasise change over time.

3-D surface

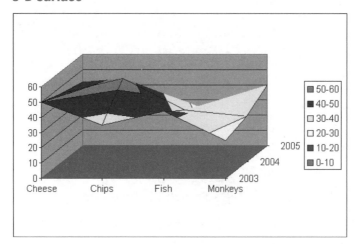

A surface chart is a bit like a 3D map. Colours and patterns show areas that are in the same range of values.

Bar chart

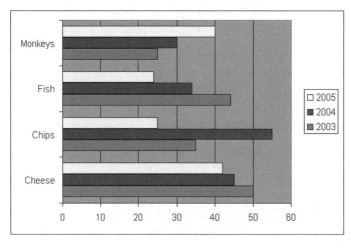

A bar chart simply compares values with each other, by displaying them as lines, or "bars".

Radar chart

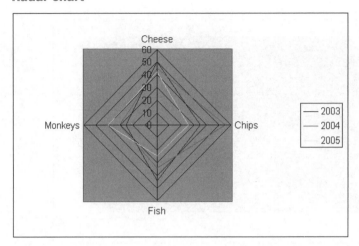

In this chart, each type of information has its own line radiating out from the centre. The further the line comes out from the centre, the higher the value.

Column chart

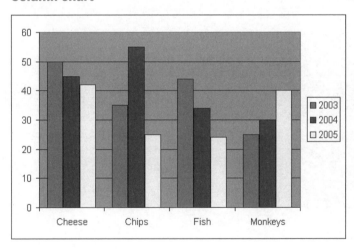

A column chart is the same as a bar chart, except the bars are vertical instead of horizontal.

6

Bubble chart

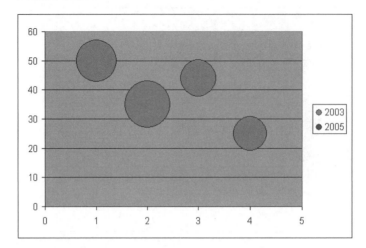

A bubble chart shows three sets of variables, represented by the two axes and the size of the bubble. The bigger the bubble, the higher the value.

Line chart

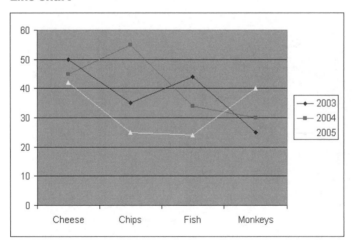

A line chart is useful for comparing overlapping figures.

Scatter chart

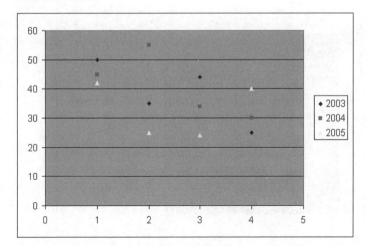

A scatter graph is useful for comparing data with the average or estimated values. This type of chart is usually used for displaying scientific data.

Pie chart

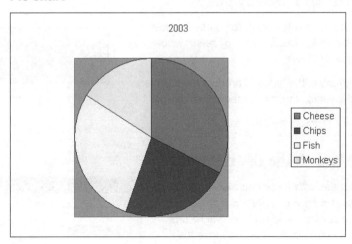

A pie chart is useful for showing one set of figures clearly.

Doughnut chart

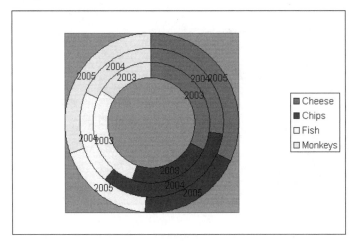

A doughnut chart is similar to a pie chart, but it can show more than one set of figures – each ring of the doughnut represents a set of figures.

6.1.2 Creating Charts with the Keyboard

1 Select the cells you wish to chart – include labels and figures, but do **not** select whole rows or columns

	2003	2004	2005
Cheese	50	45	42
Chips	35	55	25
Fish	44	34	24
Monkeys	25	30	40

In this example, the types of product are selected, as are the years, and the numbers themselves.

2 Press F11 to create the chart

6.1.3 Creating Charts with the Chart Wizard

1 Select the cells to be charted – include labels and figures, but do not select whole columns and rows, or the results will be quite bizarre – only choose the values and labels (but not the title)

2 Click on the Chart Wizard icon

3 In step 1 of the wizard, choose the chart type you require

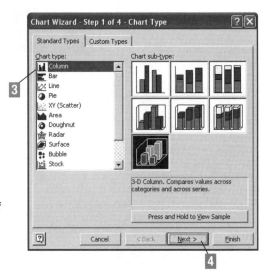

Choose a chart type from the list on the left, then choose a chart format from the examples on the right. To see an example of the chart you have selected, click and hold down the mouse button on the **Press and Hold to View Sample** button.

4 *Click on Next*

5 *In step 2 of the wizard, check that the cells you selected have produced the expected chart*

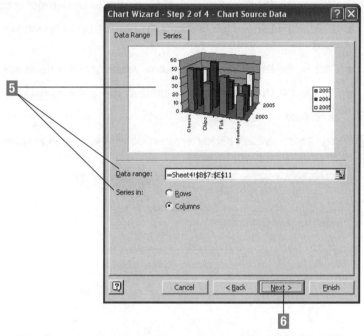

- The large area at the top shows you how your chart will look

- The **Data range** box shows you what cells you have selected

- Change the **Series in** section to decide whether the chart uses the rows or columns from your cells

6 *Click on Next*

7 *In step 3 of the wizard, change the chart options if required (see next page)*

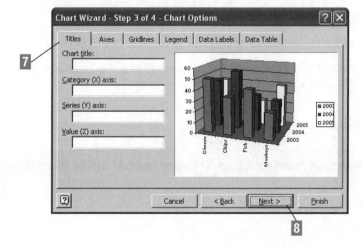

- Click on the **Titles** tab to add titles to the axes or to the whole chart

- Click on the **Axes** tab to change the scale of the axes

- Click on the **Gridlines** tab to choose whether to show major or minor gridlines

- Click on the **Legend** tab to decide the position of the legend (the chart key) on the chart

- Click on the **Data Labels** tab to show values or percentages around the bars

- Click on the **Data Table** tab to include a table of the figures you have charted

8 *Click on Next*

9 *In step 4 of the wizard, decide whether you wish your chart to appear on a new sheet or as an object next to your figures*

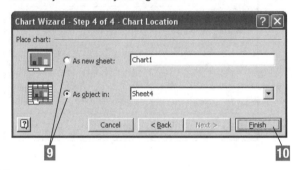

10 *Click on Finish*

6.2 Moving, Resizing and Deleting Charts

This only applies to charts which have been created using the wizard, that are on a sheet as an object.

6.2.1 Moving Charts

1 *Click on the white area of the chart to select it – black boxes will appear around the edge*

2 *Click and drag from the middle of the chart to a new location – your mouse should look like a white arrow*

6.2.2 Resizing Charts

 Your mouse must look like a double headed arrow to resize a chart! ↕

1️⃣ *Click on the chart to select it – black boxes will appear around the edge*

2️⃣ *Hover the mouse pointer over a box – your mouse pointer will change to a double headed arrow*

3️⃣ *Click and drag to make the chart larger or smaller*

6.2.3 Deleting Charts

1️⃣ *Click on the white area of the chart to select it – black boxes will appear around the edge*

2️⃣ *Press the Delete or Del key*

6.3 | Formatting Charts

6.3.1 Selecting Parts of a Pie Chart

 Black boxes appear around the part of the chart which is selected!

Click on the part of the chart you wish to select (see below)

or

Use the Chart Toolbar (see page 289)

 If you want to select one piece of pie…

You may have to click on it twice. When you first click, you will probably get the whole pie, but if you click again on the piece you want, you will get just that bit.

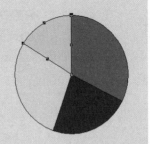

6

6.3.2 Selecting Parts of a Bar Chart

 Black boxes appear around the part of the chart which is selected!

Click on the part of the chart you wish to select

or

Use the Chart Toolbar (see page 289)

6.3.3 Formatting Part of a Chart

The instructions below describe how to format parts of charts in general. The options are different depending on which part you select.

1. *Select the part of the chart you wish to change*

2. *Click on the Format menu*

3. *Click **Selected (name of part of chart you have selected)** – for example, if you have selected the bars, the option will be **Selected Data Series***

4. *Change the options as required*

Or

1. *Select the part of the chart you wish to change*

2. *Click the Format icon on the Chart Toolbar (see page 289)*

6.3.4 Formatting a Piece of Pie

1. *Select the piece of pie you wish to change*

2. *Click on the Format menu*

3. *Click Selected Data Point*

4. *Change the options as required (see below)*

5. *If you want to change the Borders and Fill Colour, see the section on changing the colours in a chart on page 287.*

If you want to change the labels around a piece of pie, click on the Data Labels tab:

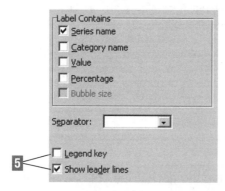

- Click in the box next to the data label you wish to show or hide

- Click **Legend key** to label the piece of pie with its colour in the legend

- Click **Show leader lines** to have a line from the label to the piece of pie

6 To rotate the pie chart, click on the Options tab, and change the number inside the **Angle of first slice** box, or use the arrows to increase or decrease the angle.

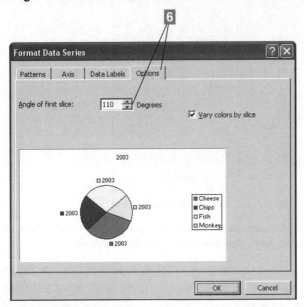

6.3.5 Formatting the Chart Background

1 *Select the white chart background (or Chart background)*

2 *Click on the Format menu*

3 *Click Selected Chart Area*

4 *Change the options as required:*

If you want to change the borders and fill colour, see the first section on page 287.

If you want to change the font, see the second section on page 287.

6.3.6 Formatting Axes

1 *Select the axis you require*

2 *Click on the Format menu*

3 *Click Selected Axis*

4 *Change the options as required (see next page)*

Changing the Line Styles

You can change the type of lines that make up the axes, and the little tick marks that divide up the values. Click on the Patterns tab:

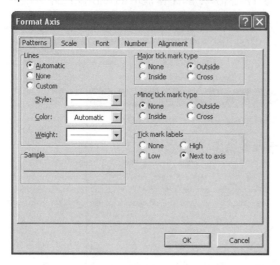

- Click in the circle next to the Axis option you require – **Automatic** chooses them for you, **None** removes them, **Custom** lets you define your own

- Click the drop down arrows to change style, colour or thickness (weight) of the line

- Major and minor tick marks are the little dividing lines on the axis, like those on a ruler – the Major ones are the bigger ones, the Minor ones are the smaller ones

- The tick mark label is the text that runs along the axis, telling you what the values or the categories are

Changing the Scale

The scale affects the distance between the numbers on the axes, and the size of your chart. For example, you might have numbers varying between 10 and 70, but you might want the chart to go up to 100, or only 80. The same chart below is shown with a maximum of 60, then 100, to show the effect changing the scale can have:

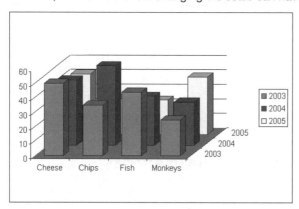

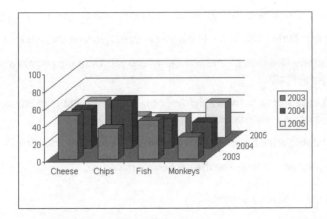

Click on the Scale tab to change the scale – you will get different options depending on which axis you choose:

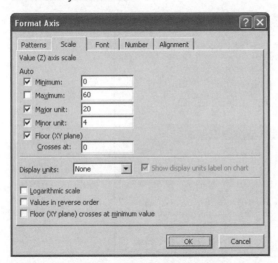

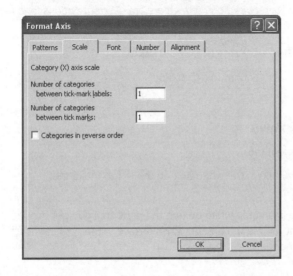

- **Minimum** and **Maximum**: the highest and lowest numbers you require on the axis

- **Major unit** and **Minor unit**: the interval you require between the labels on the axis

- **Floor (XY) plane Crosses at**: the number where you want the two axes to cross over – this is usually set to 0

- **Number of categories between tick-mark labels**: the number of labels you require – entering a value of **1** will label every category

- **Number of categories between tick marks**: the number of tick marks you require

If you want to change the font, see the section on page 287.

Changing the Number Format

1. Click on the Number tab

2. Click on the Category you require from the list on the left

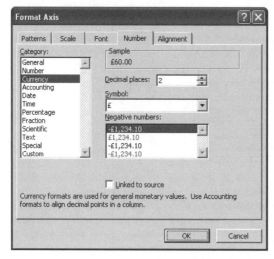

3. Change the options as required on right – there are different options for different categories

For more information about number formats

See the Number Formats section on page 265.

Changing the Alignment

Click on the Alignment tab

- Click on the vertical text in the white box on the left to make the text vertical

- Click and drag the line in the white box on the right until you get the angle you want, or use the up and down arrows in the **Degrees** box to change it

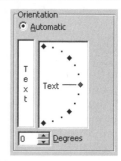

6.3.7 Changing the Colours in a Chart

1 *Select the part of the chart you wish to change*

2 *Click on the Format menu*

3 *Click **Selected (name of part of selected chart)***

4 *Click on the Patterns tab*

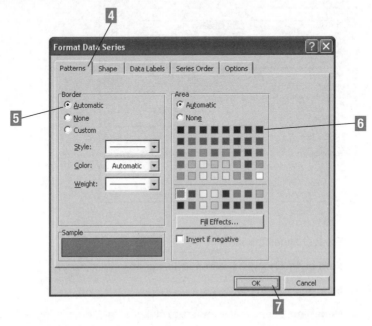

5 Change the border options from the Border section:

- **Automatic** *chooses them for you*, **None** *removes them*, **Custom** *lets you define your own*

- *For Custom borders, use the drop down arrows to create them –* **Style** *lets you choose the type of line*, **Color** *changes the colour, and* **Weight** *changes the thickness*

6 *Choose the colour in the Area section to change the fill colour – just click on the colour you like*

7 *Click OK*

6.3.8 Changing the Fonts in a Chart

You can only change the font in a part of the chart that contains text – for example, you can't change the font on the background, because it doesn't have text to change. To change the font:

1 *Select the part of the chart you wish to change*

2 *Click on the Format menu*

3 Click **Selected (part of chart you wish to change)**

4 Click on the Font tab:

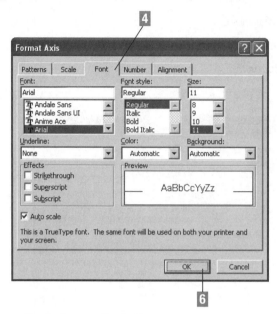

■ **Font**: changes the font

■ **Font style**: changes the font style, i.e. bold, italic, etc.

■ **Size**: changes the font size

■ **Underline**: changes the underline style – single, double, dotted, etc.

■ **Color**: changes the text colour

■ **Background**: decides whether the background of the text box is transparent (see-through) or opaque (er, not see-through)

■ **Effects**: lets you apply special effects like ~~strikethrough~~, superscript, and subscript

5 Make any changes you require

6 Click OK

6.3.9 Resizing Parts of a Chart

Only certain parts of a chart can be resized. If you cannot get a double headed arrow, then you cannot resize.

1 Select the part of the chart you wish to change – black boxes will appear around the selected part

2 Position the mouse pointer over a black box – the mouse pointer will change to a double headed arrow

3 Click and drag to resize

Choose which box you resize from carefully!

Boxes at a corner will allow you to resize both the height and the width. Boxes which are not in the corners will allow you to resize the height or the width only.

6.3.10 Moving Parts of a Chart

1. *Select the part of the chart you wish to change – black boxes will appear around it*

2. *Position the mouse pointer over a blank part in the middle – the mouse pointer will look like a white arrow*

3. *Click and drag to move*

6.4 Using the Chart Toolbar

6.4.1 Displaying the Chart Toolbar

1. *Click on the View menu*

2. *Click Toolbars – any toolbars currently displayed will be ticked*

3. *Click Chart*

6.4.2 Selecting with the Chart Toolbar

1 *Click the drop down arrow next to the Chart Objects icon*

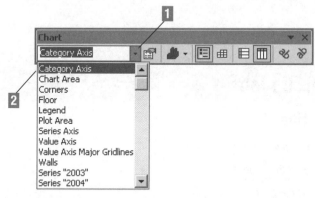

2 *Click on the part you wish to select*

6.4.3 Formatting with the Chart Toolbar

1. *Select the part of the chart you wish to format*

 2 *Click the Format icon on the chart toolbar*

6.4.4 Changing the Chart Type

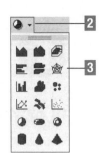

[1] *Select the white chart background*

[2] *Click on the drop down arrow next to the Chart Type icon on the chart toolbar*

[3] *Click on the chart type you prefer*

6.4.5 Show/Hide Legend

[1] *Select the white chart background*

[2] *Click on the Legend icon – this will show it if it's hidden, and hide it if it's shown*

6.4.6 Show/Hide Data Table

[1] *Select the white chart background*

[2] *Click on the Data Table icon – this will show it if it's hidden, and hide it if it's shown*

6.4.7 By Row and By Column

This lets you change the way Excel uses your data to create the chart – by row (left to right) or by column (top to bottom). If your chart looks the way you planned, then you probably don't need to use this.

[1] *Select the white chart background*

[2] *Click on the By Row icon*

or

Click on the By Column icon

6.5 Changing Chart Options

6.5.1 Changing Chart Titles

[1] *Select the white chart background*

[2] *Click on the Chart menu*

[3] *Click Chart Options*

[4] *Click on the Titles tab*

[5] *Type in the titles you require*

[6] *Click OK*

6.5.2 Adding Data Labels

⎡1⎤ *Select the white chart background*

⎡2⎤ *Click on the Chart menu*

⎡3⎤ *Click Chart Options*

⎡4⎤ *Click on the Data Labels tab*

⎡5⎤ *Click in the circle next to the type of data labels you would like to see*

⎡6⎤ *Click OK*

6.5.3 Changing the Position of the Legend

⎡1⎤ *Select the white chart background*

⎡2⎤ *Click on the Chart menu*

⎡3⎤ *Click Chart Options*

⎡4⎤ *Click on the Legend tab*

⎡5⎤ *Click in the circle next to the position you require*

⎡6⎤ *Click OK*

6.5.4 Chart Gridlines

⎡1⎤ *Select the white chart background*

⎡2⎤ *Click on the Chart menu*

⎡3⎤ *Click Chart Options*

⎡4⎤ *Click on the Gridlines tab*

⎡5⎤ *Click in the boxes next to the gridlines you would like to see*

⎡6⎤ *Click OK*

6.6 Printing Charts

6.6.1 Previewing a Chart

⎡1⎤ *Select the white chart background*

 2 *Click on the Print Preview icon*

6.6.2 Printing a Chart on its Own

⎡1⎤ *Select the white chart background*

 2 *Click on the Print icon*

6

6.6.3 Printing a Chart with the Figures

To print a chart with the numbers next to it, do not select anything! First, move the chart next to the numbers, so that you can see both of them clearly. Then just deselect the chart by clicking on an empty cell, and click the Print icon.

CHAPTER 7

Excel Quick Reference

What You'll Do

→ Get a Quick Reference to Excel

→ Discover the Standard Toolbar

→ Discover the Formatting Toolbar

7.1 What Do All the Icons Mean?

7.1.1 The Standard Toolbar

☐	Create a new, blank workbook
📂	Open a workbook
💾	Save the current workbook
📧	Email the spreadsheet to an email contact (not required for ECDL)
🔍	Search your computer for a file (not required for ECDL)
🖨	Print one copy of the active sheet
🔎	Print Preview the active sheet
ABC✓	Spell Check
✂	Cut the selected cells
📋	Copy the selected cells
📋	Paste into the current cell
🖌	Format painter
↩ ▾	Undo
↪ ▾	Redo
🌐	Insert a hyperlink to another location (not required for ECDL)
Σ	AutoSum
A↓Z	Sort Ascending
Z↓A	Sort Descending

7

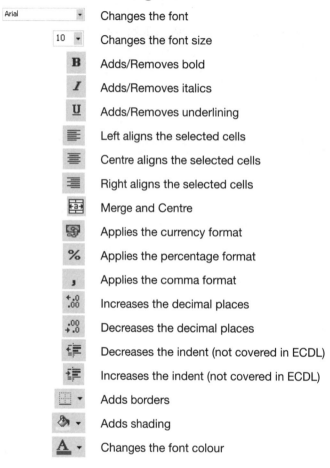

The Chart Wizard

Displays the Drawing toolbar if it is not already displayed

Zoom control

Displays the Excel Help feature

7.1.2 The Formatting Toolbar

Changes the font

Changes the font size

Adds/Removes bold

Adds/Removes italics

Adds/Removes underlining

Left aligns the selected cells

Centre aligns the selected cells

Right aligns the selected cells

Merge and Centre

Applies the currency format

Applies the percentage format

Applies the comma format

Increases the decimal places

Decreases the decimal places

Decreases the indent (not covered in ECDL)

Increases the indent (not covered in ECDL)

Adds borders

Adds shading

Changes the font colour

7.2 Glossary

7.2.1 Absolute Cell References

If you want to copy a formula to another cell, but you want to prevent Excel from adjusting the cell references, make the cell references *absolute*. Absolute cell references are indicated by a dollar sign ($).

7.2.2 Active Cell

The cell border of the active cell is darker than the other cells, and shows you which cell you are currently working on.

7.2.3 AutoFill

This feature allows you to enter a series of numbers, dates or formulae.

7.2.4 AutoFormat

This will automatically format your table, for example adding borders, shading and bold.

7.2.5 AutoSum

Automatically adds up the figures in the cells above or to the left of the active cell. If necessary, you can choose which cells you want added up.

7.2.6 Cell

This is the basic building block of the Excel worksheet. A cell is formed by the intersection of the row and column gridlines. Each cell is identified by the letter of the column and the number of the row, e.g. B7.

7.2.7 Cell Range

A group of cells that are next to each other.

7.2.8 Cell References

These are the coordinates of the cell in the worksheet, e.g. B7.

7.2.9 Chart Sheet

This is a sheet in a workbook containing a chart. The chart sheet is updated when the worksheet data is changed.

7.2.10 Fill Handle

This is a solid black square in the right hand corner of the active cell border. Using your mouse, grab the black square and drag it across to AutoFill your cells.

7.2.11 Formulae

Formulae are the basis of Excel. Formulae will do all the calculations that will normally be done by a calculator. You can use formulae to do simple calculations such as additions, subtractions, multiplication, division as well as statistical, financial and scientific calculations.

7

7.2.12 Formula Bar

This is the bar at the top of the Excel screen. It is used to enter and edit formulae and values. It also displays the formula in a particular cell.

7.2.13 Gridlines

These are the lines that you see in your spreadsheet. You can choose to print them, or leave them out.

7.2.14 Label

This is the text which usually appears next to the figures in a spreadsheet, and identifies what the figures mean.

7.2.15 Legends

A legend (also known as a key) is used in charts and graphs. Excel actually creates legends from the labels on the worksheet. The legends can be customised with borders, patterns and different fonts.

7.2.16 Mixed Cell References

In a formula there can be a combination of relative and absolute cell references. A mixed reference can look like $A1 or A$1. $A1 refers to column A regardless of the position of the cell containing the formula.

7.2.17 Paste Function

This allows you to enter commonly used calculations quickly, such as finding the average, maximum or minimum of a group of numbers.

7.2.18 Relative Cell References

Relative cell references are used in formulae where you do not wish the reference to remain constant as the formula is AutoFilled. Relative cell references do not contain the $ that is found in absolute cell references.

7.2.19 Sheets

It is possible to insert, delete, rename, move and copy sheets in Excel. It can be a worksheet, chart sheet, module sheet or dialogue sheet. A worksheet is the one used most often.

7.2.20 Worksheet

This is also called a spreadsheet. The worksheet is the primary document used in Excel. A worksheet is made up of cells in columns and rows, and is always part of a workbook.

BASIC CONCEPTS OF
INFORMATION TECHNOLOGY

1

FILE MANAGEMENT

2

WORD PROCESSING

3

SPREADSHEETS

4

DATABASES

5

PRESENTATIONS

6

INTERNET AND EMAIL

7

CHAPTER 1

Getting Started

1

What You'll Do

- → Use Databases
- → Start and Close Access
- → Open, Save and Close a Database
- → Discover the Parts of an Access Database
- → Open and Close a Database Object
- → Use a Table
- → Enter New Records

- → Select and Delete Records
- → Change the Look of a Table
- → Select and Move Columns
- → Search and Sort Records
- → Print Tables
- → Use Help in Access
- → Use Toolbars

1.1 Access

Access is a database program. That's all very well and good, but what is a database? Well, suppose you had a list made up of loads of names and addresses – that is a simple database. Access is a bit cleverer than that, though. It lets you store names and addresses, sure, but you can create clever things called relational databases, that contain lots of little databases linked together. So you could have the names and addresses database, which is linked to an employment record database, which is linked to a holiday/sick day database, which is linked to a database that records the salaries – it's as complex or as simple as you want it to be.

1.1.1 Starting Access

1. *Click on the Start button*

2. *Click on All Programs*

Microsoft
Access

3. *Click on Microsoft Access*

Or, if you have a shortcut on the desktop, double click on the shortcut

1.1.2 Closing Access

① *Click on the File menu*

② *Click Exit*

Or

Click the top X at the top right of the Access window

1.2 Opening, Saving and Closing a Database

1.2.1 Opening a Database

When you open Access, the following screen is displayed:

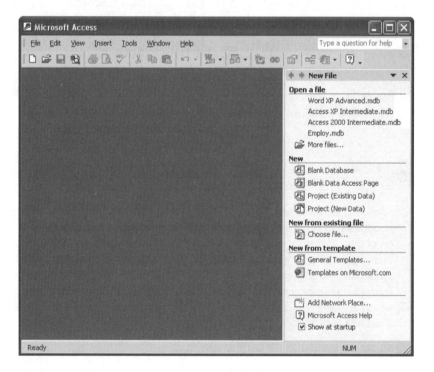

To open a database that is displayed in the Task Pane on the right of the screen, just click on the name of the file.

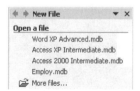

To open a database on your hard drive:

[1] *Click on the File menu*

[2] *Click Open*

   or

   Click on the Open icon

   or

   *Click on **More files** from the Task Pane*

[3] *If necessary, click on the drop down arrow next to the **Look in** box to change the folder you are in*

[4] *Double click on the database you require*

   or

   Click on the database you require

   Click Open

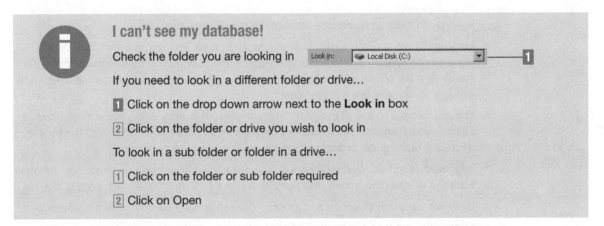

I can't see my database!

Check the folder you are looking in

If you need to look in a different folder or drive...

[1] Click on the drop down arrow next to the **Look in** box

[2] Click on the folder or drive you wish to look in

To look in a sub folder or folder in a drive...

[1] Click on the folder or sub folder required

[2] Click on Open

1.2.2 Closing a Database

[1] *Click on the File menu*

[2] *Click Close*

Or

   *Click the X at the top right of the database window – **not** the X at the top right of the Access screen!*

1.2.3 Saving a Database

Databases are not saved in the same way as Word documents, or Excel spreadsheets, etc.

■ When you create a new database it is automatically saved.

■ When you add records to a database they are automatically saved.

- When you delete or modify the information in a database, your changes are automatically saved.
- It is only when you alter the design or structure of a database that you need to save your changes.

1.3 What is a Database?

A database is a collection of information with the **information arranged in a structured way**. You have probably used paper databases to look information up, e.g. a telephone book, a card index, or a filing system.

1.3.1 The Advantages of Using Computerised Databases

If you have a lot of information to deal with, it is almost always better to use a computer rather than paper records. The main advantages are:

- You can **sort** your information into any order, e.g. a phone book on computer could be arranged in order of postcode, name of the town, area code etc.
- **Finding** people is much easier. Unlike a paper system, you are not reliant on one key piece of information, e.g. to find someone in a phone book you have to know their surname. If the phone book was on a computer, you could know their address, their first name, etc., and still use it to find them.
- You do not have to see all the information at once. The information that you wish to see can be **extracted** from the whole, e.g. all the people who live in London, all the people who are 3 months late in paying their bill, etc.
- Information can be **cross-referenced**, which would be impossible on paper, e.g. you may want to see everyone who lives in London and is also 3 months late with paying their bill.
- **Updates** are much easier on a computer. You can quickly delete or edit the information.
- Computers use **less space** than a large paper filing system.

1.3.2 Do You Need a Database?

Consider what you need a database for. Will it help you work more efficiently, or will the effort and time you put in outweigh the benefit of using it?

- **A Good Example**

  If you have a list of clients on a database, you could search through and find those clients that meet specific criteria. For example, those in Warwickshire, who have spent X amount on your product or service in the last year, but have not placed an order in the last three months. You could then send them a letter to see if they want to buy anything.

- **A Bad Example**

  A list of suppliers who you only need to look up by name. A simple card file (or table in Word) may be quicker and a lot cheaper, if all the information is simply listed in alphabetical order and is only needed in that order.

1.4 The Parts of an Access Database

1.4.1 The Database Window

When you first open a database you will see the database window. This is like the "control centre" of the database – everything you create and use will be done from here. When the database is open, this window will also be open somewhere on the screen.

- The name of the database is shown on the title bar – in this case, "Disaster".

- The Objects bar on the left shows you the seven possible parts of a database.

- At the moment you are looking at the tables – there is one table in this database, called "tblPlates".

1.4.2 What Do the Parts of a Database Do?

The seven different parts all work together to make the whole database function. Each part has a specific role in the way the database works . . .

Tables
- Tables are where **all** the **information** in your database **is stored**.

- They are the first part to be created, and no other part can function until the tables are in place.

- You can use tables to input information.

- Tables also allow you to see lots of information at once.

- A database with one table is known as a **flat-file** database.

- Most databases have more than one table. These tables will be related to each other in some way, e.g. one table for employee details, and another table for the training they go on. This is known as a **relational** database.

Queries
- Queries allow you to **extract** information from the tables. Tables contain all the information, but you may wish to take out a section from the whole, e.g. all the people who live in London, all the sales staff, etc.

- You can think of queries as the "questions" you ask of your tables.

- Queries appear as "mini" tables. The query shown below has extracted all the sales staff from a table.

Forms
- Forms are based on tables and contain the same information.

- They are used to input information in a more user-friendly way than tables.

Reports
- Reports are used to print information off from the database. They are based on the information found in tables or queries.

- Reports can also be used to produce mailing labels.

Pages
- Pages are used for adding, editing or viewing data on the web. They are like tables, but published as webpages.

Macros
- Macros are used to speed up the way a database works, e.g. you could create a macro which automatically starts your database on a specific form.

Modules
- Modules have the same function as macros. They allow you to write small programs which can run within Access to speed up your work.

1.4.3 Navigating Around the Database Window

To use different parts of the database, just click on the button you require from the Objects bar on the left. Objects of that type will appear to the right – so if you clicked on Queries, then all the Queries would appear on the right.

1.4.4 Opening a Database Object

1. *Click on the button you require, e.g. Tables*

2. *Double click on the object you require*

Or

1. *Click on the button you require, e.g. Tables*

2. *Click on the object you require*

3. *Click Open*

You can end up with lots of windows open!

When you open an object, it appears in a new window. The database window remains open behind the object window. If you open up more objects, you can end up with a lot of windows on your screen. Don't worry, this is perfectly natural, and is not at all bad for your health. If you get worried, just close the windows you don't need – but don't close the main database window, or your whole database will close!

1.4.5 Closing a Database Object

1 *Click on the File menu*

2 *Click Close*

Or

Click the X at the top of the object window

1.5 Using Tables

1.5.1 What is a Table?

■ Tables are the core of your database, and contain all the raw information. No other part of the database can function without tables.

■ Some databases store all the information in one table. These are known as **flat-file** databases.

■ More commonly, databases store the information in more than one table. These are known as **relational** databases. We will look at relationships in more detail later on.

1.5.2 Opening a Table

1 *Click on the Tables button*

2 *Click on the table you wish to open*

3 *Click Open*

Or

1 *Click on the Tables button*

2 *Double click on the table you want to open*

1.5.3 Table Jargon

■ Each table is made up of rows and columns.

■ Each row holds one complete piece of information – a **record**. The picture below shows the record for Geoff Cohen.

EMPLOYEE ID	LASTNAME	FIRSTNAME	INITIAL	GENDER	DEPARTMENT	PHONE
5	Cohen	Geoff	A	Male	SALES	(217)555-4204

- Each column holds one piece of information per record – a **field**, e.g. last name, department, gender, etc. The field names are shown in grey at the top of the table.
- Each box of the table is a **cell** and contains one piece of information.

1.5.4 Moving Around a Table

To move around cells...

Click on the cell you require

Or

Press the Tab key to move one cell to the right

Or

Use the cursor keys to move around the cells

To move around records...

Click on the record you require

Or

Use the vertical scroll bar to move up and down the records

Or

Use the record navigation buttons at the bottom left of the screen:

Going from left to right, here is what the navigation icons do:

- Move to the first record
- Move to the previous record
- Displays the current record (you can type in a record number and press Return to go to that record)
- Move to the next record
- Move to the last record
- Create a new record after the last one
- The number to the right displays the total number of records – you cannot click on this

To move around fields...

Click on the field you require

Or

Use the horizontal scroll bar to move left and right around the fields

1.5.5 Editing the Information in a Table

1 *Move to the cell you wish to change*

2 *Make any changes you require*

3 *Click outside the record you are in – the changes are automatically saved*

To quickly change everything in the cell...

1 *Position the mouse pointer at the left of the cell – it will change to a big white cross*

2 *Click the left mouse button once – the cell will be selected*

3 *Type in the new information*

4 *Click outside the record you are in – the changes are automatically saved*

When are my changes saved?

As soon as you start typing, a pencil will appear to the left of the record

As long as you can see the pencil, the information is not saved. However, as soon as you move out of this record, the pencil will disappear, and your changes are saved automatically.

When I edit the information, a drop down arrow appears...

This means that you are working with a lookup field. If you click the drop down arrow, you will get a choice of information which can go in this field, e.g. male or female for a gender field. This saves you time and helps to prevent mistakes.

I can't get out of the record I'm editing!

If you find yourself stuck in a record which Access won't let you get out of, press Escape (Esc) on the keyboard.

1.5.6 Entering New Records

 1 *Click on the New Record icon*

2 *Type in the new information*

3 *Click outside the record when you have finished – the changes are saved automatically*

What does AutoNumber mean?

Sometimes you might find a field with the word AutoNumber in. You don't have to enter information into this field yourself; Access automatically adds a number for you.

Can I add a new record anywhere in the table?

No, only in the last row of the table:

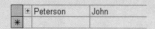

The asterisk (*) symbol shows you that this is the space for a new record.

1.5.7 Selecting Records

Click on the Record Selector to the left of the record – the mouse pointer will change to a black arrow

Or, if you would like to select several records…

1. *Click on the Record Selector to the left of the first record and hold down the mouse button*

2. *Drag over the other records you wish to select*

Can I select records that are not next to each other?

No! Usually, if you select things, then you can use the Control key to select items that are not next to each other. In an Access table, you can only select multiple records if they are next to each other.

1.5.8 Deleting Records

1. *Select the record you wish to delete (using the Record Selector to the left of the record)*

2. *Press the Delete key*

or

Click the Delete icon

When I try to delete, Access says…

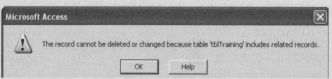

This means that you have a 'relational' database and your table is linked to another one. The person you are trying to delete has information about them in another table within this database. In order to delete them, you will have to go to the linked table first and delete them from there.

1.6 Changing the Look of a Table

1.6.1 Selecting Columns

Click on the grey bar containing the field name – the mouse will change to a black, downward pointing arrow

Or

Click and drag over several columns to select more than one

1.6.2 Changing the Width of Columns

1 *Position the mouse pointer over the grey title area to the right of the column you wish to widen – the pointer will change to a double headed arrow*

> LASTNAME ↔ FIRSTNAME

2 *Click and drag to widen the column*

or

Double click – the column will resize automatically

1.6.3 Moving Columns

1 *Select the column you wish to move*

2 *Position the mouse pointer in the middle of the grey title area – the pointer will change to a white arrow*

3 *Click and drag the column to a new location – a thick vertical black line will indicate where the column is going*

1.6.4 Saving the Layout Changes

If you change the way that your table looks, you do not have to save the changes you have made. When you close the table, Access will ask you if you want to save what you have done with the layout…

1 *Click on the File menu*

2 *Click Close*

or

Click the X at the top right of the table

3 Click Yes if you would like to keep the layout you have

or

Click No if you would like to return to the original layout

Remember that Access automatically saves the information you have keyed in! When it asks you whether you want to save, it is only referring to the layout.

1.7 Searching and Sorting Records

1.7.1 Searching

Access tables allow you to find one record at a time in order to make amendments, delete, or view a certain record quickly. However, it will not extract records from the whole table, or allow you to search based on more than one piece of information – to do that you will need to use a query.

☐1 *Click into the column you wish to search through, e.g. lastname, department*

 ☐2 *Click the Find icon*

☐3 *Type the data you wish to find next to Find What*

☐4 *Click the drop down arrow next to Match and choose the option you require – imagine that you are searching for someone whose last name is "Smith", and you have typed the word "Smith" next to Find What. Here"s what will happen with the different match options:*

  ■ **Any Part of Field**: *Will find anything that contains the word "Smith", e.g. "Smithson", "Taylor-Smith" and "Smith" itself*

  ■ **Whole Field**: *Will only find the word "Smith" and nothing else*

  ■ **Start of Field**: *Will find the word "Smith" at the beginning of the text, e.g. "Smithson", "Smith", but not "Taylor-Smith"*

☐5 *Click Find Next – the found record is highlighted in the table*

☐6 *Click Find Next again to find the next record*

When Access has finished it will display this message...

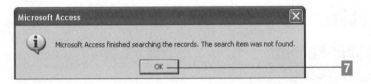

Microsoft Access

(i) Microsoft Access finished searching the records. The search item was not found.

OK

7 Click OK

8 Click Cancel to close the Find box

1.7.2 Sorting Records

You can sort records to make it easier to view or find information. In an Access table you can only sort on one field. If you want to sort on more than one you will need to use a query.

To sort records, click into the column you wish to sort, and then click on the Sort icon you require:

The first icon sorts in ascending order, the second sorts in descending order.

What do ascending and descending mean?

It depends on what you are sorting. Have a look at the list below to get an idea of how it works…

	Ascending	**Descending**
Text	A to Z	Z to A
Numbers	smallest to biggest	biggest to smallest
Dates	earliest to latest	latest to earliest

Blanks will appear at the top if you are sorting ascending, or at the bottom if you are sorting descending.

I have a field that won't sort!

Memo, OLE and Hyperlink fields do not sort (see the Specifying Data Types section on page 359 for more information on field types).

How do I save the results of my sort?

Close the table and save the layout changes when you are prompted.

1.8 Printing Tables

1.8.1 Printing All Your Records

 Click on the Print icon

1.8.2 Printing a Selection of Records

1 *Select the records you wish to print*

2 *Click on the File menu*

3 *Click Print*

4 *Click the circle next to **Selected Record(s)***

5 *Click OK*

1.8.3 Print Preview

 If you want to see the layout of what you are printing before you send it to the printer, click the Print Preview icon.

 To close print preview, click on the Close button.

1.8.4 Zooming In and Out in Print Preview

To zoom in or out of the page...

Click on the page – the mouse pointer will look like a magnifying glass

1.8.5 Moving Through the Pages

To see different pages in the preview window, use the navigation buttons:

Going from left to right, here is what each button does:

- Goes to the first page

- Goes to the previous page

- Displays the current page – you can type in a page number and press Return to go to that page

- Goes to the next page

- Goes to the last page

1.9 Using Help in Access

Access comes with a Help feature which works in exactly the same way as the help in Word – see the Help section in the Word chapters on page 46 for more details.

1.10 Toolbars

1.10.1 What are Toolbars?

Toolbars are used to carry out commands in your software. They contain pictures called icons which you click on to carry out an action:

e.g. Database toolbar:

If you cannot see the toolbar you need, you will need to turn it on using the View menu.

1.10.2 Turning Toolbars On and Off

1 *Click on the View menu*

2 *Click on the Toolbars submenu*

3 *Click on the name of the toolbar you wish to turn on or off – if it is on, it will be switched off, and if it is off, it will be switched on*

If a toolbar name has a tick next to it…

It means that the toolbar is turned on.

Queries

2.1 Creating a Simple Query

2.1.1 What is a Query?

Queries allow you to extract information from tables, e.g. all the women in the Sales department, all the staff who earn between £20,000 and £30,000 in alphabetical order.

Queries look exactly the same as tables – which is not surprising, as they are really the same thing – they just show you the information you have chosen to extract.

Queries also let you input information into the table, without having to see the whole table. If you input data into a query, it will automatically go into the table the query was based on.

Most of the time you will be producing **select queries**. These are queries that simply extract and display the information you asked for. There are other types of query but you don't need to know about them for the ECDL exam.

2.1.2 Creating a Query

There are four main steps to creating a query:

1 Choosing the table you wish to extract information from

2 Choosing the fields you wish to see in the query

3̄ Running the query to see the result

4̄ Saving the query (if required)

2.1.3 Step One: Choosing the Table

 Queries

1 *Click on the Queries button in the database window*

2 *Double click on* **Create query in Design view** *– the Show Table box will appear*

🗗 Create query in Design view

or

Click on New

Click on Design View

Click OK – the Show Table box will appear

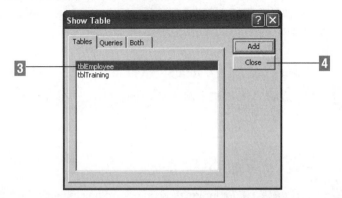

3 *Double click on the table you wish to use – the table will appear in the background*

4 *Click Close*

I didn't add a table before I clicked Close...

Click on the Show Table icon to bring the box back!

I added the same table more than once...

It's very easy to double click on the same table more than once, or forget to close the Show Table box. If you have added the same table twice, click on the second table

 and press the Delete key!

Using more than one table...

If you have two or more tables you want to get results from, just add them in when you see the Show Table box. They will show up above the query boxes as normal, and you can choose the fields you need from any table, and carry out the query as normal.

2.1.4 Step Two: Choosing the Fields

You are now in the Design View of the query. It is here that you get to ask Access for the fields you wish to see.

Double click on the field you wish to see from the list within the table – the field will jump to the query grid

Or

Click and drag the field you require to the Field row in the query grid

I can't see all the fields I've added...

If you add lots of fields to the query grid, you will need to use the horizontal scroll bar to see them all.

I've added the wrong field...

See page 318 for information on how to delete fields.

How can I add all the fields at once?

Double click the * at the top of the list of fields.

2.1.5 Step Three: Running a Query

You are still in Design View, and this is the place where you ask Access for the information you wish to see. You now want to see the answer, and that's where running the query comes in. Running the query takes you out of Design View and into Datasheet View, where you can see the records that match what you've asked for:

! *Click on the Run icon*

Or

⊞ ▾ *Click the Datasheet View icon*

What is the difference between the Run icon and the Datasheet icon?

At this stage – nothing! It's only when you get to more advanced queries that the difference will become clear.

Why can I see "expr" next to some of my fields?

You've probably added the same field more than once! You need to return to Design View and delete one of the fields – see page 318 for how to delete fields.

What will happen if I change the data I can see in the query?

The table will also change! Think of the query as the same as the table – you are just seeing less of it. So if you change the data in the query, the data in the table will change as well.

2.1.6 Saving a Query

1. *Click on the Save icon*

2. *Enter a name for the query*

3. *Click OK*

Give queries a consistent name...

e.g. start the name off with the letters QRY, qry or Query. That way you will know that it's a query whenever you come across it.

2.1.7 Closing a Query

1. *Click on the File menu*

2. *Click Close*

   or

   Click the X at the top right of the query

2.2 | Changing the View

2.2.1 What are Views?

There are two views which you will need to use in a query:

- **Design View**: This is where you add the table and the fields that you wish to see in the query. You can think of it as the place where you ask Access what you want to see.

- **Datasheet View**: This is where you can see the answer. The Datasheet View looks just like the table.

You will also see another view available – **SQL view**. This shows how the query will look in SQL code. However, you will not need to use it unless you are interested in using code to program your database – it's not covered in ECDL, and quite frankly, your life is a lot less complicated and more interesting without it. So don't worry about it. You're not missing anything.

2.2.2 Switching to Design View

Click on the Design View icon

2.2.3 Switching to Datasheet View

Click on the Datasheet View icon

2.3 | Editing a Query

You must be in Design View to edit a query!

Design View allows you to edit the question which you are asking Access. Datasheet View allows you to see the answer.

2.3.1 Selecting Fields in Design View

1 Position the mouse on the grey bar just above the field in the query grid – the pointer will change to a black, downward-pointing arrow

2 Click once with the left mouse button

2.3.2 Deleting Fields

1 Ensure that you are in Design View

2 Select the field you wish to delete

3 Press the Delete key

2.3.3 Moving Fields

1. *Ensure that you are in Design View*

2. *Select the field you wish to move*

3. *Position the mouse in the middle of the grey bar just above the field in the query grid*

4. *Click and drag to a new position – a vertical black line will show where you are going*

2.3.4 Printing Queries

1. *Open the query you wish to print*

2. *Click on the Print icon*

To obtain a print preview of your query…

Click on the Print Preview icon

2.4 Adding Criteria to Queries

2.4.1 What are Criteria?

So far you have created queries that have pulled out certain fields from the table. However, it is more likely that you will want to pull out certain records, e.g. all the **females**, all the people in the **Sales** department, all the people who earn **over £20,000**. The text in bold is known as criteria, and they can easily be added to a query.

2.4.2 Searching for Records on One Criterion

1. *Create a new query as normal*

2. *Add the fields you wish to see in Design View*

3. *Type in the criterion you wish to use on the Criteria row, under the relevant field name – the criterion will get quotation marks around it when you click outside*

4. *Run the query as normal*

e.g. Finding females. The word "female" is typed on the Criteria row under the Gender field:

Field:	GENDER
Table:	tblEmployee
Sort:	
Show:	☑
Criteria:	"female"
or:	

e.g. Finding people in the Sales department. The word "sales" is typed on the Criteria row under the Department field…

Are criteria case sensitive?

No, you can type in whatever case you like, as long as you spell it correctly!

Why is my query not showing anything?

The biggest mistake with adding criteria is spelling the criteria incorrectly, or using a term which is not in the table. For example, let's say you want to find the females in this table:

	EMPLOYEE ID	LASTNAME	FIRSTNAME	INITIAL	GENDER
+	5	Cohen	Geoff	A	Male
+	9	Dean	Christine	W	Female
+	12	Egan	Michelle	P	Female
+	33	Orlando	John	S	Male
+	21	Kaufman	Lisa	C	Female

If you type the word "females" as your criterion, you won't find anybody, because the text in the table is "female" without an "s" on the end!

It may also be that you have stray criteria left over from another time when you ran this query that are affecting your result.

2.4.3 Searching for Records Which Do NOT Meet a Criterion

You may want to find records which are **not** something, e.g. all the people who do **not** work in the Sales department.

1. *Create a new query as normal*

2. *Add the fields you wish to see in Design View*

3. *Type the word **NOT** in front of your criterion underneath the field you wish to find it in – your criterion will get quotation marks around it, once you click outside*

4. *Run the query as normal*

2.4.4 Searching for Records Where Information is Missing

You may have forgotten to add information in various fields when you were inputting them. Or you may have left certain information deliberately blank when you were inputting because you did not have the information to hand at the time. If you would like to find the blanks in a field:

1. *Create your query as normal*

2. *Add the fields you wish to see in Design View*

3. *Type the word "NULL" into the criteria row of the field you wish to find blanks in (this will change to "Is null" once you have clicked outside!)*

   The example on the left will find people whose last name has been left blank.

4. *Run your query as normal*

2.5 Numbers, Dates and Wildcards

So far, the criteria you have added have not allowed you to make comparisons. You may want to find people who earn more or less than a certain figure, or people who started before or after a certain date. This section will show you how.

2.5.1 Using Numbers

Below are examples of criteria which can be added to make comparisons with numbers, e.g. greater than, less than, between, etc. In the examples below, the number 100 has been used to show you how it works:

What do you want to find?	This is what you type in the criteria row:
Numbers greater than 100	>100
Numbers less than 100	<100
Numbers greater than or equal to 100	>=100
Numbers less than or equal to 100	<=100
Between 1 and 100	Between 1 and 100

When using numbers as criteria...

Just type the number – you do not have to include pound signs, percentage symbols, etc.

2.5.2 Using Dates

Below are examples of criteria which can be added to make comparisons with dates, e.g. before, after, between, etc. In the examples below, the date 1/1/2000 has been used to show you how it works:

What do you want to find?	This is what you type in the criteria row:
Dates after 1/1/2000	>1/1/2000
Dates before 1/1/2000	<1/1/2000
Dates after or equal to 1/1/2000	>=1/1/2000
Dates before or equal to 1/1/2000	<=1/1/2000
Dates between 1/1/2000 and 31/12/2000	Between 1/1/2000 and 31/12/2000

Can I type dates with full stops?

No! Access won't let you, and you will get an error message. Always use slashes, like this: 1/1/2000

Access will put hashes (#) around your dates!

In the same way as criteria get quotation marks when you click outside, dates will get hash marks (#) around them.

How do I remember whether to use greater than or less than?

Imagine that Access takes the 1/1/1900 as 1. Every subsequent day goes up by an integer of one, so 2/1/1900 is 2, 3/1/1900 is 3 etc. The bigger the number the later the date. So if you want to find earlier dates it will be less than, and if you want to find later dates it will be greater than.

2.5.3 Using a Wildcard

Wildcards allow you to search for partial information in a field, e.g. finding words that start with a certain letter, finding words that end with a certain letter, finding dates that end in a certain year, etc. A wildcard is just an asterisk (*), and can be placed wherever there is blank information to be filled in. The table below shows examples of wildcards:

What do you want to find?	This is what you type in the criteria row:
Words beginning with **Ke**	Ke*
Words ending in **son**	*son
Dates ending in the year 1984	*/*/84

Access will add the word "Like" and quotation marks around criteria with wildcards!

In the same way that criteria get quotation marks around them when you click outside, wildcards will display this text.

2.6 Adding More Than One Criterion

2.6.1 What are AND and OR?

Often you will want to add more than one criterion, e.g. all the **females** who work in the **Sales** department, all the **males** who earn **under £20,000** etc. If you have more than one criterion, you must specify whether the relationship between them is AND or OR:

- **AND** means you will find records which match **both** criteria

  e.g. only females who work in Sales

  only males who earn over £20,000

- **OR** means that you will find records which match **either** of the criteria

  e.g. all the females, and all the people who work in Sales

  all the males, and all the people who earn over £20,000

You can't have ANDs on the same field!

e.g. Female AND Male will not give you anybody, because no-one can be both female and male at the same time.

ORs are usually on the same field

e.g. Manchester OR London will return all the records which are either Manchester or London. If you said London AND Manchester, you will not get anything because you are asking Access to find you records which have both Manchester and London in the same field. You can't be in Manchester and London at the same time.

2.6.2 Using AND

1. *Create your query as normal*

2. *Add the fields you wish to see in Design View*

3. *Type your first criterion onto the Criteria row under the relevant field*

4. *Enter any other criteria **on the same Criteria row as the first** and under the relevant field*

5. *Run your query as normal*

The example will show all the females in the Sales department:

GENDER	DEPARTMENT
tblEmployee	tblEmployee
☑	☑
"female"	"sales"

2.6.3 Using OR

1. Create your query as normal

2. Add the fields you wish to see in Design View

3. Type your first criterion onto the first Criteria row under the relevant field

4. Type any additional criteria **on a different Criteria row** under the relevant field

5. Run your query as normal

The example will show all the females, and all the people in the Sales department:

GENDER	DEPARTMENT
tblEmployee	tblEmployee
☑	☑
"female"	
	"sales"

2.6.4 Some Examples of Queries with Multiple Criteria

This will find all the females in the Executive department who were hired after 1/1/80 – i.e. Female AND executive AND after 1/1/80:

GENDER	DEPARTMENT	DATE HIRED
tblEmployee	tblEmployee	tblEmployee
☑	☑	☑
"female"	"executive"	>#01/01/1980#

This will find all the executive staff and all the sales staff – i.e. executive OR sales:

DEPARTMENT
tblEmployee
☑
"executive"
"sales"

This will find all the females who are executives and all the males who are salespeople – i.e. (female AND executive) OR (male AND salesperson):

GENDER	DEPARTMENT
tblEmployee	tblEmployee
☑	☑
"female"	"executive"
"male"	"sales"

2.7 Sorting Queries

2.7.1 Sorting in Datasheet View

As well as choosing to see certain records, you can also change the order in which the information is displayed. To do this, you need to sort the query. You can sort in either Datasheet or Design View.

What's the difference between sorting in Datasheet View and sorting in Design View?

In Datasheet View you can only sort by one field.
In Design View you can sort on more than one field.

2.7.2 Sorting on One Field in Datasheet View

[1] *Click into the column you wish to sort*

[2] *Click on the sort button you require*

  Sort ascending

Or Sort descending

2.7.3 Sorting on One Field in Design View

[1] *Click into the Sort row for the field you wish to sort*

[2] *Click the drop down arrow which appears*

[3] *Click Ascending or Descending*

[4] *Run your query as normal*

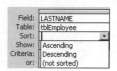

Field:	LASTNAME
Table:	tblEmployee
Sort:	
Show:	Ascending
Criteria:	Descending
or:	(not sorted)

How do I remove the sort order?

This is done in the same way as sorting a field. Click the drop down arrow in the sort box, and then click on **Not Sorted** to remove the sort order.

2.7.4 What Does Sorting on More Than One Field Mean?

Let's imagine that you wish to sort a query by the **Lastname** field. If lots of people have the same last name, then you would probably want to sort their first names within that, as in this example:

LASTNAME	FIRSTNAME
Pope	Jan
Rizzo	Ann
Rodan	Bill
Sanders	Kathy
Skye	Jim
Smith	Bob
Smith	Fred
Smith	Jane
Smith	Kim
Young	Sandy
Youngblood	Dick
Zambini	Rick

Imagine that you need to produce a list of the people who work in different departments. You could sort by the Department field first, and then within that sort by the person's last name, like this:

DEPARTMENT	LASTNAME
FINANCE	Collins
FINANCE	Smith
FINANCE	Smith
FINANCE	Smith
SALES	Adams
SALES	Bicksby
SALES	Campbell
SALES	Cohen
SALES	Drasin
SALES	Drendon
SALES	Egan
SALES	Gilbert

2.7.5 Sorting on More Than One Field in Design View

The field which is your first choice for sorting must be to the left!

In the query grid, the field which is your first choice for sorting must be on the left of any other fields you wish to sort.

For example, sorting by **department** and then by **lastname** – the Department field must be to the left of Lastname:

DEPARTMENT	LASTNAME
tblEmployee	tblEmployee
Ascending	Ascending
☑	☑

For information about moving fields in Design View, see the section about moving fields on page 319.

1 *Ensure that the field which is your first choice for ordering is on the left*

2 *Click into the Sort row for your first field*

3 *Click the drop down arrow*

4 *Click Ascending or Descending*

5 *Click into the Sort row for your second field*

6 *Click Ascending or Descending*

7 *Run your query as normal*

2.8 Showing/Hiding Fields

2.8.1 Showing/Hiding Fields

The Design View of a query also allows you to hide fields before you run it. This can be useful if you want to keep certain information confidential, e.g. salary.

1 *Create your query as normal*

2 *Add the fields you require in Design View*

3 *Click the box on the Show row under the field you require*

(A ticked box will show, a blank box will be hidden)

In this example, the Gender field will show, but the Salary field will be hidden:

GENDER	SALARY
tblEmployee	tblEmployee
☑	☐

4 *Run your query as normal*

Adding Filters

2.9.1 What are Filters?

A filter is a way of filtering out the records you want to see, based on criteria which you set, e.g. all the people in the Sales department. It's a bit like using criteria in queries except quicker and easier, and that can't be bad.

Filters, however, can be applied to a table, a query or a form. When you apply them, Access will just show you the selected records you have chosen to see.

2.9.2 Filtering by Selection

1 *Open the table, query or form you wish to filter*

2 *Select the information which you would like to see from any record*

In the example you will get all the people in the Sales department:

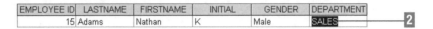

 3 *Click the Filter by Selection icon*

4 *You can see whether records have been filtered by checking next to the navigation buttons. In the example below, the selected record has been filtered:*

Do you have to select the whole field?

No! You can also select:

- The first part of the field, e.g. selecting **LASTNAME** **And**erson will filter all the records which begin with the letters "And" such as Anderson, Andrews, etc.
- Any part of the field, e.g. selecting **LASTNAME** **And**er**son** will filter all the records which contain the letters "der" anywhere within them such as Anderson, Sanderson, etc.

Can I filter records which have been filtered?

Yes! If you have more than one criterion which you would like to apply, you can apply another filter to the filtered records.

2.9.3 Excluding by Selection

This will allow you to filter records which do **not** meet the criteria you specify:

1. *Open the table, query or form you wish to filter*

2. *Select the information which you would **not** like to see from any record*

3. *Right click over the selection – a menu will appear*

4. *Click Filter Excluding Selection*

2.9.4 Removing Filters

 Click on the Remove Filter icon

2.10 Filtering by Form

Filter by Form allows you to do more complex filtering than Filter by Selection. It creates a form, which you use to fill out the criteria you require.

2.10.1 Using Filter by Form with More Than One Criterion

1. *Open the table, query or form you wish to filter*

2. *Click on the Filter by Form icon – a form will appear for you to fill in*

   If you have used filters before, Access will remember the last thing you filtered and add this as your criteria

3. *Click into the field you wish to add criteria to*

4. *Click the down arrow and choose the criteria you wish to add*

   or

   Type in the criteria you wish to add

5. *Click on the Apply Filter icon*

2.10.2 Using AND with Filter by Form

1. *Open the table, query or form you wish to filter*

2. *Click on the Filter by Form icon – a form will appear for you to fill in. As before, if you have used filters before, Access will remember the last thing you filtered and add this as your criteria*

3. *Enter the criteria you require underneath the appropriate fields – this example will find all the females in the Sales department:*

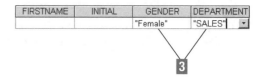

4. *Click on the Apply Filter icon*

2.10.3 Using OR with Filter by Form

|1| *Open the table, query or form you wish to filter*

|2| *Click on the Filter by Form icon – a form will appear for you to fill in. If you have used filters before, Access will remember the last thing you filtered and add this as your criteria*

|3| *Enter your first criterion underneath the appropriate field*

 |4| *Click the OR tab at the bottom of the form*

|5| *Enter your next criterion underneath the appropriate field*

|6| *Repeat steps 4 and 5 if you have more criteria*

|7| *Click on the Apply Filter icon*

 You can use NULL and NOT in Filter by Form…

If you would like to filter the blanks in a field, type the word **null** into the form underneath the relevant field.

If you would like to find records which do **not** meet the criterion you specify, type the word "not" before the criterion, e.g. **not Sales**

2.10.4 Saving a Filter as a Query

|1| *Click on the Filter by Form icon*

|2| *Enter your criteria as required*

 |3| *Click on the Save as Query icon*

|4| *Enter a name for your query*

|5| *Click OK*

You can access your query from the queries in the Database window.

2.10.5 Deleting Criteria

|1| *Select the criteria you wish to delete*

|2| *Press the Delete key*

CHAPTER 3

Forms

What You'll Do

→ Use Forms

→ Navigate Around Records

→ Edit and Add Records

→ Print, Close and Delete Forms

→ Create a Form Using Form Wizard

→ Change Form Design

→ Look at the Parts of a Form

→ Select Controls and Labels

→ Resize, Move and Delete Controls and Labels

→ Save Design Changes to a Form

3.1 Using Forms

3.1.1 What are Forms?

Forms are based on tables or queries. They show the same information, but they look nicer.

Okay, they're more useful than that – you can use them to:

- Input data in a more user-friendly way than inputting data directly into a table or query.

- View individual records on the screen (rather than multiple records like a table or query).

- Input data into more than one table at once.

- Prevent users from having to access the tables in your database. The tables are the structure of your database, and if they are accidentally deleted, or their design is accidentally changed, it could ruin everything. Forms give people a way of inputting data without giving them access to the tables.

3.1.2 Opening a Form

🔲 Forms 1 Click on the Forms button

2 Click the form you wish to open

🔲 Open 3 Click Open

Or

1. *Click on the Forms button*

2. *Double click the form you wish to open*

3.1.3 Navigating Around Records

Click the required button at the bottom of the form:

|◀ ◀ | 8   ▶ | ▶| | ▶*| of 50

Going from left to right, here is what the buttons do:

- Move to the first record
- Move to the previous record
- Move to the next record
- Move to the last record

3.1.4 Editing a Record

1. *Go to the record you wish to edit*

2. *Click on the field you wish to change*

3. *Make your changes as required*

When are my changes saved?

Just like in a table, as soon as you move onto another record the changes will be saved. So be careful!

3.1.5 Adding a New Record

▶*   *Click on the New Record icon*

3.1.6 Changing the Orientation

1. *Click on the File menu*

2. *Click Page Setup*

3. *Click on the Page tab*

4. *Click in the circle next to Landscape*

    or

    Click in the circle next to Portrait

5. *Click OK*

3.1.7 Printing a Form

Click on the Print icon

3.1.8 Closing a Form

Click the X on the form window

You will not be asked to save!

If you have only typed data in, Access will not ask you if you want to save the form.

3.1.9 Deleting a Form

1 *Click on the Forms button*

2 *Select the form you want to delete*

3 *Click on the Delete Form icon*

4 *Click Yes*

3.1.10 Deleting a Record

1 *In Form View, go to the record you wish to delete*

2 *Click on the Delete icon on the toolbar*

3.2 Creating a Form Using the Form Wizard

3.2.1 Ways of Creating a Form

There are seven ways of creating a form:

- **Design View**: will allow you to create the form completely from scratch with no help from Access whatsoever. This gives you more control, but can be scary.
- **Form Wizard**: will take you through a series of steps to help you create your form. This is much easier, but you don't have as much control.
- **AutoForm Columnar**: will instantly create a form where each record is shown on a different screen.
- **AutoForm Tabular**: will instantly create a form where several records are shown in tabular format.
- **AutoForm Datasheet**: will instantly create a form that looks the same as the table.
- **Chart Wizard**: will allow you to create a chart on a form.
- **Pivot Table Wizard**: will allow you to create a pivot table on a form.

The only way we will deal with this is by using the Form Wizard – it has enough control to be useful, but isn't too difficult.

3.2.2 Creating a Form Using the Form Wizard

1 *Click on the Forms button*

2 *Double click on Create form by using wizard*

       📄   Create form by using wizard

or

Click New

Click Form Wizard

Click OK

3 *Click the drop down arrow under Table/Queries*

4 *Click on the table or query to base your form on*

5 *Double click on the fields you wish to see on the form underneath Available Fields – they will jump over to the Selected Fields column*

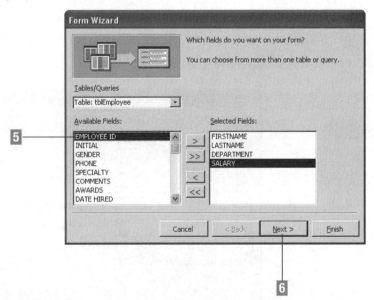

What if I add the wrong field?

1 Click on the field you wish to remove underneath Selected Fields

2 Click on the left pointing arrow `<`

6 *Click Next*

7 *Click in the circle next to the layout you require:*

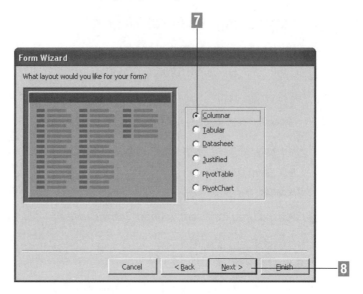

- **Columnar** will show you one record at a time on the screen

- **Tabular** will show you multiple records at a time on the screen

- **Datasheet** and **Justified** create a form with the same layout as the table

8 *Click Next*

9 *Click on the style you require*

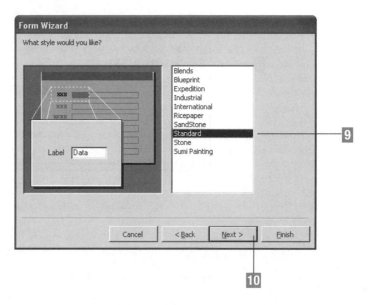

10 *Click Next*

11 *Type a name for your form – give your form a descriptive name, i.e. include the word "Form" in the name*

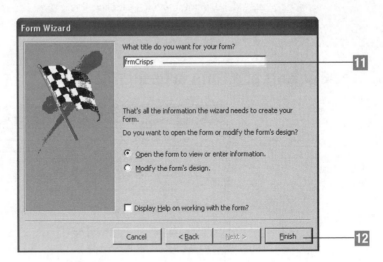

12 *Click Finish*

When is my form saved?

As soon as you click Finish!

3.3 Changing Form Design

3.3.1 The Views

There are three views to a form:

■ **Form View**: where you can edit and view records.

■ **Datasheet View**: where you can edit and view records in table format.

■ **Design View**: where you can edit the way your form looks and works.

3.3.2 Changing the View

1 *Click the drop down arrow next to the view button*

2 *Click on the view you require*

The view button looks different depending on which view you are in!

When you are in Form View it looks like this: 🖳 ▾

When you are in Design View it looks like this: 🖼 ▾

However, it is always the first button on the toolbar.

3.3.3 The Elements of a Form in Design View

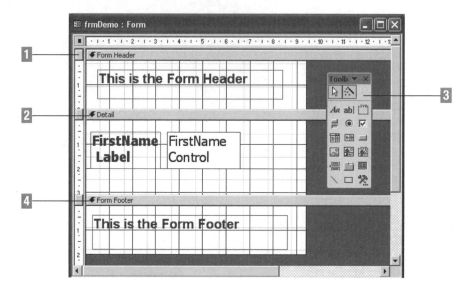

1 The top box is the form header

2 The middle box is the Detail area:

- Firstname *Label* – this looks the same in Design View as in Form View, and tells you what type of field you are entering

- Firstname *Control* – this is where the actual information appears in Form View, e.g. Mark, Simon etc., and is where you will type in the field information

3 The Toolbox is the floating toolbar with all your form buttons on

4 The bottom box is the form footer

I can't see the Toolbox!

Ensure you are in Design View, and click on the Toolbox icon at the top of the screen

3.4 The Parts of a Form

3.4.1 What are the Parts of a Form?

There are three parts to a form:

- **Form Header**: often used for titles. This appears at the top of every page in the form.

- **Detail**: where all the data appears.

- **Form Footer**: often used for record numbers etc. This appears at the bottom of every page in the form.

3.4.2 Selecting a Part

☐ *Ensure you are in Design View*

☐ *Click on the grey bar representing the part you require – the grey bar will go darker when it is selected*

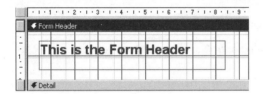

3.4.3 Resizing the Height

☐ *Ensure you are in Design View*

☐ *Position the mouse at the bottom border of the part you wish to resize*

e.g. resizing the detail – the mouse pointer will change to a double headed arrow

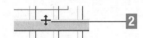

☐ *Click and drag to resize*

3.4.4 Resizing the Width

☐ *Ensure you are in Design View*

☐ *Position the mouse at the right hand border of the part you wish to resize – the mouse pointer will change to a double headed arrow*

☐ *Click and drag to resize*

3.5 | Controls and Labels

3.5.1 What are Controls and Labels?

- A control is a box where data will appear in Form View

- A label is a box that describes the control, and looks the same in Design View as it does in Form View.

 How can I tell the difference between a control and a label?

In Design View, the control and label often look identical. It is up to you to switch back to Form View and check which box shows the actual data, and which just shows the label.

3.5.2 Selecting a Control or Label

Ensure you are in Design View:

Click anywhere on the control, or anywhere on the label

 Why does it look like both the control and the label are selected?

The control and its associated label are always linked. You will probably want to move them together, otherwise your control may lose its label.

3.5.3 Selecting Several Controls and Labels

1. *Ensure you are in Design View*
2. *Click on the first control/label you require*
3. *Hold down Shift on the keyboard*
4. *Click on the remaining control(s)/label(s) you require*
5. *Release the Shift key*

 What if I accidentally select a control or label?

To remove something from a selection...

1. Hold down Shift
2. Click on the control or label you want to remove from the selection

3.5.4 Moving a Control or Label Separately

1. *Ensure you are in Design View*

2. *Select the control/label*

 3. *Position the mouse over the big box at the top left until the mouse pointer changes to a pointing hand*

4. *Click and drag the control/label to a new position*

3.5.5 Moving a Control with its Label

1. *Ensure you are in Design View*

2. *Select the control/label*

 3. *Position the mouse on the border of the selected control/label until the mouse pointer changes to an open hand*

4. *Click and drag the control/label to a new position*

3.5.6 Resizing a Control or Label

1. *Ensure you are in Design View*

2. *Select the control/label*

3. *Hover your mouse pointer over a box until the mouse pointer changes to a double headed arrow*

4. *Click and drag the control/label to resize*

3.5.7 Deleting a Control and Label

1. *Ensure you are in Design View*

2. *Select the control*

3. *Press the Delete key*

3.5.8 Deleting a Label on its Own

1. *Ensure you are in Design View*

2. *Select the label*

3. *Press the Delete key*

3.5.9 Adding Text to a Form Header or Footer

1. *Ensure you are in Design View*

2. *Resize the Header or Footer to make space for your text*

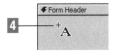 **3** *Click on the Label icon in the Toolbox*

4 *Your mouse pointer should change to a cross with "A" next to it*

5 *Click and drag to draw the label*

6 *Type in your text*

7 *Click away from the label to deselect it*

3.5.10 Editing Text

You can only edit the text in labels. The text inside a control is just the name of the field where it gets its data from, and will show the actual data when you are in Form View.

1 *Ensure you are in Design View*

2 *Select the label*

3 *Click in the middle of the label – a cursor will appear*

4 *Edit the text as normal*

5 *Press Return*

6 *Click OK*

3.6 Saving Design Changes to a Form

3.6.1 Saving Changes

Access does not save your design changes automatically; you will have to do that yourself. To save the design changes, click on the Save icon.

CHAPTER 4

Reports

What You'll Do

→ Use Reports

→ Open a Report

→ Change the Print Preview

→ Move Between the Pages

→ Close a Report

→ Create a Report

→ Change the Design of a Report

→ Discover the Parts of a Report

→ Create Summary Options

4.1 Using Reports

4.1.1 What are Reports?

Reports are used to print off the information from your database in a presentable format. They are based on tables or queries. Base a report on a query if you only want to show certain records in your report, rather than every record in the tables. You can use reports to:

- Group information under key headings

- Calculate totals and work out statistical information

- Produce mailing labels

4.1.2 Opening a Report

Reports

1 Click on the Reports button

2 Click on the report you wish to open

3 Click Open

Or

1 Click on the Reports button

2 Double click the report you wish to open

4.1.3 Changing the Print Preview

When you open a report you will be taken to the Print Preview. To change the way the Print Preview looks, use the toolbar:

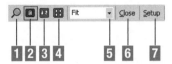

Going from left to right, here is what each icon means:

1 *Zooms in or out of the report*

2 *Shows one full page*

3 *Shows two full pages*

4 *Click this icon and drag over the grid to view multiple pages*

5 *Click the drop down arrow to change the zoom level*

6 *Closes the report*

7 *Goes to the page setup*

4.1.4 Moving Between the Pages

Click the navigation buttons at the bottom of the screen:

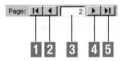

Going from left to right, here is what each icon means:

1 *Go to the first page*

2 *Go to the previous page*

3 *Displays the current page – you can type in a page number and press Return to go to that page*

4 *Go to the next page*

5 *Go to the last page*

4.1.5 Printing a Report

To print the whole report, just click once on the Print icon.

4.1.6 Printing a Selection of Pages

⒈ *Click on the File menu*

⒉ *Click on Print*

⒊ *Click in the circle before Pages*

⒋ *Change the page numbers in the From and To boxes*

⒌ *Click OK*

4.1.7 Changing the Orientation of your Report

⒈ *Click File*

⒉ *Click Page Setup*

⒊ *Click Page tab*

⒋ *Click the circle next to Landscape*

or

Click the circle next to Portrait

⒌ *Click OK*

4.1.8 Changing the Paper Size

⒈ *Click File*

⒉ *Click Page Setup*

⒊ *Click Page tab*

⒋ *Click the down arrow next to Size*

⒌ *Select the Paper Size you require*

⒍ *Click OK*

4.1.9 Closing a Report

Click on the X icon at the top of the report window

Or

Click Close

4.2.1 The Ways of Creating a Report

There are several different ways of creating a report:

- **Design View**: will allow you to create the report from scratch with no help from Access.

- **Report Wizard**: will allow you to create a report with help from the Access Report Wizard. You can choose which fields you wish to see on the report.

- **AutoReport Columnar**: will create an instant report based on the query or table you specify, with the each record laid out in a column. You cannot choose which fields you wish to see.

- **AutoReport Tabular**: will create an instant report based on the query or table you specify, with all the records laid out in tabular format. You cannot choose which fields you wish to see.

- **Chart Wizard**: will create a chart with help from the Chart Wizard.

- **Label Wizard**: will create mailing labels with help from the Label Wizard.

4.2.2 Creating a Report with the Report Wizard

1️⃣ *Click on the Reports button*

2️⃣ *Double click Create report by using wizard*

    📄   Create report by using wizard ──── 2️⃣

or

Click New

Click Report Wizard

Click OK

3️⃣ *Click the drop down arrow under Tables/Queries*

4️⃣ *Click on the table or query you wish to base the report on*

5️⃣ *Double click the fields you wish to see on your report from underneath Available Fields – they will jump over to the Selected Fields column*

6️⃣ *Click Next*

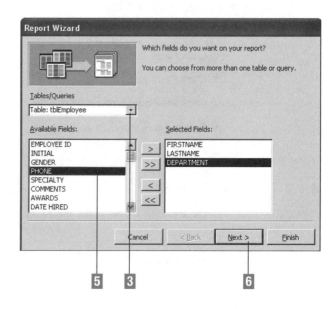

7 *If required, double click on the field(s) you wish to group by, e.g. Department*

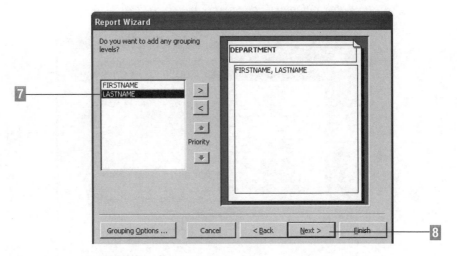

8 *Click Next*

9 *If required, click the drop down arrow and click on the field you wish to sort by*

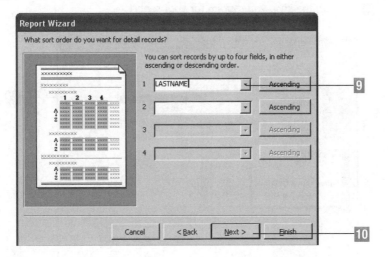

10 *Click Next*

11 *Click the circles next to the layout options you require for your report (the options will be slightly different if you are grouping by a field)*

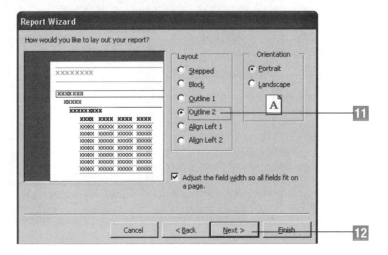

12 *Click Next*

13 *Click on the style you require for your report*

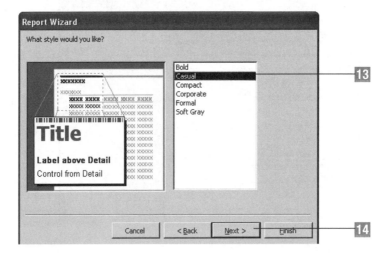

14 *Click Next*

15 *Type in a title for your report (this will appear as the title of the report)*

16 *Click Finish*

4.3 Changing the Design of a Report

4.3.1 What are the Views?

There are three views to a report:

- **Print Preview**: where you can view the report as it will appear when printed.

- **Design View**: where you can change how the report is designed.

- **Layout View**: in which you can see the layout of your report with some sample information. You probably won't need to use this view very often.

4.3.2 Changing the View

1 *Click the drop down arrow next to the view button*

2 *Click the view you require*

The view button will look different depending on which view you are in!

When you are in Print Preview it looks like this:

When you are in Design View it looks like this:

However, it is always the first button on the toolbar.

4.4 The Parts of a Report

4.4.1 What are the Parts of a Report in Design View?

- **Report Header**: which appears at the top of the report.

- **Page Header**: which appears at the top of every page in the report.

- **Detail**: which contains the actual records from the table.

- **Page Footer**: which appears at the bottom of every page in the report.

- **Report Footer**: which appears at the end of the report.

Sometimes reports can have extra headers and footers depending on whether information has been grouped. For example, in the report below the information has been grouped by department. The department field therefore appears in the "department header". Every time there is a new department, this header will appear.

reportFishcake

DEPARTMENT	FINANCE
LASTNAME	**FIRSTNAME**
	Todd
	Dominique
Collins	Sara
Smith	Jane
Smith	Bob
Smith	Fred

DEPARTMENT	SALES
LASTNAME	**FIRSTNAME**
Adams	Nathan
Bicksby	Becky
Campbell	Susan
Cohen	Geoff

4.4.2 Changing Labels and Controls on a Report

Changing Labels and Controls on a Report…

… is exactly the same as changing them in the Design View of a form, including adding text and editing text. If you would like to format these elements of the report, follow the instructions starting on page 338.

4.5 Summary Options on a Report

4.5.1 What are Summary Options?

You can use the report wizard to summarise number or currency fields on your report. They will allow you to produce:

- Totals

- Averages

- Maximum Number

- Minimum Number

If your report is grouped, you can also obtain subtotals, sub-averages, etc., based on each group.

For example, the report below has used Summary Options to find the total salary, the average salary, the maximum salary, and the minimum salary for each department:

DEPARTMENT	FIRSTNAME	LASTNAME	SALARY
EXECUTIVE			
	Christine	Dean	14500
	Debbie	Anderson	12000
	Debbie	Anderson	12000
	Lori	Dickerson	49000
	Vicky	Goreman	59000
	Lena	Barnett	12250
	Mary	Hamby	11500
	Rick	Zambini	79500
	Robert	Newman	52000
	Marilyn	Keegan	16500
	Sandy	Beman	35000
	Harry	Eivera	10500

Summary for 'DEPARTMENT' = EXECUTIVE (12 detail records)

		Sum	363750
		Avg	30312.5
		Min	10500
		Max	79500

The Summary Options for salary are shown at the bottom right of the report – the Sum, the Average, the Minimum and the Maximum.

4.5.2 Creating Summary Options

[1] Click on the Reports button

[2] Click Create report by using wizard

[3] Click the drop down arrow under Tables/Queries

[4] Click on the table or query you wish to base this report on

[5] Double click the fields you wish to see on the report

[6] Click Next

[7] Double click the field(s) you wish to group by if required

If you wish to create subtotals for a set of records, you will have to group by the field you wish to find subtotals for

[8] Click Next

[9] If required, choose the field(s) to sort by if required by clicking the drop down arrow

[10] Click the Summary Options button

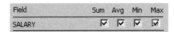

[11] Tick the boxes next to the field summary values you require

Field	Sum	Avg	Min	Max
SALARY	☑	☑	☑	☑

[12] Choose the options you require underneath Show

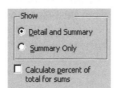

[13] Click OK

[14] Click Next

[15] Choose the layout you require

[16] Click Next

[17] Click the style you require

[18] Click Next

[19] Type the title you require for your report

[20] Click Finish

CHAPTER 5

Creating a Simple Database

What You'll Do

- Create a Simple Database
- Create a Database without Wizards
- Create a Database Using Database Wizard
- Use the Switchboard
- Create Tables
- Change the View of a Table
- Edit, Delete and Move Fields
- Set Field Properties
- Change Field Size
- Set an Input Mask
- Add a Caption
- Set the Validation Rule and Validation Text
- Index a Field

5.1 Planning a Database

5.1.1 What is the Purpose of My Database?

Designing databases can be a complex business. The more time and thought you put into the planning stage, the more effective your database will be later.

To get an idea of what you will need, ask yourself the following questions:

- What do you want the database to do for you?
- What will other people need the database to do?
- Do you already use some paper forms in a manual system? If you do, this information could be valuable.

5.1.2 The Key Question – What Information Do I Want out of My Database?

Start working on paper first!

- List all of the information that you want to get out
- Spend time ensuring that you have thought of everything

Make sure there is a separate field for each piece of data you wish to sort or extract…

For example, if you create a field called name which includes both the first name and the last name, you will not be able to sort it alphabetically by the last name. It will also be difficult to extract people whose last name is, for example, "Smith". When you create the query you will have to use wildcards.

5.1.3 The Golden Rule

The Golden Rule is…

Information should **NEVER** need to be entered twice!

The greatest mistake in designing a database is creating something where information is duplicated in different places. This makes your database almost impossible to work with. Here are some examples. Let's suppose you need a database to do the following:

- Hold information about **employees and which training course(s) they are going on**.

- Be able to produce a list of the people's names and the course(s) they are going on.

- Be able to produce a list of the courses and the people who are going on that course.

5.1.4 Example One – Duplicating Records

The temptation is to cram all this information into one table. You would probably decide that the following fields are crucial: *Lastname*, *Firstname*, *Course*.

But look what happens when you create a table with these fields and start to input data – Honor Blackman is going on three courses, which means her details have to be entered three times:

Firstname	Lastname	Department	Course
Bob	Hoskins	Geezer	Word 2000
Roger	Moore	Espionage	Excel XP
Honor	Blackman	Aerial Display	Word XP
Honour	Blackman	Aerial Display	Excel XP
Honor	Blackman	Geezer	Access 2000
Michael	Caine	Geezer	Word XP

This can cause all sorts of difficulties. Consider the following . . .

- You will waste time entering the same details again and again.

- Because you are inputting the same details again and again, you increase the chances of making a mistake in one of them. Look at the three records for Honor Blackman above. One of them has spelt "Honor" wrong, and another has put her in a different department. When you write a query to find people called "Honor Blackman" you are not going to find the record which is spelt "Honour". When you write a query to find "Honor Blackman" you will not know whether she is in the Geezer or Aerial Display department, as the table above says that she is in both.

- Let's imagine that you want to update the details for Honor Blackman. You will have to change her details three times, once for each record that she appears in.

- Imagine that you wish to sort this table into order of last name. You will not be able to produce a coherent alphabetical list of the people, because they will be duplicated again and again.

- Imagine that you want to know how many employees you have. You will not be able to count them easily because they are duplicated so many times.

- Imagine that you want to produce a coherent list of the courses. Many of the people in the table above are attending the Word XP course. This means that Word XP is duplicated many times. So you will only be able to produce a list with lots of duplication. This becomes even more complicated when you consider that you will probably need the dates, the times and the location of these courses etc.

5.1.5 Example Two – Duplicating Fields

In the last example you saw how duplicating records causes problems. However, it is still tempting to get all the information into one table. At this point, people may decide to duplicate the course field instead, like this:

Firstname	Lastname	Department	Course1	Course2	Course3
Bob	Hoskins	Geezer	Word 2000		
Roger	Moore	Espionage	Excel XP	Word 2000	
Honor	Blackman	Aerial Display	Word XP	Excel XP	Access 2000
Michael	Caine	Geezer	Word XP		

Although this may solve the problem incurred by duplicating the records, it creates plenty more problems of its own . . .

- Imagine that you want to find all the people who are on the Word 2000 course. When you create a query, you don't know whether "Word 2000" has been input into Course 1, Course 2, Course 3 etc., so you have to add all the course fields to the query and add the criterion "Word 2000" to all of them. The relationship between the criteria has to be OR so you will have to add each criterion on a different line. If you have 60 course fields, this is going to make a very complicated query!

- Imagine that you want an alphabetical list of all the courses. As the course names are spread out over several different fields, there is no way of doing this.

- Look at the number of blank fields which there are in this table. Most people may only be going on one or two courses, and yet you have a table with three course fields, and most of them are blank! This creates a very unwieldy table.

- You probably won't just want the course name, as in the picture above, but the date, the location, the price etc. You will end up having to create several duplicated fields for all this information as well.

5.1.6 The Solution – a Relational Database

If you find that you are duplicating records or duplicating fields then you almost certainly need a **relational** database. In other words, a database with **more than one table** and where those tables are **related** to each other in some way. The database we have been looking at causes problems because . . .

One person can go on **many courses**

Because there are many courses we have no choice but to duplicate either the course field itself, or the records to match up to each of the many courses the person is going on.

Some other examples may be . . .

- **One organisation** has **many contacts**

- **One artist** has **many albums**

- **One club** has **many members**

- **One doctor** has **many patients**

When this situation arises you need two tables, a table for the **one** side (e.g. people), and a table for the **many** side (e.g. courses). We will look at this again when we create relationships (see the next chapter).

5.2 Creating a New Database

5.2.1 Creating a New Database without Wizards

1. Click on the File menu

2. Click on New

   or

   Click on the New icon

3. Click on Blank Database in the task pane

4. Change the folder to save the database in, if required

5. Type in a filename for your database

6. Click Create – the Database window will appear

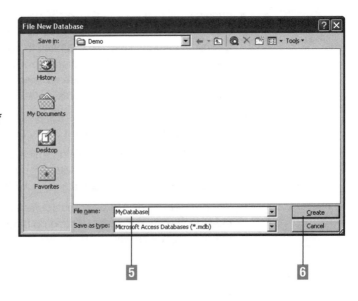

5.3 Creating a Database with the Database Wizard

5.3.1 Creating a New Database with Wizards

1 *Click on the File menu*

2 *Click on New*

> *or*

> *Click on the New icon*

3 *In the New File task pane, click on **General Templates** under **New from template***

4 *Click on the Databases tab*

5 *Click on the type of database you require, e.g. Asset Tracking*

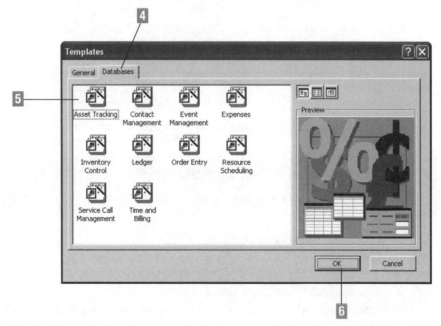

6 *Click OK*

7 *Change the folder to save the database in, if required*

8 *Type the filename for your database*

9 *Click Create – the Wizard will start*

What will my database store?

The first step of the wizard will tell you the type of information you will be able to store in the database.

The Asset Tracking database will store:

- Asset information
- Asset depreciation history
- Asset maintenance history
- Information about employees
- Department information
- Vendor information

10 *Click on Next – the next step will show you the tables and fields in the database*

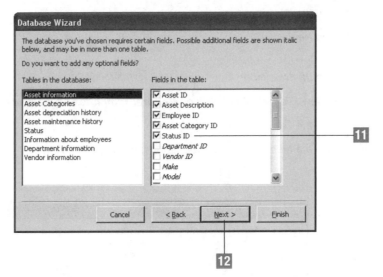

11 *Click in the box next to any fields you wish to add – they are ticked when included*

Why can't I remove some of the fields?

If you try to click into a box to remove a field from a table you may see this error message:

This means that the field you have tried to remove is required in the table.

12 *Click on Next*

13 *Click on the style you would like your database to use for forms*

14 *Click on Next*

15 *Click on the style you would like your database to use for reports*

16 *Click on Next*

17 *Type a title for your database*

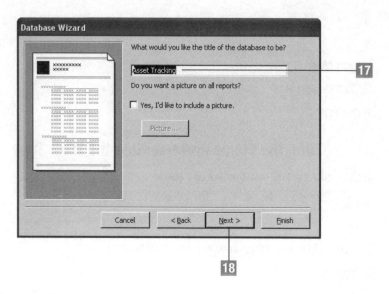

18 *Click on Next*

19 *Click on Finish – Access will create your database after a few seconds*

5.3.2 Using the Switchboard

When Access creates your database using a wizard, you will find that you have a switchboard. This helps you to use the database, and helps to keep the data protected. Just click on the button next to the function you require.

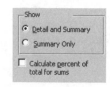

5.4 Creating Tables

5.4.1 The Four Steps

Creating a table without using a wizard has four main steps:

- Creating a table

- Creating the fields and deciding the data types

- Deciding on a primary key field if needed

- Saving the table

5.4.2 Step One – Creating a Table

Tables   **1** *Click on the Tables button*

2 *Double click on* **Create table in Design View**

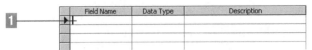

Or

1 *Click New*

2 *Click Design View*

3 *Click OK*

5.4.3 Step Two – Creating the Fields and Deciding the Data Type

1 *Click into the first row under Field Name*

Field Name	Data Type	Description

2 *Type in your first field name, e.g. OrganisationID*

3 *Press Tab*

   or

   Click into the Data Type column

4 *If required, click the drop down arrow and change the data type (see next section)*

5 *Press Tab*

   or

   Click into the Description column

6 *If required, type in a description for this field (e.g. what the field is for)*

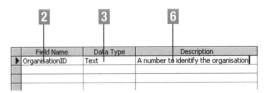

Field Name	Data Type	Description
OrganisationID	Text	A number to identify the organisation

Access will not allow the following characters in field names:

. (full-stop)   ! (exclamation point)   [ ] (brackets)   ` (grave accent)

It is good practice to not include spaces in field names…

Although you can use spaces in field names and it will not usually cause problems, it can cause conflicts if you use Visual Basic for Applications with Access.

5.4.4 Specifying Data Types

You must specify what data type each of the fields in your table should be...

Data type	What does it store?	Example	Extra information
Text	Letters or numbers	Firstname Lastname	Holds up to 255 characters. Most of your fields will probably be text.
Memo	Letters or numbers	Comments	Holds up to 64,000 characters. It is usually used when you need to add a lot of text.
Number	Numbers	Number of staff	Holds numbers which you intend to sort numerically, or perform calculations on.
Date/Time	Dates and times	Date hired Order date	Holds dates which you can then sort into date order and perform calculations on.
Currency	Monetary values	Salary	Formats numbers as currency and allows you to perform calculations on those numbers.
AutoNumber	A number which Access generates automatically for each record	ID Number	Used mostly as a primary key field, because the number will be unique for each record. Even if the record is deleted, the number goes with it.
Yes/No	A field which gives you the choice of "yes" or "no"	Full-time	e.g.
OLE Object	OLE objects are generally graphics, e.g. photographs, logos	Logo Product preview	Holds up to 1 gigabyte (limited by disk space).
Hyperlink	Links to somewhere else that your computer has access to, e.g. a Word document, a website	Company website	When you click on the data in this field it will link you to somewhere else.
Lookup Wizard	A field that allows you to choose from a drop down list	Gender Department	e.g.

Is a phone number a number data type?

No! Phone numbers, part numbers, or numbers on which you don't intend to do calculations are **text**! If you make them numbers, you will not be able to have a "0" at the start of your phone numbers!

5.4.5 Step Three – the Primary Key

What is the primary key?

- A special field that **uniquely** identifies each record in the table. In other words there is different information in that field for each record, e.g. id number, product code. You could not use something like "lastname" as the primary key because some people are likely to have the same lastname. The primary key must be unique to each record.

- It is good practice to identify a primary key for each table, although you do not have to if you think you do not need one.

- If you are creating relationships then there **must** be a primary key in the table which is **one** side of the relationship.

1 *Click into the field you want to become a primary key*

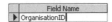

 2 *Click on the Primary Key icon – a key will appear next to the field*

If you do not create a primary key you will be asked about it when you save the table!

See the next section for more details.

5.4.6 Saving the Table

You must save tables before you can input data into them...

1 *Click on the Save button*

2 *Type a name for the table, e.g. Table Organisations or tblOrganisations*

3 *Click OK*

What should I call my table?

When saving a table it is good practice to identify it as a table in the name, e.g. table organisations, table students, table employees. Most people would type tblOrganisations, tblStudents, or tblEmployees, for example.

If you didn't create a primary key…

… Access would ask you if you want to create one when saving.

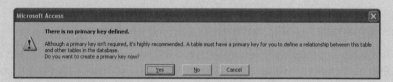

If you say yes, you will end up with an extra field in your table called "ID".

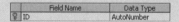

To delete this field, see page 362.

5.5 Changing the View of a Table

5.5.1 What are the Views of a Table?

There are two views to a table:

- **Design View**: where you can add, edit or delete fields and change the way your table works.
- **Datasheet View**: where you can input data.

5.5.2 Changing the View

1 Click the drop down arrow next to the view button

2 Click on the view you require

The view icon looks different depending on which view you are in!

When you are in Design View it will look like this:

When you are in Datasheet View it will look like this:

5.6 Changing Table Design

5.6.1 Editing a Field

1 *Ensure you are in Design View*

2 *Click into the field you wish to edit*

3 *Make any changes you require*

4 *Click Save, or Access will warn you to save when you leave Design View*

Access tells me that some data may be deleted...

If you have already typed information into the field in Datasheet view, then editing the field may create changes that render the existing information invalid, for example, if you change the data type from text to number.

5.6.2 Deleting a Field

1 *Ensure you are in Design View*

 2 *Click on the grey bar next to the field you wish to delete – it will become highlighted*

3 *Press Delete*

4 *Click Save, or Access will warn you to save when you leave Design View*

You will be warned twice about deleting the primary key!

If you delete the primary key, Access will not only warn you that you are deleting a field, but also that it is the primary key for the table.

5.6.3 Moving Fields

1 *Ensure you are in Design View*

2 *Click on the grey bar next to the field you wish to delete – it will become highlighted to indicate that it is selected*

3 *Position the mouse pointer on the grey bar next to the field*

4 *Click and drag the field to a new location*

5 *Click Save, or Access will warn you to save when you leave Design View*

5.7 Field Properties

5.7.1 What are Field Properties?

Field properties are a way of limiting the information which people can type into your table – useful if you want to try and minimise the possibility of mistakes. For example, you can use them to:

- Limit the number of characters allowed into a field, e.g. allowing only 10 characters for postcode

- Specify a default, or automatic value, e.g. "London" in the town field, if most of your addresses are in London

- Change the way that data appears, e.g. formatting a date which is typed in as **1/1/06** to appear as **01 January 2006**

5.7.2 Setting Field Properties

You can change the field properties at any time, but…

… if you change them after you have already inputted data to the table, you may lose some of the information. If existing data doesn't fit the new requirements, Access may just delete it.

1 *Ensure you are in Design View of the table*

2 *Click into the field you wish to set properties for*

3 *Change the properties as required (see next sections)*

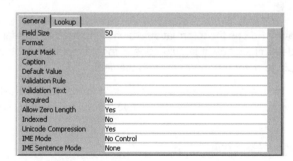

4 *Click on the Save icon*

Field properties change depending on the data type!

e.g. fields with a text data type will have different properties available than a field with a number date type, etc.

5.7.3 Changing Field Size

What does it mean? The maximum number of characters which people can input into a field (including spaces).

When am I likely to use it? For text fields where there is always a limited number of characters, e.g. postcode, phone number.

1 *Click into the Field Size box*

Field Size	12

2 *Change the number to the maximum number allowed for your field*

5.7.4 Changing Format

What does it mean? Changes the way in which the data appears.

When am I likely to use it? For dates or numbers which you wish to appear differently from the way they are inputted, e.g. numbers which you wish to become percentages, dates which you wish to become long dates, 01 Jan 1999.

1 *Click in the Format box*

2 *Click the drop down arrow*

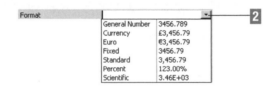

3 *Click on the format you require*

5.7.5 Setting an Input Mask

What does it mean? Forces the information which is inputted to appear in a certain way. The input mask determines how it should appear, for example an input mask of "0000" would force people to enter four numbers into the field.

When am I likely to use it? When there is a standard format for the field in question, e.g. National Insurance numbers which are always two letters, followed by six numbers and then one letter.

1 *Click into the Input Mask box*

2 *Type in the input mask you require, e.g. LL000000L for a National Insurance number*

These are the symbols you are most likely to use in your input mask:

0	Number which must be filled in
9	Number which does not have to be filled in
#	Number or space which does not have to be filled in and can include plus or minus signs
L	Letter which must be filled in
?	Letter which does not need to be filled in
A	Letter or number which must be filled in
a	Letter or number which does not need to be filled in
&	Any character or space which must be filled in
C	Any character or space which does not have to be filled in
<	All characters which follow this will be converted to lowercase (the symbol does not show when you input data)
>	All characters which follow this will be converted to uppercase (the symbol does not show when you input data)

5.7.6 Adding a Caption

What does it mean? The text which appears at the top of the column in Datasheet View.

When am I likely to use it? When you want the text at the top of the column to be different from the actual field name.

1 *Click into the Caption box*

2 *Type the caption you require*

5.7.7 Changing the Default Value

What does it mean? Text which is already typed into the field before you start to input data (you can still type something else, though).

When am I likely to use it? When you often type the same data into a field, e.g. if most of your records contain "London"' in the address, you could change the default for town/city to "London".

1 *Click into the Default Value box*

2 *Type the default you require*

5.7.8 Setting the Validation Rule and Validation Text

What does it mean? Setting a rule for the data which can be inputted into a field. The validation text is the error message which will be displayed if the rule is broken.

When am I likely to use it? One example would be a credit limit. Imagine that nobody can have a credit limit over £50,000. You can set the validation rule as <50000, which forces Access to only accept numbers which are less than 50,000.

1 *Click into the Validation Rule box*

2 *Enter the validation rule, e.g. <50000*

3 *Click into the Validation Text box*

4 *Type the error message you wish to appear if people break the rule, e.g. "Please enter a figure of less than £50,000"*

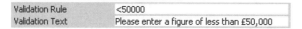

| Validation Rule | <50000 |
| Validation Text | Please enter a figure of less than £50,000 |

5.7.9 Making a Field Required

What does it mean? People must enter something into this field when they create a new record.

When am I likely to use it? When you have a field which you do not want to be left blank, e.g. organisation name, phone number etc.

1 *Click into the Required box*

2 *Click the drop down arrow*

3 *Click Yes*

If you do not fill in a required field in Datasheet View, Access will display the following message:

5.7.10 Allowing Zero Length

What does it mean? Allows you to leave a field blank on purpose.

When am I likely to use it? When you have a field which you know is to be left blank.

1 *Click into the Zero Length box*

2 *Click the drop down arrow*

3 *Click Yes*

5.7.11 Indexing a Field

What does it mean? Access keeps a sorted copy of this field in the background which speeds up sorting and grouping the data in this field.

When am I likely to use it? On fields which you are likely to sort often in a very large database.

1. *Click into the Indexed box*

2. *Click **Yes (No Duplicates)** if this field is to be unique to each record, e.g. the primary key*

   or

   *Click Yes **(Duplicated OK)** if this field will contain duplicates*

5.7.12 AutoNumber Property: New Values

What does it mean? The way in which AutoNumber generates the next number. Usually it goes up by one each time.

When am I likely to use it? When you do not want the AutoNumber to go up by one each time.

1. *Click into the New Values box*

2. *Click the drop down arrow*

3. *Click Random*

5.7.13 Number Property: Decimal

What does it mean? Determines how many decimal places are to appear to the right of the decimal point.

When am I likely to use it? When you need to specify a certain number of decimal points for a number field.

1. *Click into the Decimal Places box*

2. *Click the drop down arrow*

3. *Click on the number of decimal places you require*

5.7.14 Text, Memo or Hyperlink: Unicode Compression

What does it mean? Reduces the amount of space needed to store information in a text, memo or hyperlink field. It is on by default.

When am I likely to use it? If you want to minimise the amount of space needed to store that field.

1. *Click into the Unicode Compression box*

2. *Click the drop down arrow*

3. *Click on Yes or No*

CHAPTER 6

Relationships

What You'll Do

→ Discover Types of Relationship

→ Create a One-to-Many Relationship

→ Discover Cascade Update

→ Discover Cascade Delete

→ Close the Relationships Window

→ Create a One-to-One Relationship

6.1 What are Relationships?

6.1.1 What is a Relational Database?

A relational database is simply **a database with two or more tables which are linked together**. In fact, very few databases (if they are designed correctly) hold their information in just one table.

You know you need a relational database when you find that you are duplicating records or duplicating fields. This makes your database almost impossible to work with.

6.1.2 The Types of Relationship

There are three types of relationship . . .

One-to-One

This is the least common type of relationship. It is used when you have special information which you would like to keep separate from the main table. This can be for security reasons, or because you will rarely need to refer to it, or because the information does not apply to every record in the main table.

Some examples of one-to-one relationships . . .

- Main table contains information about all the staff. Another table is created holding information about the staff football team. This information is not appropriate for the main table so is kept separately. A one-to-one relationship is created between the two.
- Main table contains information about all staff. A separate table holds information about their previous employer. This information rarely needs to be referred to, so is kept separately with a one-to-one relationship between the two.

One-to-Many

This is probably the easiest and most common type of relationship. It is needed when there is one thing which can have many things attached to it.

Some examples of one-to-many . . .

- One organisation can have many contacts
- One employee can go on many courses
- One supplier can have many products
- One album can have many songs
- One doctor can have many patients
- One teacher can have many students

Many-to-Many

However, it is also common to have a situation where a one-to-many comes back on itself. Take the example of *one employee can go on many courses*. In actual fact it doesn't end there, because *one course can be attended by many employees*. The same thing happens with something like products and customers. *One product can have many customers* but it is also true to say that *one customer can buy many products*. If you find that a one-to-many can be reversed in this way, you may need a many-to-many relationship. Many-to-many relationships are not required for the ECDL exams.

Some examples of many-to-many . . .

- One organisation can have many contacts/One contact can work for many organisations
- One product can have many customers/One customer can buy many products
- One employee can go on many courses/One course can be attended by many employees
- One teacher can have many students/One student can have many teachers

6.2 Creating a One-to-Many Relationship

6.2.1 One-to-Many Relationships – the theory

In a one-to-many relationship there are **two tables** . . .

- A table to hold the **one** side of the relationship

- A table to hold the **many** side of the relationship

The two tables are linked together by a **matching field** which holds the same information in both tables. In the example both tables contain the Employee ID field. This is what links the two tables.

This is the **One** table. It holds information about the employees:

	EMPLOYEE ID	LASTNAME	FIRSTNAME
+	1	Smith	Kim
+	2	Beman	Sandy
+	3	Bicksby	Becky
+	4	Campbell	Susan
+	5	Cohen	Geoff

This is the **Many** table. It holds information about the courses the employees are going on:

EMPLOYEE ID	TRAINING COURSE
1	Access Advanced
2	Access Essentials
3	Talking Proper
4	Embroidery
5	Access Advanced

- In the one side table this is known as the **primary key**.

  This has to be unique to each record. In the example above, each employee has their own unique **Employee ID** number.

- In the many side table this is known as the **foreign key**.

  This matches the number in the one side table. In the example above, each course has an employee ID number which relates back to one of the employees in the one side table. So the first record in the courses table says that employee ID number 1 is going on Access Advanced. Looking at the employee table shows us that employee ID number 1 is Kim Smith.

Why does the primary key have to be unique?

If the primary key is not unique to each record, the many table will get confused about which record it is matched to in the one table.

Let's imagine that you decide to use Firstname as the primary key in the following table:

LASTNAME	FIRSTNAME
Lucas	John
Montovan	John
Peterson	John
Orlando	John
Sanders	Kathy
Loftus	Kathy
Keegan	Keith

When we get to the many table it isn't clear which John is going on the Access Advanced course. Is it Lucas, Montovan, Peterson or Orlando?

Firstname	TRAINING COURSE
John	Access Advanced
Kathy	Access Essentials
Keith	Talking Proper

In fact, Access would not allow you to create this situation for real. If you made Firstname the primary key, everybody would have to have a different first name in order for Access to allow it!

6.2.2 What Do You Need Before You Can Create the Relationship?

Before you set up a one-to-many relationship you must have the following in your database . . .

- A table which is to be the one side with a unique field defined as the primary key

- A table which is to be the many side with a field which has the same name and data type as the primary key field in the one table (this is known as the foreign key)

The primary key and the foreign key must have a matching data type

Use the table below as a guide:

Primary Key Data Type	Foreign Key Data Type
Text	Text
Number	Number with the same field size as the primary key
AutoNumber	Number with a Field Size of Long Integer (the foreign key can't be AutoNumber as well otherwise it will just go 1,2,3 etc. – and that defeats the point of the many table!)

6.2.3 Creating a One-to-Many Relationship

[1] *Close all tables, queries, and so on, until you can just see the database window*

[2] *Click on the relationships icon*

    – the Show Table box should appear (if not, click on the Show Table icon)

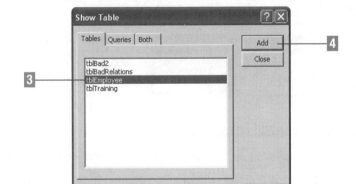

[3] *Click on the table you wish to add*

[4] *Click on Add*

[5] *Repeat steps 3 and 4 for any more tables you wish to add*

[6] *Click Close*

7 *Click on the primary key field in the One table – this will appear in bold*

8 *Click and drag the primary key field to the matching field in the Many table – a white box will appear when you are in the right place*

9 *Click in the box next to Enforce Referential Integrity, so that it is ticked*

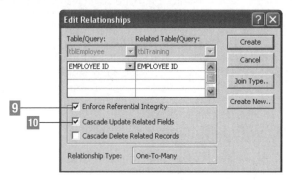

10 *Click in the box next to Cascade Update Related Fields, so that it is ticked*

11 *Click Create – the relationship will be created, and you will see the join in the Relationships window*

6.2.4 What is Referential Integrity?

Referential integrity makes the relationship between tables safer by . . .

■ **Ensuring that the relationship between records remains valid**

In other words, all the information in the many table must match something in the one table. Imagine that this table is your one table:

	EMPLOYEE ID	LASTNAME	FIRSTNAME
+	1	Smith	Kim
+	2	Beman	Sandy
+	3	Bicksby	Becky
+	4	Campbell	Susan
+	5	Cohen	Geoff

You could not create a record with an employee ID of 6 in the many table, because employee ID 6 does not exist in the one table.

■ **Ensuring that you do not accidentally delete related data**

With referential integrity turned on you cannot delete a record from the one table if it has related records in the many table. You must delete the records in the many table first.

The only exception to this is if Cascade Delete is turned on (see below).

6.2.5 What Does Cascade Update Mean?

If you change the primary key in the one table then all the records in the many table update to have the new primary key. It is useful to turn this on just in case you do change the primary key in the future.

6.2.6 What Does Cascade Delete Mean?

This negates the part of referential integrity which forces you to delete the records in the many table before you can delete the record in the one table.

If you turn Cascade Delete on then you can delete the record in the one table and all its related records in the many table will be deleted.

It is not a good idea to turn this on, except when you want to delete a lot of records from the one table, otherwise you may accidentally delete a lot of data.

6.2.7 Closing the Relationships Window

1 *Click the X button at the top right of the Relationships window*

2 *Click Yes – you are only being asked to save the layout changes, not the relationship. This is saved as soon as you create it!*

6.2.8 How Do I Input Data into the Many Table?

Just open the Many table, and enter the data. You will find that you have to remember the primary key information in order to input it correctly.

6

6.3 Creating a One-to-One Relationship

6.3.1 One-to-One Relationships – the Theory

A one-to-one relationship is rarely needed. However, you can use it to store information in a separate table from the main one, either because you want to keep it secure or because you will rarely have to refer to it.

There are two tables . . .

- A main table which has a unique field defined as the primary key

- A related table which has a field with the same name and data type as the primary key in the main table, **and which is also set as a primary key**.

In the example below the main table holds information about employees, and the related table holds information about their previous employer. The Employee ID field is present in both of the tables and is what links the two together:

	EMPLOYEE ID	LASTNAME	FIRSTNAME
+	1	Smith	Kim
+	2	Beman	Sandy
+	3	Bicksby	Becky
+	4	Campbell	Susan
+	5	Cohen	Geoff

EMPLOYEE ID	Previous Organisation
1	Gladrags Inc
2	Radio Norwich
3	The Cake Shop
4	Spimm Industries

As both of the Employee ID fields are primary keys there can only be one employee to one previous employer.

6.3.2 What Do You Need to Create a One-to-One Relationship?

Before you can create a one-to-one relationship between two tables you need to have the following . . .

- A main table with a unique field defined as the primary key

- Another table with a field with the same name and data type as the primary key in the other table, which is also defined as a primary key

6.3.3 Creating a One-to-One Relationship

1 *Close all tables, queries, and so on, until you can just see the database window*

2 *Click the Relationships icon*

3 *Ensure that you can see the tables you wish to add – if you can't, click the Show Table icon, double click the tables you want to add, then click Close*

4 *Click the primary key field in the main table*

5 *Drag the primary key field to the matching field in the second table – a box will appear when you are in the correct place*

6 *Tick the box next to Enforce Referential Integrity*

7 *Tick the box next to Cascade Update Related Fields*

8 *Click Create*

9 *Close the Relationships window*

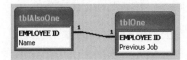

CHAPTER 7

Quick Reference

Step One: Decide ...
- Decide what info do I want out?
- Work backwards, and decide what info you need to go in!

Step Two: Decide (On Paper) ...
- What tables do you need?
- What fields do you need? Which ones should be lookups?

Step Three: Consult!
- It's crucial you take time to talk to anyone who might use your database or need to take info from it!

Step Four: Create the Database
- Create a new database and name it

Step Five: Create Tables
- Create your tables and your fields
- Create lookups

Step Six: Relationships
- Determine the relationships between your tables
- Key in a few "dummy" records

Step Seven: Queries
- Create your most important queries (this will test whether you have put in everything that you need)

Step Eight: Forms and Reports
- Create your forms
- Create your reports

Step Nine: Test!
- Test your database again
- Consult everyone and make sure that nothing has been missed!
- Delete the "dummy" records and key in your real info

Step Ten: Written Record
- Make a written record of the tables, fields, lookups and relationships in your database

CHAPTER 1

Getting Started

What You'll Do

→ Get Started in PowerPoint

→ Start and Exit PowerPoint

→ Adjust the Areas of the Screen

→ Create a Blank Presentation

→ Choose the Layout

→ Use a Design Template

→ Save a Presentation

→ Open and Close a Presentation

→ Change the Zoom Control

→ Display and Hide Toolbars

→ Use Help in PowerPoint

1.1 What is PowerPoint?

1.1.1 What is it for?

PowerPoint is for producing presentations on...

- Acetates (overhead projector slides)

- 35mm slides

- Paper

- The computer screen

- The Internet

All of these are created in exactly the same way!

The only difference comes at the end when you wish to give the presentation. You could print onto acetate or paper, run the slide show on the screen, upload your presentation to the Internet, or send your presentation to a specialist shop to create 35mm slides.

It can also produce extra documents related to your presentation...

- Speaker's notes

- Audience handouts

1.1.2 PowerPoint Jargon

Every presentation you produce is made up of slides. Slide is a generic term that can mean any of the types of presentation listed in the previous section.

A presentation

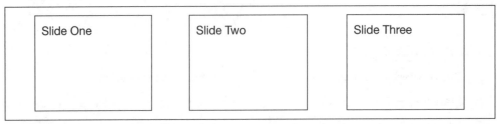

1.2 Starting and Exiting PowerPoint

1.2.1 Starting PowerPoint

[1] *Click on the Start button*

[2] *Click on All Programs*

Microsoft
PowerPoint

[3] *Click Microsoft PowerPoint*

Or, if you have a shortcut on your desktop, double click the shortcut.

1.2.2 Exiting PowerPoint

[1] *Click on the File menu*

[2] *Click Exit*

Or

Click on the X at the top right hand corner of the screen

1.3 The PowerPoint Screen in Normal View

Here is a picture of the PowerPoint screen in Normal view. The screen can look very different depending on which view you are in! (see page 393)...

1 *The blue bar at the top is the title bar*

2 *Underneath that is the menu bar*

3 *Underneath that is the Standard toolbar*

4 *Underneath that is the Formatting toolbar*

5 *The large white bar on the left is the thumbnail view area*

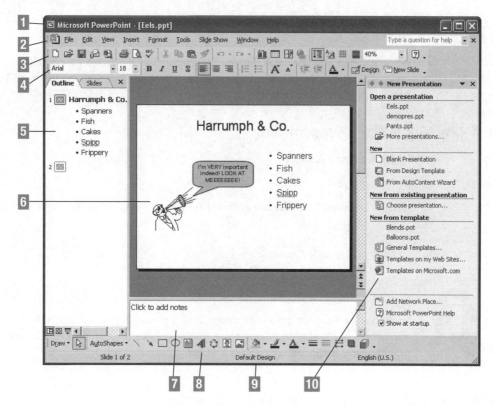

6 *The large area in the middle is the slide view area*

7 *Just under that is the speaker's notes area*

8 *Under that is the drawing toolbar*

9 *Under that, right at the bottom, is the status bar*

10 *Last, but not least, on the right, is the Task Pane, where you will access most of PowerPoint's features*

1.3.1 Adjusting the Areas of the Screen

There are three main areas of the screen in Normal view…

- Outline view area
- Slide view area
- Speaker's notes

At different times in your work, you will want to concentrate on different areas. To make an area bigger or smaller…

1 *Position your mouse at the edge of an area – the mouse pointer will change to a double headed arrow*

2 *Click and drag*

1.4 Creating a New Presentation

When you first start PowerPoint, you will be given a new, blank presentation to start with. If you have closed this, or opened another file and then closed it, you will need to create another presentation if you want a new file.

1.4.1 Creating a Blank Presentation

1. *Click on the File menu*

2. *Click on New*

New

□ Blank Presentation

3. *Click on Blank Presentation from the Task Pane – you will be given a new, blank file*

Or

Click on the New Presentation icon

---

i **Should I use the menu or the icon?**

The icon is the quickest way of creating a new presentation, but using the menu gives you access to PowerPoint's design templates, where you can choose colours and pictures for the backgrounds of your slides.

1.4.2 Choosing the Layout

Once you have chosen Blank Presentation, the Task Pane will change to the Slide Layout pane. To choose a slide layout, just pick one that you like, and click on it!

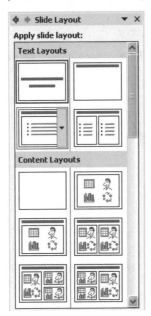

1.4.3 Using a Design Template

Design templates are preset designs that include colours, images, backgrounds, and so on. They will not add anything, just change the appearance. To apply a design template…

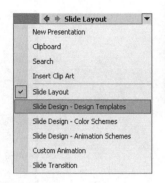

1. *Click on the drop down arrow at the top of the Task Pane*

2. *Choose Slide Design – Design Templates*

3. *Click on the template you wish to use*

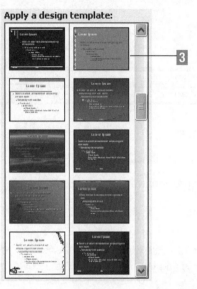

1.5 Saving a Presentation

1.5.1 Saving a Presentation

1. *Click on the Save icon*

   or

   Click on the File menu

   Click on Save

2. *Type a filename (maximum of 255 characters) into the **File name** box*

3. *Change the location in the **Save in** box if required, by clicking on the drop down arrow next to it*

4. *Click Save*

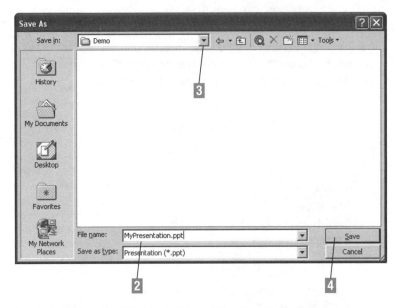

1.5.2 Saving a Presentation After You Have Made Changes

Just click on the Save icon – the previous version is overwritten.

Save regularly!

Click on the Save icon at regular intervals when you are working. If you forget to save for a long time, you are in danger of losing your work if there is a power cut.

1.5.3 Saving a Copy of a Presentation Using Save As

Use Save As if you want to save a copy of your file under a different name, or in a different place.

1 *Click File*

2 *Click Save As*

3 *Type in a new filename (if required)*

4 *Change the Save in box to a different folder (if required)*

5 *Click Save*

1.5.4 Saving As a Different Format

When you save your presentation it is saved in the default format for PowerPoint XP. In other words, the computer knows that it came from PowerPoint XP and it will only open it if you have PowerPoint 97, 2000 or XP on your computer. However, you may want to use your presentation to do something different – in which case you will need to save it in a different format. Below are some examples of when you might do this:

- As an earlier version of PowerPoint, so the presentation can be opened in earlier versions

- As a format that will be compatible across different programs/software, e.g. text file or RTF (Rich Text Format). In PowerPoint this will mean saving the text you can see in Outline view only

- As HTML for the World Wide Web

- As a template to reuse the format again

- As an image file, e.g. WMF (Windows Metafile) or GIF (Graphics Interchange Format). This will enable you to save a slide as an image. You will not be able to edit once you have saved in this format

    1 *Click on the File menu*

    2 *Click Save As*

    3 *Click on the drop down arrow to the right of the **Save as type** box (scrolling to see all the options if necessary)*

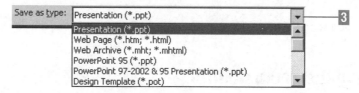

    4 *Choose the type of file you want to save as*

    5 *Click Save*

1.6 Opening and Closing a Presentation

1.6.1 Opening a Presentation

    1 *Click on the Open icon*

    2 *Click the drop down arrow next to the **Look in** box, and go to the drive and folder where your file is saved*

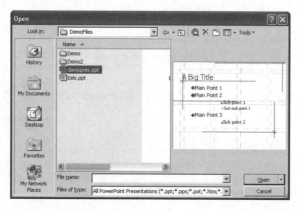

3 *Click on the file/folder you require*

4 *Click Open*

1.6.2 Opening Multiple Files

To open more than one file, just repeat the process – open one file, then open another one. They will appear as buttons on your taskbar, which you can click to switch between them:

1.6.3 Closing a Presentation

1 *Click on the File menu*

2 *Click Close*

Or

Click on the bottom X at the top right hand corner of the screen

---

1.7   Changing the Zoom Control

1.7.1 What Is the Zoom Control?

The zoom control allows you to zoom in and look at your presentation close up, or zoom out to look at your presentation from a distance.

1.7.2 Changing the Zoom with the Icon

1 *Click the drop down arrow next to the Zoom icon*

2 *Click on the zoom level you require*

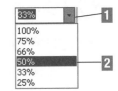

1.7.3 Changing the Zoom with the Menu

1 *Click on the View menu*

2 *Click Zoom*

3 *Click in the circle next to the zoom level you require*

or

Click the up and down arrows next to the percentage box

4 *Click OK*

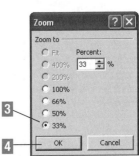

1.8 Toolbars

You can choose which toolbars you want displayed according to what you are working on.

1.8.1 Displaying Toolbars

1. *Click on the View menu*

2. *Click on Toolbars*

3. *Click on the name of the toolbar you want to display*

1.8.2 Hiding Toolbars

1. *Click on the View menu*

2. *Click on Toolbars*

3. *Click on the name of the toolbar you want to hide*

Hidden or displayed?

You can tell which toolbars are currently displayed. The toolbars that are displayed have a tick next to them, the toolbars that are hidden do not. So if the toolbar you want is ticked, it is somewhere on the screen.

1.9 Using Help in PowerPoint

PowerPoint comes with a Help feature which works in exactly the same way as the help in Word – see the Help section in the Word chapters on page 46 for more details.

CHAPTER 2

Basic Operations

What You'll Do

→ Move Around a Presentation

→ Change Basic Preferences

→ Add Text to Slides

→ Create New Slides

→ Change the View

→ Use the Slide Sorter View

→ Change the Size of Slides

→ Change the Orientation of Slides

→ Print Slides

→ Select Text and Placeholders

→ Move, Resize and Delete Placeholders

→ Move and Copy Text

→ Move, Copy and Delete Slides

→ Create Speaker's Notes

2.1 | Moving Around a Presentation

2.1.1 Where Am I?

Slide 2 of 6   Check the status bar at the bottom of the screen – it tells you what slide you are on, and how many slides you have.

2.1.2 Moving Around with the Scroll Bar

To move to the next slide, click the double headed down arrows

To move to the previous slide, click the double headed up arrows

2.1.3 Moving Around with the Keyboard

To move to the **next slide**, press Page Down (sometimes called PgDn)

To move to the **previous slide**, press Page Up (sometimes called PgUp)

To move to the **first slide**, press Ctrl and Home

To move to the **last slide**, press Ctrl and End

2.1.4 To Move to Individual Slides

1 *Use the Slide Sorter view (see page 395)*

Or

2 *Click into the slide required in the thumbnail view area*

(see page 395)

1 ▦ **Harrumph & Co.**
- Spanners
- Fish
- Cakes
- Spigo
- Frippery

2 ▦ **Our Plan**
- More hats
- Er, that's it

2.2 Changing Basic Preferences

2.2.1 About PowerPoint's General Options

PowerPoint XP has a number of basic preferences which you can change to personalise the program to your taste. For instance, you can change the folder to which your presentations will be automatically opened from and saved to (the default folder). You can also update the user name associated with the program. To access these options . . .

2.2.2 Changing the Default Folder

1 *Click on the Tools menu*

2 *Click on Options*

3 *Click on the Save tab*

4 *Click in the box under Default file location*

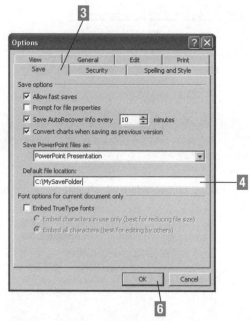

5 *Type in the drive and folder you wish to save to*

6 *Click OK*

2.2.3 Changing the User Name

⌷1⌷ *Click on the Tools menu*

⌷2⌷ *Click on Options*

⌷3⌷ *Click on the General tab*

⌷4⌷ *Click in the box next to Name*

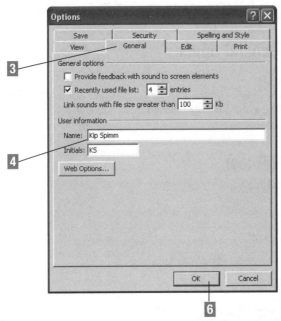

⌷5⌷ Type in the new user name

⌷6⌷ Click OK

2.3 Adding Text to Slides

2.3.1 What are Slide Layouts?

Every slide has a layout containing placeholders which you can enter text into. There are two layouts shown below:

Title Slide Layout

Bulleted List Layout

2.3.2 What are Placeholders?

Every layout has placeholder for each item that you will put on your slides. These will always give instructions on how to add information.

Text Placeholder

- Click to add text

Chart Placeholder

Double click to add chart

ClipArt Placeholder

Double click to add clip art

Media Clip Placeholder

Double click to add media clip

2.3.3 Adding Text to Placeholders

1. *Click inside the placeholder you want to add text to – diagonal lines will appear around the edge*

2. *Start typing!*

3. *Click outside the placeholder when you have finished*

PowerPoint does the formatting for you!

PowerPoint comes with preset formatting depending on the template you have chosen. Titles will be bigger, subtitles and bulleted lists will be smaller. There will be different alignments and there will be different fonts.

You can change the formatting on individual slides, but you may lose consistency with the rest of the slides in the presentation. If you wish to change the formatting consistently use the master slides (see page 411).

Moving to the next placeholder with the keyboard

Press Escape (Esc), then press Tab.

2.3.4 Creating Bulleted Lists

1. *Click into the bulleted list placeholder*

2. *Type your first point*

3. *Press Return to start a new point*

2.3.5 Changing the Layout

Once a slide is created it is easy to change your mind about its layout…

1. *Select the slide you wish to change*

2. *Click on the Format menu*

3. *Click on Slide Layout*

4. *Click on the required new layout in the Task Pane*

2.3.6 Editing the Text in Placeholders

1. *Click inside the placeholder you want to change – diagonal lines will appear around the edge*

2. *Make any changes you require*

2.3.7 Creating New Areas for Text

If the placeholders on your slide do not give you all the space you need for text, you can draw a text box.

1. *Click on the Text Box icon on the drawing toolbar*

2. *Position the mouse on the slide where you require extra text*

3. *Click and drag the shape of the text box you require*

4. *Start typing – text will wrap inside the box*

2.4 Creating New Slides

2.4.1 Creating New Slides

1. *Move to the slide which will appear before the new one*

2. *Click on the New Slide icon*

3. *Click on the layout you require from the Task Pane*

You can also press Ctrl and M to add a new slide!

Don't create a new presentation by mistake!

Lots of people fall into the trap of creating new slides by clicking on the New icon, or by going to File and New. This won't just create a new slide, it will also create a new presentation – leaving all of your existing slides stranded. If you have done this, close down the new presentation, and you should end up back in the old one where you can add a new slide as normal.

2.5 The Different Views of PowerPoint

2.5.1 Changing the View

[1] *Click on the View menu*

[2] *Click on the view you require*

Or

Click on the required icon from the bottom left of the screen

Going from left to right, the icons will take you to a different view:

- *Normal view*
- *Slide Sorter view*
- *Slide Show view (runs the slide show)*

2.5.2 Normal View

Normal view is the one that you will work in most of the time. It offers you three different areas:

- Slide view area where you can see your slide
- Thumbnail view area where you can see all the text in your presentation
- Speaker's notes area where you can write your own notes on the slides

Each of these areas can be adjusted according to your preference. In Normal view, you can…

- Add text
- Add pictures
- Create speaker's notes

On the left in Normal view is the thumbnail area – it is sometimes called the Outline Pane, although it is still technically the Normal view. This shows you an outline of your presentation. You can click on the slides to switch between them, or just get a general idea of how things look. Click on the icons at the top to switch between the image or text versions.

In the text version, you can add text into the small, outlined slides – just click on them and type as normal, pressing Return to add new lines.

1 Harrumph & Co.
- Spanners
- Fish
- Cakes
- Spi00
- Frippery

2 Our Plan
- More hats
- Er, that's it

2.5.3 Slide Sorter View

Slide Sorter view shows you all your slides as if they were laid out on a table. You cannot add text or pictures in Slide Sorter view, but you can…

- Change the order of slides
- Delete slides
- Add transition and animation effects (see pages 434 and 436)

2.5.4 Slide Show View

Slide Show view is used for giving an on-screen presentation. When you have finished creating your presentation, this is what you will use to present the show – or you can use it to make sure it works before standing up in front of 300 people…

2.6 Normal View

2.6.1 Getting to Normal View

This is the view that PowerPoint will open in. If you have changed views…

Click on the Normal View icon (see page 393)

Or

1 *Click on the View menu*

2 *Click on Normal*

2.6.2 The Three Panes

Slide pane: In the Slide pane, you can see one slide at a time. You can…

- See individual slides in detail
- Work with pictures
- Work with diagrams

Outline pane: Use the Outline pane to work with the text in your presentation. You can…

- Add or delete text
- Move text around

Notes pane: The Notes pane is for adding your speaker's notes to the slides.

Michael Caine: An acting legend, well known for his portrayal of Alfie in "Alfie", Charlie in "The Italian Job", and Peachy Carnahan in "The Man Who Would Be King" (possibly his best role). He has absolutely nothing to do with PowerPoint, but his last name rhymes with "pane", so I thought I'd mention him here to break up the monotony of all this talk of slides and panes. Now, back to work.

2.7 Slide Sorter View

2.7.1 Getting to the Slide Sorter View

1. *Click on the View menu*
2. *Click Slide Sorter*

Or

Click on the Slide Sorter View icon (see page 393)

2.7.2 Selecting Slides in Slide Sorter View

Click on the slide you require – a dark border will appear around the edge.

Or, if you would like to select several slides…

1. *Click on the first slide you require*
2. *Hold down the Shift key*
3. *Click on the other slides you require*

Or, if you would like to select all of the slides…

Press Ctrl and A

2.7.3 Moving Slides in Slide Sorter View

1. *Select the slide(s) you wish to appear in the summary*
2. *Click and drag to a new location – a vertical grey line indicates where your slide will be placed*

2.7.4 Deleting Slides in Slide Sorter View

1. *Select the slide(s) you wish to delete*
2. *Press Delete*

2.7.5 Creating a Summary Slide

The summary slide will lift the titles off any slides which you select, and turn them into a bulleted list, which you can use as an agenda or as a conclusion.

1. *Select the slides you wish to appear in the summary*

 2. *Click on the Summary Slide icon*

2.8 Page Setup

2.8.1 Changing the Size of Slides for Different Presentations

For most cases, you will be presenting the slide show on a screen. But sometimes, the slides might be printed on 35mm slides, or overhead projector plastic sheets. To change the slide format...

1. *Click on the File menu*

2. *Click Page Setup*

3. *Click the drop down arrow underneath the **Slides sized for** box*

4. *Click on the type of presentation you are creating*

5. *Click OK*

2.8.2 Creating Custom Sized Slides

1. *Click on the File menu*

2. *Click Page Setup*

3. *Change the width and height as required – click into the boxes and type new numbers, or use the up and down arrows*

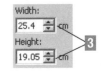

4. *Click OK*

2.8.3 Changing the Orientation of Your Slides, Outlines, or Notes Pages

1. *Click on the File menu*

2. *Click Page Setup*

3. *Click into the white circle next to the orientation you require*

4. *Click OK*

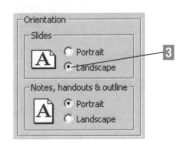

Can I make some slides portrait, and some slides landscape?

Not in the same presentation. All the slides must be portrait or landscape.

2.9 Printing Slides

2.9.1 Previewing in Greyscale

If you only have a black and white printer and would like to see what your presentation looks like in black and white before you print…

1 *Click on the **Color/Grayscale** icon*

2 *Choose whether you want to see colour, greyscale, or pure black and white*

3 *Repeat steps 1 to 2 to return to colour*

2.9.2 Printing All the Slides

Click on the Print icon

2.9.3 Print Options

1 *Click on the File menu*

2 *Click Print*

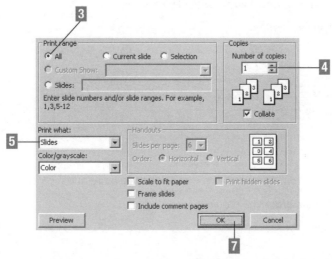

3 *Change the **Print range** options as required:*

■ Click on **All** to print all slides, **Current slide** to print the slide you are on, or **Selection** to print whatever you have selected

■ Click on **Slides** and type in the slides you want to print – if you want to print slide 5, type in **5**; for slides 4 to 19, type **4-19**; for slide 3, slide 12 and slides 15 to 22, type **3**, **12**, **15-22**

4 Change the **Copies** options as required – type in the number of copies you require, or use the up and down arrows

5 Click the drop down arrow by the **Print what** box and choose what you want to print – e.g. handouts, slides, speaker's notes, or outline

6 Change any other options as required:

- **Grayscale** prints out in black and white and shades of grey, **Pure black and white** prints out in just black and white

- **Scale to fit paper** reduces or enlarges the slide to fit the sheet of paper

- **Frame slides** prints a border around the slides

- **Collate** lets you change the order of pages – if you are not sure, leave it ticked. Ticked will print out a 3 page presentation in this order: 1, 2, 3, then 1, 2, 3 Unticked will print out in this order: 1, 1, 2, 2, 3, 3.

7 Click OK

2.9.4 Printing Handouts

You can print out handouts for your audience to write their notes on. They will include miniatures of the slides in your presentation.

1 Click on the File menu

2 Click on Print

3 Click the drop down arrow under **Print what**

4 Click on Handouts

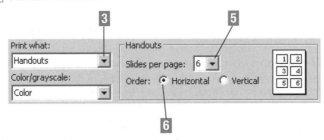

5 Click the drop down arrow next to **Slides per page** and click on the number you require

6 Choose the order you require

7 Click OK

2.9.5 Printing Speaker's Notes or Outline View

If you would just like the outline text of your presentation (as it appears in the outline page), or you would like to print out the notes you have typed in the notes pane...

1. Click on the File menu

2. Click Print

3. Click the drop down arrow underneath the **Print what** box

4. Click on the option you require

5. Click OK

2.10 Selecting Text and Placeholders

2.10.1 Why Select?

- To format text or placeholders
- To move text or placeholders
- To resize placeholders
- To delete placeholders

Unless you select beforehand, PowerPoint does not know what you are trying to work with!

2.10.2 Working with Text Inside a Placeholder

1. Click inside the placeholder you want to change – diagonal lines will appear

2. Make your changes to the text

A Big Title|

2.10.3 Selecting the Whole of a Placeholder

1. Click inside the placeholder you want to change – diagonal lines appear

2. Click on the diagonal lines – dotted lines appear

3. Make your changes to the placeholder

A Big Title

2.10.4 Selecting Text

1. Click inside the placeholder you want to change – diagonal lines will appear

2. Click and drag over the text you require – the text will go white, with a black background

3. Make any change to your text

2.10.5 Deselecting Text or Placeholders

Click outside the placeholder into any blank space – the text will go back to normal

2.11 Moving, Resizing and Deleting Placeholders

These will work with any placeholder – text, pictures, clip art, and so on.

2.11.1 Moving Placeholders

1. *Select the whole placeholder – dotted lines appear around the edge*
2. *Position the mouse over the dotted line – mouse pointer will change to a four headed arrow*
3. *Click and drag to a new location*

2.11.2 Resizing Placeholders

1. *Select the whole placeholder, making sure that dotted lines appear around the edge – if they are diagonal lines, click on them once to make them dotted*
2. *Position the mouse over a resizing handle – it will change to a double headed arrow*
3. *Click and drag to resize – dragging from a corner will resize the box proportionally, and dragging from a middle handle will stretch or squash the shape of the box*

2.11.3 Deleting Placeholders

1. *Select the whole placeholder – dotted lines will appear around the edge*
2. *Press Delete*

2.12 Moving and Copying Text

2.12.1 Moving Text Using the Icons

1. *Select the text you would like to move*
2. *Click on the Cut icon – the text is moved to the Windows Clipboard*
3. *Position the cursor in the place you would like to move the text to*
4. *Click on the Paste icon*

2.12.2 Copying Text Using the Icons

1. *Select the text you would like to copy*
2. *Click on the Copy icon – the text is copied to the Windows Clipboard*
3. *Position the cursor in the place you would like to copy the text to*
4. *Click on the Paste icon*

2.12.3 Moving Text Using the Menu

1 *Select the text you want to move*

2 *Click on the Edit menu*

3 *Click on Cut*

4 *Click where you want to put your text*

5 *Click on the Edit menu*

6 *Click on Paste – the text will have moved to the new location*

2.12.4 Copying Text Using the Menu

1 *Select the text you want to move*

2 *Click on the Edit menu*

3 *Click on Copy*

4 *Click where you want to put your text*

5 *Click on the Edit menu*

6 *Click on Paste – the text will be in both the new and the original location*

2.12.5 Viewing the Clipboard

When you either cut or copy text in PowerPoint XP, it is stored on the clipboard. To view the clipboard . . .

1 *Click on the Edit menu*

2 *Click on Office Clipboard*

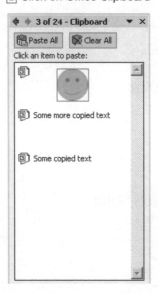

2.12.6 Using the Clipboard

To paste items from the clipboard . . .

|1| *Click where you would like to put the item*

|2| *Place the mouse pointer over the item you want to paste*

|3| *Click on it*

 Eventually the Clipboard will get full up

Once you have cut or copied 24 items, the clipboard will get full. Click on the Clear All icon to empty it.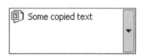

2.12.7 Deleting Text

|1| *Select the text you wish to delete*

|2| *Press the Delete or Del key*

2.13 Moving, Copying and Deleting Slides

2.13.1 Moving Slides

You can move slides in both Normal view (using the thumbnails pane on the left of the window) and Slide Sorter view. Whichever you choose, the process of moving the slides is the same . . .

|1| *Click on the slide to move, holding down the mouse button – a blue border will appear around the slide*

|2| *Drag the slide to its new location – a line indicates where the slide will be placed*

|3| *Release the mouse button to place the slide*

2.13.2 Selecting Several Slides Next to Each Other

|1| *Click on the first slide*

|2| *Hold down the Shift key*

|3| *Click on the last slide*

2.13.3 Selecting Several Slides Not Next to Each Other

|1| *Click on the first slide*

|2| *Hold down the Control key*

|3| *Click on all the other slides you want to select*

2.13.4 Copying Slides

1. *Go to Slide Sorter view*

2. *Click on the slide you wish to copy*

3. *Click on the Copy icon*

4. *Click between the two slides where you want the copied slide to appear*

5. *Click on the Paste icon*

Or

1. *Click on the slide you wish to copy*

2. *Click on the Edit menu*

3. *Click on Copy*

4. *Click between the two slides where you want the copied slide to appear*

5. *Click on the Edit menu*

6. *Click on Paste*

2.13.5 Moving Slides Between Presentations

1. *Go to Slide Sorter view*

2. *Click on the slide you wish to copy*

3. *Click on the Cut (to move) or Copy (to copy) icon*

4. *Switch to the window of the presentation you want to move/copy the slide to*

5. *Click between the two slides where you want the slide to appear*

6. *Click on the Paste icon*

Or

1. *Click on the slide you wish to copy*

2. *Click on the Edit menu*

3. *Click on Cut or Copy*

4. *Switch to the window of the presentation you want to move/copy the slide to*

5. *Click between the two slides where you want the slide to appear*

6. *Click on the Edit menu*

7. *Click on Paste*

Moving and copying using the keyboard

There are some handy keyboard shortcuts you can use to move or copy items. Simply select whatever you wish to cut or copy and press the Control key and X to cut, or Control and C to copy. Then just press Control and P to paste.

2.13.6 Deleting Slides

1. *Go to Slide Sorter view*

2. *Click on the slide you wish to delete*

3. *Press the Delete or Del key*

2.14 Creating Speaker's Notes

2.14.1 Where Can I Type My Notes?

You can type notes to accompany your presentation, which will only be viewable by you. To do this, you need to be in Normal view. You can type your notes into the Notes pane, which you'll find at the bottom of the screen.

2.14.2 Getting to the Notes Pane

1. *Click on the View menu*

2. *Click Normal*

3. *Click in the Notes pane*

2.14.3 Adding Notes

1. *Go to the slide you wish to add notes to*

2. *Click inside the Notes pane*

3. *Start typing!*

Start typing your notes in here

2.14.4 Resizing the Notes Pane

If you're typing in a lot of notes, you can easily increase the size of the Notes pane . . .

1. *Position the cursor over the top border of the Notes pane – the cursor will look like a double arrow*

2. *Click and drag the Notes pane to the size you want*

CHAPTER 3

Formatting Slides

What You'll Do

→ Format Slides

→ Change the Appearance of Text

→ Change the Style of Bullets and Numbering

→ Change the Background

3

3.1 Changing the Appearance of Text

Use the master slides for consistent formatting!

If you wish to change all the slides in your presentation, go to a master slide (see the section starting on page 411 for more on master slides).

3.1.1 Making Text Bold, Italic, Underlined or Shadowed

[1] *Select the text or placeholder you want to change*

[2] *Click on the icon you require (shown below) – it will look pushed in when clicked*

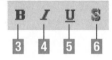

Going from left to right, here is what each icon does:

[3] **Bold**

[4] *Italic*

[5] <u>Underline</u>

[6] Shadow

To remove any of these effects, just click the icon again – it will no longer look pushed in.

3.1.2 Changing the Fonts

⬚1 *Select the text or placeholder to change*

⬚2 *Click the drop down arrow next to the Font box*

⬚3 *Click on the font you require – use the scroll bar to see more fonts if necessary*

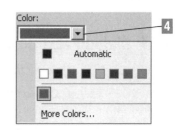

3.1.3 Changing the Size of Text

⬚1 *Select the text or placeholder to change*

⬚2 *Click the drop down arrow next to the Font Size box*

⬚3 *Click on the size you require – use the scroll bar to see more sizes if necessary*

Or

⬚4 *Select the text or placeholder to change*

⬚5 *Click on the Increase or Decrease Font Size icons – the big A increases the size, the small A decreases it*

3.1.4 Changing Font Colour

⬚1 *Select the text or placeholder you wish to change*

⬚2 *Click on the Format menu*

⬚3 *Click Font*

⬚4 *Click on the drop down arrow next to* **Color**

⬚5 *Click on the colour you require*

   or

   Click on More Colors

   Click on the Standard tab

   Click on the colour you require

⬚6 *Click OK*

ⓘ **My text doesn't look the right colour…**

The text will not look right until you deselect it. If it is still selected, it will look very wrong indeed.

3.1.5 Changing Case

This is a quick and easy way to change the case of your text, and save retyping. There are five case options:

- This is sentence case

- this is lowercase

- THIS IS UPPERCASE

- This Is Title Case

- tHIS iS tOGGLE cASE

  1. *Select the text you want to change*

  2. *Click on the Format menu*

  3. *Click Change Case – the Change Case dialog box will appear (see right)*

  4. *Click in the circle to the left of the option you want*

  5. *Click OK*

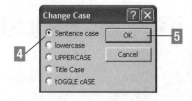

Title Case

In titles it is customary not to capitalise prepositions – e.g. **and**, **or**, **but**, **to**, etc.

Toggle case

If you choose toggle case, all of your upper case letters will be swapped for lower case, and vice versa.

3.1.6 Changing Line Spacing

1. *Select the text or placeholder you want to change*

2. *Click on the Format menu*

3. *Click Line Spacing*

4. *Change the options as required:*

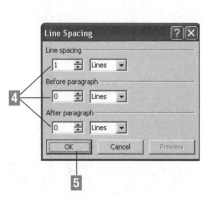

   - **Line spacing**: the amount of space between the lines

   - **Before paragraph**: the amount of space between the paragraphs

   - **After paragraph**: the amount of space after the paragraphs

5. *Click OK*

3.1.7 Changing the Alignment

Changing the alignment changes the position of the text inside the placeholder. Text can be aligned either to the left of the placeholder, in the centre of the placeholder, or to the right of the placeholder.

☐1 *Select the text or placeholder to change*

☐2 *Click on the alignment option you require – the first icon aligns the text to the left, the next one centres it, and the last one aligns it to the right*

3.2 Bullets and Numbering

Use the master slides for consistent formatting!

If you wish to change the bullets for all the slides in your presentation, go to a master slide (see the sections on master slides, starting on page 411).

3.2.1 Changing the Style of Bullet Points

☐1 *Select the text or placeholder you want to change*

☐2 *Click on the Format menu*

☐3 *Click Bullets and Numbering*

☐4 *If necessary, click on the **Bulleted** tab*

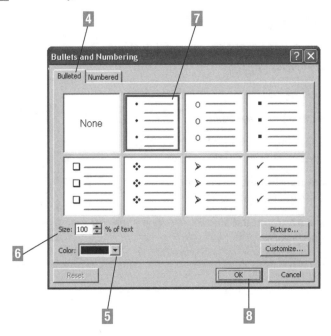

5 *If required, click on the drop down arrow next to **Color** and click on the colour you require*

6 *If required, click into the box next to **Size** and choose the size you require*

7 *Click on the bullet style you require*

8 *Click OK*

3.2.2 Choosing Another Character

If you don't like any of the bullet styles, go to the Bullets and Numbering dialog box, and then…

1 *Click on **Customize***

2 *If required, click the drop down arrow next to **Font** and choose the font you require*

3 *Click on the symbol you require*

4 *Click OK*

5 *Click OK*

3.2.3 Removing Bullets

1 *Select the paragraph you want to remove bullets from*

2 *Click on the Bullets icon to remove bullets*

3.3 Changing the Background

3.3.1 Changing the Colour of the Background

1 *If you are in Slide Sorter view, select at least one slide*

2 *Click on the Format menu*

3 *Click Background*

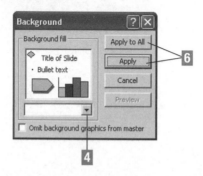

4 *Click the drop down arrow underneath the preview*

⑤ *Click on a colour from those pictured (these are from the current colour scheme)*

or

Click on More Colors

Click on a colour from the Standard tab

Click OK

⑥ *Click on Apply to All to change all the slides*

or

Click on Apply to change selected slides

CHAPTER 4

Masters and Templates

What You'll Do

→ Work with Masters and Templates

→ Use the Slide Master

→ Close the Slide Master

→ Make Changes to the Slide Master

→ Use the Title Master

→ Close the Title Master

→ Make Changes to the Title Master

→ Use the Handout Master

→ Close the Handout Master

→ Make Changes to the Handout Master

→ Use the Notes Master

→ Close the Notes Master

→ Make Changes to the Notes Master

→ Apply a Template

→ Undo and Redo

→ Spell Check

4

4.1 Using the Master Slides

4.1.1 What are the Master Slides?

The master slides are there to save you time and give consistency to your presentation. When you make a change on a master, it changes all the slides. You can use them to . . .

■ Change the fonts

■ Change the bullet style

■ Change the position of placeholders

■ Change the graphics in the background of your slides

■ Add a logo to the background

■ Change the position of slide numbering, the date or footer information

This saves you a lot of time and effort in keeping your presentation consistent.

4.1.2 Why Use a Master Slide?

Whatever you do on a master slide will affect everything consistently . . .

Change the slide master ....All your slides will change accordingly

Change the title master....................................All your title slides will change

Change the handout master ....All your handouts will change

Change the notes master ....All your speaker's notes pages will change

4.2 The Slide Master

4.2.1 Which Slide Does the Slide Master Affect?

Anything you do on the slide master will affect every slide, except those with the title slide layout.

There are two exceptions to this rule:

■ If you change the fonts on the slide master, ALL the slides in the presentation change.

■ If you have used the blank presentation template, you will not have access to a title master, and anything you do on the slide master will affect ALL the slides in the presentation.

4.2.2 Getting to the Slide Master

1 *Click on the View menu*

2 *Click Master*

3 *Click Slide Master*

4.2.3 The Slide Master

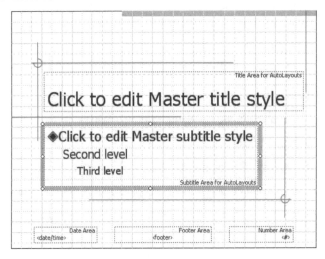

Master title style: How all your titles will look

Master subtitle style: How all your main points will look

Second level, Third level etc: How all your sub-points will look

The date and time will appear on the bottom left if you have added them

The footer will appear on the bottom centre if you have added one

The page/slide number will appear on the bottom right if you have added them

You can also add any template graphics – these will appear on every slide

You can ignore the date area, footer area and number area if you have not added these to your slides

To find out how to add information to these areas see page 439.

4.2.4 Closing the Slide Master

[1] *Click on the View menu*

[2] *Click on the view you wish to return to*

Or

Click on a slide view icon from the bottom left of the screen

Or

Click **Close Master View** *from the Master toolbar*

4.2.5 Making Changes to the Slide Master

You can change the Slide Master just like you would change a normal slide.

4.3 The Title Master

4.3.1 Which Slide Does the Title Master Affect?

Anything you do on the Title Master will affect every slide which has the Title Slide layout.

The Title Master is not available if you have used the blank presentation template. If you have a more complicated template, you can make the title slides look different from the other slides in the presentation, which will give them more emphasis.

4.3.2 Getting to the Title Master

[1] *Click on the View menu*

[2] *Click Master*

[3] *Click Title Master*

Or

[1] *Select any slide which has the title slide layout*

[2] *Hold down the Shift key*

[3] *Click on the Normal View icon*

4.3.3 The Title Master

This works in the same way as the Slide Master, but everything you do here will change any slide based on the Title Slide layout.

 You can ignore the date area, footer area and number area if you have not added these to your slides

To find out how to add information to these areas, see page 439.

4.3.4 Closing the Title Master

[1] *Click on the View menu*

[2] *Click on the view you wish to return to*

Or

Click on a slide view icon from the bottom of the screen

Or

*Click **Close Master View** from the Master toolbar*

4.3.5 Making Changes on the Title Master

You can change the Title Master just like you would change a normal slide.

4.4 The Handout Master

4.4.1 What Does the Handout Master Affect?

Anything you do on the handout master will affect your audience handouts.

4.4.2 Getting to the Handout Master

[1] *Click on the View menu*

[2] *Click Master*

[3] *Click Handout Master*

4.4.3 The Handout Master

Click on the handout you require from the Handout Master toolbar.

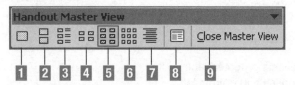

Going from left to right, here is what each icon means:

[1] One slide per page

[2] Two slides per page

[3] Three slides per page

[4] Four slides per page

[5] Six slides per page

[6] Nine slides per page

[7] Outline

[8] Handout Master Layout

[9] Close the Handout Master view

4.4.4 Closing the Handout Master

$\boxed{1}$ *Click on the View menu*

$\boxed{2}$ *Click on the view you wish to return to*

Or

Click on a slide view icon from the bottom of the screen

Or

*Click **Close Master View** from the Master toolbar*

4.4.5 Making Changes on the Handout Master

You can change the Handout Master just like you would change a normal slide.

4.5 The Notes Master

4.5.1 What Does the Notes Master Affect?

Anything you do on the notes master will affect your speaker's notes (see page 404).

4.5.2 Getting to the Notes Master

$\boxed{1}$ *Click on the View menu*

$\boxed{2}$ *Click Master*

$\boxed{3}$ *Click Notes Master*

4.5.3 The Notes Master

- If you added headers or footers, they will appear at the top left and bottom left

- The miniature slide in the top half of the page can be moved or resized

- The notes area in the bottom half of the page can also be moved or resized

- The text in the notes area shows how your main and sub-points will look on your notes

4.5.4 Closing the Notes Master

$\boxed{1}$ *Click on the View menu*

$\boxed{2}$ *Click on the view you wish to return to*

Or

> *Click on a slide view icon from the bottom of the screen*

Or

`Close Master View`   *Click **Close Master View** from the master toolbar*

4.5.5 Making Changes on the Notes Master

You can change the Notes Master just like you would change a normal slide.

4.6   Applying a Template

4.6.1 What are Design Templates?

Design templates are pre-set formats that add graphics, colours and fonts consistently onto all the slides in your presentation. The design template will decide how the following elements look . . .

- Fonts and formatting
- Bullet points
- Background graphics

`Blue Diagonal`

The design template you are currently using will appear on the status bar at the bottom right of the screen.

4.6.2 Applying a Design Template

`Design`

1 *Click on the Design icon*

   or

   Click on the Format menu
   Click on Slide Design

2 *Click on the template you require*

You can change your mind later on – if you have already applied a Design Template, simply repeat the above steps, and choose a different one.

Apply a design template:

4.7 Undo and Redo

Undo and Redo work in exactly the same way as they do in Word. See Chapter 1 in the Word module, starting on page 115.

4.8 Spell Checking

PowerPoint comes with a spell checker which works in exactly the same way as the one in Word. See Chapter 3 in the Word module on Spelling and Grammar, starting on page 165.

5.1 Creating a Chart

5.1.1 Creating Charts

1 Create a new slide

2 Click on the Chart layout

3 Click OK

4 Double click the chart area – you will be taken to the chart Datasheet View (see the next section)

Or

1 Go to the slide you wish to add a chart to in Slide View

2 Click on the Chart icon – you will be taken to the chart Datasheet View (see the next section)

My chart has got in the way of everything else!

When you add a chart with the icon it will go right in the middle of the slide. You will then have to move and resize it yourself (see page 422).

Or

1. *Go to the slide you wish to add a chart to in Slide View*

2. *Click on the Insert menu*

3. *Click Chart – you will be taken to the chart Datasheet View (see next section)*

5.2 The Datasheet

5.2.1 What is the Datasheet?

The datasheet contains the text and figures that your chart is based on. When you create a new chart, PowerPoint inserts dummy text and figures to help you get an idea of what to do. When you double click a chart, you are taken into the Datasheet View so that you can change the figures and chart options.

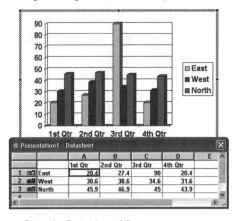

Chart in Datasheet View

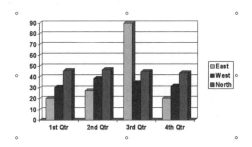

Chart in normal PowerPoint view

5.2.2 Switching from the Chart to PowerPoint

Once you have finished your chart, you will need to come out of it and go back to PowerPoint . . .

Click outside the diagonal lines around the chart to go back to PowerPoint

5.2.3 Switching from PowerPoint to the Datasheet View

If you need to edit your chart, just double click in the middle of the chart to go back to it.

5.2.4 Deleting Information from the Datasheet

You must delete the dummy information using the following method, otherwise stray bits tend to crop up where they are not wanted.

[1] *Click the grey box in the top left corner to select the whole datasheet*

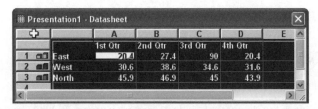

[2] *Press Delete*

5.2.5 Moving Around the Datasheet

Press the cursor keys on the keyboard to move around the cells

or

Click on the cell you require

or

Press the Tab key to move one cell to the right

or

Press the Enter key to move down one cell

5.2.6 Adding Information into the Datasheet

The information you wish to chart should be typed into the datasheet.

■ Labels across the top must start directly underneath "A"

■ Labels down the left hand side must start directly next to "1"

[1] *Click into the cell where you wish to start typing*

[2] *Start typing*

PowerPoint will "build" the chart in the background as you type the figures.

The first row and the first column are "frozen"

The headings for the figures in your datasheet are always held in the first row and the first column. These two areas remain on the screen if you scroll across or down. This can sometimes make it look as if you have lost some of the figures you have typed. However, if you scroll back to the left or back up towards the top, they should reappear.

5.2.7 Resizing the Datasheet

[1] *Position the mouse at a corner of the datasheet – the mouse pointer will change to a double headed black arrow*

[2] *Click and drag to resize the datasheet*

5.2.8 Show/Hide the Datasheet

 Click on the Show/Hide datasheet icon

Or

☐1 *Click on the View menu*

☐2 *Click Datasheet*

You can also close the datasheet to hide it – just click on the X at the top right of the datasheet.

5.3 Moving, Resizing and Deleting a Chart

You must be in PowerPoint!

In order to move, resize or delete the chart on the slide, you must be in PowerPoint and not the Datasheet View.

5.3.1 Moving the Chart

☐1 *Select the chart – white circles will appear around the edge*

☐2 *Position the mouse pointer in the middle of the chart*

☐3 *Click and drag it to a new location*

5.3.2 Resizing the Chart

☐1 *Select the chart – white circles will appear around the edge*

☐2 *Position the mouse over a white circle*

☐3 *Click and drag to increase or decrease the size*

5.3.3 Deleting the Chart

☐1 *Select the chart – white circles will appear around the edge*

☐2 *Press Delete*

5.4 Working with Charts

To select parts of a graph you must be in the Datasheet View!

Once you are in a chart, they work in exactly the same way as charts in Excel. See the Chart section starting on page 273.

5.5 Creating an Organisation Chart

5.5.1 What is an Organisation Chart?

An organisation chart is used to create hierarchical charts which display the structure of an organisation.

5.5.2 Adding an Organisation Chart Using the Slide Layout

[1] *Create a new slide*

[2] *Choose Organisation Chart layout*

[3] *Click OK*

[4] *Double click the organisation chart placeholder*

[5] *Choose the type of chart you want*

[6] *Click OK*

Or

[1] *Select the slide you wish to add an organisation chart to*

[2] *Click on the Insert menu*

[3] *Click on Diagram*

[4] *Choose the type of chart you want*

[5] *Click OK*

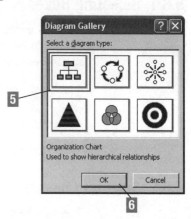

When you have inserted an organisation chart, a new toolbar will appear above the chart.

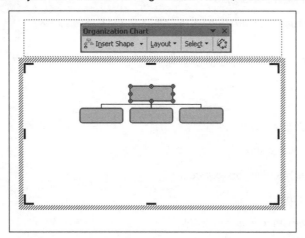

5.5.3 Switching from the Organisation Chart to PowerPoint

Once you have finished your chart you will need to come out of the organisation chart and go back into PowerPoint. To do this, just click outside the area of the organisation chart.

5.5.4 Switching from PowerPoint to the Organisation Chart

If you need to edit your organisation chart, just click on it once.

5.6 | Selecting Parts of an Organisation Chart

5.6.1 Selecting Boxes

Just click on the box you require, making sure to click on the edge of the box. If you click on the middle, then you will go into the text editing mode. If this happens, just click on the diagonal lines to select it.

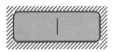

Text editing mode

Normal selection

5.6.2 Selecting Several Boxes

1 *Select the first box you require*

2 *Hold down Shift*

3 *Click on any other boxes you require – the boxes will go black*

5.6.3 Selecting Shapes

1 *Click on at least one shape*

2 *Click the drop down arrow next to Select on the Organisation Chart toolbar*

3 *Click on the shapes you wish to select*

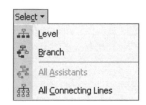

5.6.4 Selecting Lines

Click on the line you require

Or, to select several lines . . .

1 *Click on the first line you require*

2 *Hold down the Shift key*

3 *Click on any other lines you require*

5.7　Working with Organisation Charts

5.7.1　Adding Information to a Box

1. *Click into the box you wish to add information to*
2. *Type in the name*
3. *Press Enter on the keyboard*
4. *Type in the job title*
5. *Press Enter and type comments if required*
6. *Click outside the box when you have finished*
   or
   Click into the next box you wish to add text to

5.7.2　Amending Existing Text

1. *Click on the box you wish to change*
2. *Edit the text as normal*

5.7.3　Adding Extra Boxes

1. *Click on the box you want to add the new box next to or under*
2. *Click on the drop down arrow next to Insert Shape on the Organisation Chart toolbar*
3. *Click on the type of worker you wish to add*

5.7.4　Deleting Boxes

1. *Select the box(es) you wish to delete*
2. *Press Delete*

5.7.5　Moving Boxes

1. *Click and drag the box required*
2. *Move the box over the box you wish to add it to*
3. *Release the mouse*

CHAPTER 6

Graphics

What You'll Do

→ Add Pictures to Slides

→ Insert Pictures with the Slide Layout

→ Work with Pictures

→ Display the Drawing Toolbar

→ Draw Shapes

→ Flip Objects

→ Rotate Objects

→ Align Shapes to Each Other

→ Align Shapes Relative to Each Slide

→ Distribute Objects Evenly

6.1 Adding Pictures to Slides

6.1.1 Inserting Pictures with the Slide Layout

1. *If necessary, create a new slide*

2. *Choose a layout with a placeholder for Clip Art*

3. *Double click the placeholder for Clip Art – you will be taken to the Clip Art task pane*

Or

1. *Move to the slide you wish to add a picture to in Slide View*

2. *Click on the Clip Art icon on the drawing toolbar – you will be taken to the Clip Art task pane*

Or

1. *Move to the slide you wish to add a picture to in Slide View*

2. *Click on the Insert menu*

3. *Click Picture*

4. *Click Clip Art – you will be taken to the ClipArt task pane*

The Clip Art task pane works in exactly the same way as the one in Word. See the section starting on page 191.

6.1.2 Inserting Pictures that are Not Clip Art

If you wish to insert a picture file that is not part of the Clip Art collection, such as a logo or a scanned image . . .

Inserting a Picture From File . . .

1 *Move to the slide you wish to add a picture to in Slide View*

2 *Click on the Insert menu*

3 *Click Picture*

4 *Click From File*

5 *Change the **Look in** box to the folder where your picture is saved*

6 *Click on your picture file*

7 *Click Insert*

Inserting a Picture From Scanner . . .

1 *Move to the slide you wish to add a picture to in Slide View*

2 *Click on the Insert menu*

3 *Click Picture*

4 *Click From Scanner or Camera – you will be taken to your scanning software*

5 *Scan the picture as normal*

6.2 Working with Pictures

Once you have inserted Clip Art or pictures in PowerPoint, they work in exactly the same way as they do in Word. See the section starting on page 193.

There are two slight differences in PowerPoint:

If you inserted the Clip Art using the placeholder, and then delete the Clip Art . . .

You will still see the placeholder when your Clip Art is deleted. This will not print, and it will not show during an on-screen show. To get rid of it, change the layout, delete the placeholder or add a different piece of Clip Art.

6.2.1 Displaying the Drawing Toolbar

You can use the Drawing toolbar to draw shapes and diagrams on your slide. When displayed, it is usually at the bottom of the PowerPoint screen. If it is not already displayed . . .

1. Click on the View menu

2. Click Toolbars

3. Click Drawing – if there is a tick next to it, it is already turned on

6.2.2 Drawing Shapes

The Drawing toolbar works in exactly the same way as it does in Word. See the section on drawing shapes starting on page 186.

6.3 Rotation and Ordering

6.3.1 Flipping Objects

1. Select the shape(s) you require

Draw ▼ 2. Click Draw

3. Click Rotate or Flip

4. Click Flip Horizontal

or

Click Flip Vertical

6.3.2 Rotating Objects

1. Select the shape(s) you want to rotate

2. Hover the mouse pointer over the green circle – the rotate symbol will appear

3. Click and drag to turn the shape

Or

1. Select the shape(s) to rotate

2. Click Draw

3. Click Rotate or Flip

4. Click Rotate Left

or

Click Rotate Right

Or use the menu to rotate a shape more exactly . . .

1. Select the shape(s) to rotate

2. Click on the Format menu

3. Click Object or AutoShape

4 *Click on the Size tab*

5 *Change the rotation options as required – type in the angle you want to rotate by, or use the up and down arrows*

6 *Click OK*

6.3.3 Changing the Ordering

If you have several objects on a page that are on top of each other, they form a kind of "queue". Whichever object you can see on top is at the front of the queue, and whichever object you can see underneath all the others is at the back of the queue. In this diagram there are three circles, and their number corresponds to their position in the queue:

You can change this order using the **send to back/bring to front** commands, or the **send backward/bring forward** commands. Let's imagine that you decide to send the 1st circle to the back. The circle will go to the back of the queue, behind the other two circles:

If, however, you sent the same circle backward it would just go one stage behind in the queue, rather than all the way to the back. In other words, it would go behind the 2nd circle, but not behind the 3rd:

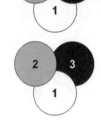

1 *Select the object you wish to move*

2 *Click Draw*

3 *Click on Order*

4 *Click Send to Back*

   or

   Click Bring to Front

   or

   Click Send Backward

   or

   Click Bring Forward

6.4   Alignment

6.4.1 Aligning Shapes to Each Other

If you wish to line shapes up on the slide, you can choose to line them up to each other or relative to the slide. Overleaf are some diagrams of two shapes aligned to each other in different ways:

Horizontal alignment for shapes that are side by side:

| Align | Top | | Align | Middle | | Align | Bottom |

Vertical alignment for shapes that are above each other:

| Align | | Align | | Align |
| Left | | Centre | | Right |

1. *Select the shapes you wish to align to each other*

2. *Click Draw*

3. *Click Align and Distribute*

4. *Make sure the **Relative to Slide** option is not ticked*

5. *Click on the Alignment you require*

All my shapes have appeared on top of each other!

This means you've chosen the wrong type of alignment for the way your shapes are positioned on the slide. If your shapes are side by side you need align top, align middle or align bottom. If your shapes are above each other, you need align left, align centre, or align right.

If I align two shapes to each other, which one will move?

If you align top, the shapes will line up to whichever shape is higher up on the slide. If you align left, the shapes will line up to whichever shape is furthest left on the slide etc.

6.4.2 Aligning Shapes Relative to the Slide

Sometimes you may want to line shapes up to the left of the slide, or with the top of the slide, etc., rather than lining them up to another shape. In these instances, you need to turn **Relative to Slide** on . . .

1. *Select the shapes you wish to align*

2. *Click Draw*

3. *Click Align or Distribute*

4. *If **Relative to Slide** is ticked, go on to step 8*

   *If **Relative to Slide** is not ticked, go on to step 5*

5. *Click Relative to Slide*

6 *Click Draw*

7 *Click Align or Distribute*

8 *Click on the Alignment you require*

6.4.3 Distributing Objects Evenly

The Distribute Evenly feature allows you to space objects out evenly. The spacing can be even between the shapes at either end, or spaced out evenly across the slide. In the following image, the first row of arrows is spaced evenly in relation to each other. The second row is spaced evenly in relation to the slide.

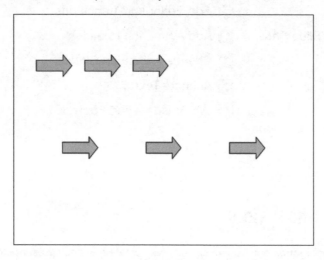

1 *Select the shapes to distribute evenly*

2 *Click Draw*

3 *Click Align or Distribute*

4 *Tick **Relative to Slide** if you wish the shapes to be distributed relative to the slide*
or

*Leave **Relative to Slide** unticked if you wish the shapes to be distributed relative to each other*

Click Distribute Horizontally if your shapes are side by side
or

Click Distribute Vertically if your shapes are above each other

6

CHAPTER 7

On-Screen Shows

What You'll Do

→ Use the Slide Show View

→ Run Your Slide Show

→ Go to the Next Slide in Slide Show View

→ Hide and Unhide Slides

→ Add Slide Transitions

→ Create or Change Slide Transitions

→ Advance Slides Automatically

→ Add Sounds to Transitions

→ Add Animation to Slides

→ Change Animation Effects

→ Animate Text

→ Use Headers and Footers

7.1 Using the Slide Show View

This is it, your big moment. You've slaved away creating a fancy presentation, you've checked it twice, plugged in the big projector, set up the screen, and the audience are sitting there patiently, waiting for you to impress them. It's time to run the slide show . . .

7.1.1 Running Your Slide Show

1. *Select the slide you want to start from*

2. *Click on the View menu*

3. *Click on the Slide Show menu*

Or

1. *Select the slide you want to start from*

2. *Click on the Slide Show menu*

3. *Click View Show*

Or

1. *Select the slide you wish to start from*

2. *Click on the Slide Show View icon at the bottom left of the screen*

7.1.2 Using Slide Show Options During a Slide Show

1 *Click on the upward pointing arrow at the bottom left of the slide*

or

Right click on the slide

2 *Click on the option you require from the menu*

7.1.3 Going to the Next Slide in Slide Show View

Click the mouse on a blank part of the slide

Or

Press the right cursor key

7.1.4 Going to the Previous Slide in Slide Show View

Press the left cursor key

Or

1 *Bring up the slide show options (see above)*

2 *Click Previous*

7.1.5 Going to Any Slide in Slide Show View

1 *Bring up the slide show options*

2 *Click Go*

3 *Click By Title*

Click on the slide you wish to go to

or

Click Slide Navigator

Click on the slide you wish to go to

Click Go To

7.1.6 Closing Slide Show View Before the Show is Over

Press Escape (Esc) on the keyboard

Or

1 *Bring up the slide show options*

2 *Click End Show*

7

7.1.7 Hiding and Unhiding Slides

By hiding slides, you can prevent them appearing in your slide show . . .

1️⃣ *Go into Slide Sorter view*

2️⃣ *Select the slide(s) you wish to hide*

3️⃣ *Click on the Slide Show menu*

4️⃣ *Select Hide Slide to hide the slide, or to unhide an already hidden slide – the slide number will now have a box around it and a line through it*

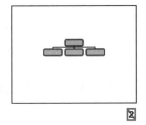

7.1.8 Hiding the Mouse in Slide Show View

1️⃣ Bring up the slide show options (see page 433)

2️⃣ Click Pointer Options

3️⃣ Click Hidden

To turn the mouse back on . . .

1️⃣ Right click the mouse

2️⃣ Click Pointer Options

3️⃣ Click Arrow

7.2 Adding Slide Transitions

7.2.1 What are Slide Transitions?

This refers to the way slides come onto the screen during an on-screen show.

7.2.2 Creating or Changing Slide Transitions in Slide Sorter View

This method is the same whether you want to add a transition, or change an existing transition.

1️⃣ *Switch to Slide Sorter view*

2️⃣ *Select the slide you wish to add a transition to*

📇 T̲ransition   3️⃣ *Click on the Transition icon – the Slide Transition task pane will appear*

4️⃣ *Click on the transition you require – scroll down to see more transitions if necessary*

or

Click No Transition at the top of the list, to remove the transition effect

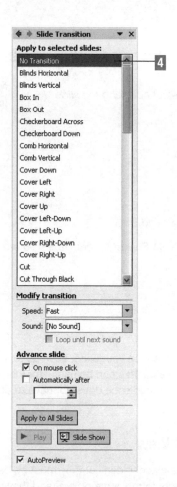

7.2.3 Modifying the Speed of Transitions

In the Slide Transition task pane . . .

☐1 *Select the slide(s) you wish to adjust*

☐2 *Click on the drop down arrow next to Speed*

☐3 *Select from either Slow, Medium or Fast*

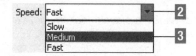

7.2.4 Advance Slides Automatically

Slides are set by default to advance when you click the mouse button. To change this, open the Slide Transition task pane . . .

1 Select the slide(s) you wish to adjust

2 Click in the box next to **Automatically after**, so that a tick appears in the box

3 Click on the up and down arrows to select how long the slide stays on screen

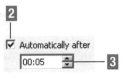

7.2.5 Add Sound to Transitions

In the Slide Transition task pane

1 Select the slide(s) you wish to adjust

2 Click on the drop down arrow next to Sound

3 Select a sound from the list, or choose **No Sound** to remove the sound

7.3 Adding Animation to Slides

7.3.1 What are Animation Effects?

Animation effects can be applied to any object on your slide, such as text or a picture. Once it is animated it will "fly" onto the screen. This can be useful for long bulleted lists. Each point can fly in separately, so that your audience does not have to concentrate on the whole list at once.

7.3.2 Creating Animation Effects in Normal View

This will only affect objects which are in a placeholder, i.e. they must be part of the slide's original layout. You can keep adding effects to the same object, and they will all happen in sequence. Don't go overboard though – you don't want your audience waiting half an hour while a bullet point goes through 87 different animations. No matter how exciting you think it is, it never hurts to keep things simple . . .

1 Switch to Normal view

2 Click on the Slide Show menu

3 Click on Custom Animation – the Custom Animation Task Pane will appear

4 Select the object(s) you wish to change – a placeholder, image, etc.

5 Click on Add Effect

6 Click on the type of animation you require

- Entrance – makes the object appear

- Emphasis – makes the object stand out from the others

- Exit – makes the object disappear

- Motion Paths – makes the object follow a certain path

7 *Click on the animation you require – or click on More Effects to see more animations, click on the one you want, then click OK*

8 *To change how the animation starts, click the drop down arrow next to Start – you can have it play when you click the mouse, at the same time as the other effects, or after the others*

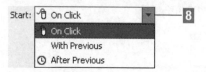

9 *To change the speed of the effect, click on the drop down arrow next to Speed, and choose the option you require*

10 *Repeat steps 4 to 9 for any other objects you wish to animate*

11 *Click Play to see how the finished effect looks*

7.3.3 Changing Animation Effects

If you have added too many animation effects to one object, you may want to change or remove some of them.

1 *Click on the Slide Show menu*

2 *Click Custom Animation*

3 *Select the object you wish to change in Normal view*

4 *Select the animation from the list that you want to change or remove*

5 *Click **Change** to change the effect (and then follow steps 6 to 11 in the previous section)*

Or

*Click **Remove** to remove the effect*

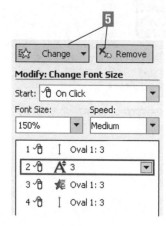

7.3.4 Animating Text

If you animate a text placeholder, you can change the way that the text comes onto the screen. From the Custom Animation task pane . . .

⎡1⎤ *Select the text animation you wish to change from the list*

2 *Click on the drop down arrow next to it*

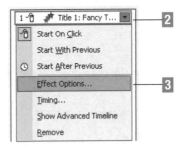

3 *Click on Effect Options*

4 *Click on the Effect tab*

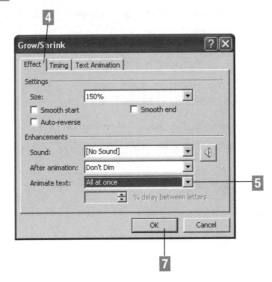

5 *Click the drop down arrow next to **Animate text***

⎡6⎤ *Click the option you require (all at once, word by word, or letter by letter)*

7 *Click OK*

CHAPTER 8

Headers and Footers

8.1 Headers and Footers

8.1.1 What are Headers and Footers for?

Headers and Footers can be used to display information such as page numbers, the date, and other information that you want repeated on every slide or page. On slides, you can only have footers, and not headers. Footers appear at the bottom of the slides so they are less conspicuous during presentations. Headers and footers can appear at the top and bottom of every page for notes and handouts only.

Headers and Footers are stored on the Master Slides

If you wish to make changes to headers and footers, go to the Slide Master or Title Master (see page 412–415).

8.1.2 Adding Footers onto Your Slides

1. *If necessary, select the slide(s) you want to change*

2. *Click on the View menu*

3. *Click Header and Footer*

4. *Click on the Slide tab (if you are not there already)*

5. *Tick the **Date and time** box if required:*

   *Choose **Update automatically** to have the date updated each time you open or print the presentation, and click on the drop down arrow to choose a date format*

   or

   *Type in a fixed date underneath **Fixed***

6. *Tick the **Slide number** box if required – this will automatically number all your slides*

7. *If required, tick the **Footer** box, and type your footer information into the white box*

8. *Click Apply to All to change all the slides*

   or

   Click Apply to change selected slides

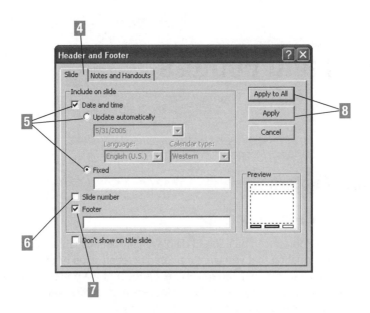

Where will my footers appear?

The black boxes with the thick outlines in the Preview box will show you where your footers will appear.

What about headers?

Repeat the steps in the previous section, clicking the Notes and Handouts tab in step 4. Click into the Header box in step 7, and follow the rest of the steps.

CHAPTER 1

Introduction to the Internet

What You'll Do

→ Discover the Internet

→ Discover Web Security

→ Discover Email

1.1 What is the Internet?

1.1.1 What is the Internet?

- The Internet is a **network of computers connected to each other through the telephone system**.

- It is not intangible, but **a physical structure** that connects computers together.

1.1.2 The Main Parts of the Internet

The Internet has two main parts:

- The World Wide Web (WWW)

- Email

1.1.3 What is the World Wide Web?

Here are just some of the things you can do over the World Wide Web:

- **Read pages of information**
  People throughout the world have produced webpages on their computers. Other people can then read that information if they are also connected to the Internet.

- **E-Commerce**
  You can shop for goods over the World Wide Web. Things like books and last-minute flight deals are available.

- **Download software**
  You can download files from the web onto your computer. All sorts of stuff is available from games, to pictures, to trial versions of new software. Once they are downloaded, they can be used on your computer.

- **Chat**
  Some webpages allow you to chat with other people who are connected to the Internet at the same time as you. You can type messages to each other which appear on the screen immediately.

1.1.4 Web Browsers

A web browser is a program that lets you look at webpages and websites. Some common browsers are Internet Explorer, Firefox, and Opera.

1.1.5 Web Terms

You will come across lots of strange words when learning about the Internet. Here are some of the more important ones:

- http – this is one of the languages used on the Internet to help computers to communicate, and stands for **h**yper **t**ext **t**ransfer **p**rotocol.

- ftp – this is a similar language, used for transferring files – it stands for **f**ile **t**ransfer **p**rotocol.

- URL (Uniform Resource Locator) – the address of a website – for example, the URL of the BBC's website is www.bbc.co.uk.

- Hyperlink – how people get around on the web. When you click on a hyperlink, you are taken to another page, or a different website. If you are on a page with no hyperlinks, it's not that easy to get somewhere else.

- ISP – Internet Service Provider. To get access to the web, you must pay a fee to an ISP who will connect you up. It's a bit like having a telephone – you can buy a phone, but you need to pay the telephone company to let you connect to the telephone lines.

1.1.6 What is Email?

- Email is a way of sending and receiving messages over the Internet.

- It is cheaper and faster than the traditional postal system.

- Email also allows you access to **Usenet**, otherwise known as **Newsgroups**. This is a bit like a collection of notice boards which you can send emails to. They are then posted up where other people can read them and reply. There are newsgroups on virtually every topic you can think of.

1.2 Web Security

1.2.1 Cookies

A cookie is a text file placed on your hard drive by a website. It is used to keep track of your preferences for the site, or to remember your login details to save you logging in every time. Cookies should not store sensitive information like bank details, or credit card numbers.

1.2.2 Cache

The cache is a store of pages you have visited recently. Browsers keep these files to make your web browsing quicker – but it means people using your machine can see where you have been! So don't go looking at anything you shouldn't . . .

1.2.3 Protected Websites

A protected website is one that you log into using a user name and password. This stops people seeing your private details.

1.2.4 Digital Certificates

A digital certificate is used on a file download or protected webpage, so you know if the site is safe to download from. Some files with no certificate are safe, but you use them at your own risk.

1.2.5 Encryption

Encryption stops people reading things they shouldn't. An encrypted file has a special code applied to it, so if someone tries to read it without the secret code, it will look like nonsense. Once you apply the secret code, the file is magically made readable.

1.2.6 Viruses

A virus is a nasty program designed to attack your PC or just annoy you. Be very careful when downloading files from the Internet: always check them with a virus checker before running or opening them. If you're not sure about this, ask your IT department to do it for you.

1.2.7 Credit Card Fraud

Some websites will ask for your credit card details, then sell them or use them to buy things illegally. Make sure the website has a gold padlock in the browser status bar at the bottom – double check that the site is a proper, respectable one before handing over any details.

1.2.8 Firewalls

A firewall is a big wall of fire to keep out snakes and tigers. It is also a word used to describe a software program that stops people sneaking on to your PC when you're connected to the Internet. Some people like looking out for unprotected machines, so they can poke around and see what's on there. A firewall can stop them getting in.

CHAPTER 2

Getting Started on the Web

What You'll Do

→ Get Started on the Web

→ Start Internet Explorer

→ Use Help in Internet Explorer

→ Switch Toolbars On and Off

→ Go to a Webpage

→ Type in a URL

→ Clear the History

→ Browse the World Wide Web

→ Open Pages in a New Window

→ Download from a Link

→ Complete a Web Form

→ Use the Back Button

→ Use the Forward Button

→ Use the Home, Stop and Refresh Buttons

→ Guess Webpages

2.1 Internet Explorer

2.1.1 Starting Internet Explorer

1 *Click the Start button*

2 *Click on All Programs*

3 *Click on Internet Explorer*

Internet
Explorer

Or

Double click on the desktop shortcut

2.1.2 Closing Internet Explorer

To close it, just click on the big X at the top right of the Internet Explorer window.

2.1.3 The Screen

Part of the screen	What does it do?
1 *Title Bar*	Tells you the title of the webpage you are looking at.
2 *Menu Bar*	Gives you access to the commands available in Internet Explorer. All commands are grouped under the menus.
3 *Standard Buttons Toolbar*	The icons on the Standard toolbar provide a quick way of carrying out standard commands.
4 *Links Toolbar*	The icons on the Links toolbar provide a quick way of accessing webpages you frequently visit.
5 *Scroll Bars*	The vertical scroll bar allows you to move through a long webpage, whilst the horizontal scroll bar allows you to move across a wide webpage.
6 *Address Bar*	Can be used to enter the address of a website you want to visit. Will also display the address of a website you are currently viewing.
7 *Status Bar*	Displays messages, such as the progress on connecting to a website. The right hand side will indicate the security settings for the webpage you are looking at.

2.2 | Using Help in Internet Explorer

Internet Explorer comes with a Help feature which works in exactly the same way as the help in Word – see the Help section in the Word chapters on page 46 for more details.

2.3 | Toolbars

2.3.1 Switching Toolbars On and Off

1 *Click on the View menu*

2 *Click on Toolbars – a list will appear*

3 *Click on the toolbar you would like to turn on or off – a tick appears before toolbars that are switched on*

2.3.2 The Standard Buttons Toolbar

This toolbar gives you quick access to some of the standard commands available from the menus.

Going from left to right, here is what each icon does:

1 Goes back to the previous page

2 Goes forward to the next page (you cannot use this unless you have gone back at least one page)

3 Stops the page loading

4 Refreshes the page, or loads it again

5 Goes to the Home page

6 Uses Microsoft's search facility

7 Displays the Favourites list (a list of sites you have bookmarked)

8 Displays the Media options (not required for ECDL)

9 Displays the History list (sites you have recently visited)

10 Lets you read or send email

11 Prints the current page

12 Lets you edit the page with another piece of software (not required for ECDL)

13 Lets you link up to a discussion server (not required for ECDL)

14 Displays the Research tool (not required for ECDL)

15 Runs Microsoft Messenger (not required for ECDL)

2.3.3 The Address Bar

1 *This toolbar is used to enter the address of websites you want to visit. You can also use it to revisit websites (see page 450).*

1

2.4 Going to a Webpage

2.4.1 Typing in the URL

If you know the URL (the website address) of a webpage it is easy to get to:

1 *Click into the Address bar – the existing URL will go blue*

2 *Delete any existing address*

3 *Type the address you require, e.g. www.bbc.co.uk*

4 *Press Enter or click Go – Internet Explorer will eventually load the page*

Watch the symbol at the top right....

At the top right hand corner of the screen you will see an Internet Explorer symbol:

If you can see this moving, then Internet Explorer is busy downloading your webpage. If it has stopped doing anything, then you may need to request your page again by clicking the Refresh button.

How much longer do I have to wait?

If you check the status bar at the bottom left of the screen, you will often see an indicator of how much has been downloaded already.

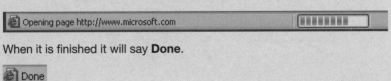

When it is finished it will say **Done**.

Error messages

You may get error messages after you request the page. This can be for several reasons: the page may no longer exist, one of the servers that you need may be broken, or too many people may be trying to get the same page as you.

If you get an error, wait for a while and then try again.

2.4.2 What If I Don't Know the Address?

If you don't know the address, you can guess it (see page 453) or use a search engine (see page 456).

2.4.3 Matches in the Address Bar

If you have typed in an address before, a list will probably appear as you begin to type. Just click on the site you want to visit to save time.

2.4.4 Accessing a Web Address You Have Already Visited

To return to an address that you have typed in recently . . .

1 *Click the drop down arrow at the end of the Address bar*

2 *Click on the address you require*

2.4.5 Clearing the History

If you do not want other people to see what sites you have been to when they click the drop down arrow on the Address bar, you can clear the history:

1 *Click on the Tools menu*

2 *Click on Internet Options (may just be called Options depending on your browser version)*

3 *Click Clear History*

4 *Click Yes*

5 *Click OK*

Browsing the World Wide Web

2.5.1 The Home Page

- When you first connect to a site you will see its home page.

- This is like the front cover of a magazine which welcomes you in and gives you an idea of what you can expect to find inside.

- The Home page will usually contain links to other pages in the site.

Links are usually underlined text (usually blue), or pictures – the mouse pointer will turn into a pointing hand when you hover it over a link. Use the scroll bar to see more of the page if necessary.

2.5.2 How Can I Tell Where the Links Are?

There are two sorts of links:

- **Hypertext Links**
  Which is underlined text, often coloured blue

- **Hypermedia Links**
  Which are pictures that link you to somewhere else

 When you pass your mouse over a link it will look like a pointing hand.

2.5.3 Using Links

1 *Position the mouse over the hyperlink you require*

2 *Click when the mouse looks like a hand – the page you are linking to will open*

2.5.4 Opening Pages in a New Window

1 *Right click on the link*

2 *Click on* **Open in New Window**

| Open |
| Open in New Window |
| Save Target As... |
| Print Target |
| Cut |
| Copy |
| Copy Shortcut |
| Paste |
| Add to Favorites... |
| Properties |

2.5.5 Downloading from a Link

1 *Right click on the link*

2 *Click on* **Save Target As**

3 *Choose a save location*

4 *Click Save*

2.5.6 Completing a Web Form

Web forms let you type in information, to log in, or buy things, or sign up for newsletters, and so on. There are several types of items in forms:

What they are	What they look like	What to do
Text boxes		Click inside the box with the mouse, and type something
Buttons	Click Me!	Click on the button
Radio buttons	⦿ Option 1 ◯ Option 2	Click inside the circle – only one can be selected at a time
Check boxes	☑ Option 1 ☑ Option 2	Click inside the box – many can be selected at a time

2.5.7 The Back Button

To go back over pages you have seen already this session, click on the Back button.

2.5.8 Going Back a Long Way

1 *Click the drop down arrow next to the Back button*

2 *Click on the site you require*

2.5.9 The Forward Button

To go forward again, once you have been back, click on the Forward button.

2.5.10 Going Forward a Long Way

1 *Click the drop down arrow next to the Forward button*

2 *Click on the site you require*

2.5.11 The Home Button

The Home button takes you to your default home page. By default, this is usually Microsoft's site, or the shop you bought your PC from, but you can set it to whatever you want (see page 459). Click on the Home button to go to the home page.

2.5.12 The Stop Button

The Stop button stops a page downloading. Click on it if . . .

■ A page is taking a long time to appear on the screen.

■ You think you might have typed in the wrong address.

  ■ Internet Explorer is going somewhere you don't want it to!

2.5.13 The Refresh Button

The Refresh button tells Internet Explorer to go and download the webpage you are looking at from the server. Click on it if . . .

- Internet Explorer hasn't finished downloading the page and seems to have stopped doing anything.

- You think the page may have changed since you downloaded it the first time.

2.6 Guessing Webpages

When to guess web addresses . . .

Accessing a webpage is easy if you know the address. If you don't know it, it is sometimes useful to try guessing. You'll be surprised how often this is quicker and less frustrating than using a search engine to find it!

2.6.1 The Structure of a Web Address

Part	Hypertext Transfer Protocol, World Wide Web	Domain name	Org type	Country
Example	http://www.	happy.	co.	uk
What it means	This lets the browser know that you want to visit a website	This is the **domain** name – it indicates the name of the organisation	Identifies the type of organisation. In this example, a commercial company	Identifies the country the site is registered in

2.6.2 The Prefix http://www.

- Most web addresses have this at the start.
- Some large companies, like Microsoft, seem to have managed to drop the www part.

2.6.3 The Domain Names

- This identifies the organisation that owns the site, e.g. BBC, Channel4, etc.
- The only difficulty is that organisations can abbreviate their names. At Happy Computers, the domain name is "Happy", but it could just as easily have been "HappyComputers", "Happy-Computers", or "Happyc".

2.6.4 Organisation Type

On UK sites the domain name is followed by a code that helps people identify what sort of organisation it is. The most common are . . .

Abbreviation	Stands for	Examples
co.	Company	Commercial, profit making
org.	Non-profit organisation	Charities, Unions, Trusts
ac.	Academic institution	Universities, Colleges and Schools
gov.	Government	Government, Councils, Parliament Sites, Heritage Sites

2.6.5 Example of Countries

Code	Country
uk	United Kingdom
de	Germany
fr	France
es	Spain

2.6.6 The Large Exception – the USA

The only big exceptions to the location and organisational info above are sites registered in the States.

- American sites do NOT need a country code at the end.

- There are different organisational codes (see below).

Abbreviation	Stands for . . .
.com	Commercial in the US
.org	Non-profit organisation in the US
.edu	Academic institution in the US

Tips for guessing sites

- Sometimes organisations which you would expect to have a .co.uk address actually end in .com, e.g. www.channel4.com – it's worth trying .com if you can't find it with .co.uk

- It's always a good idea to guess the address of a site. If, however, after a few tries you still haven't found it, give up and use a search engine (see page 456).

Typing a web address quickly

If you type in a domain name and then press Ctrl and Enter, Internet Explorer will automatically add the http://www at the start and .com at the end.

More exceptions . . .

There will be exceptions, of course, to any and all of these rules. But it's always worth having a guess.

2

CHAPTER 3

Using Search Engines

What You'll Do

→ Use Search Engines

→ Get to a Search Engine

→ Search for Words or Phrases

3.1 Introduction to Search Engines

3.1.1 What are Search Engines?

Search Engines are ordinary websites with huge databases hidden behind them. The databases contain information about webpages and websites on the WWW. If you wanted to find pages about monkeys, or cheese, you could use a search engine to find them, instead of trying to guess some bizarre, complicated address.

3.1.2 Using Search Engines

■ All search engines have a search box similar to the one shown below.

■ To find information, you click into the search box and type in **keywords** to describe what you are looking for. So, if you wanted to find information on Shakespeare's tragedies you might type something like this . . .

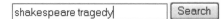

■ The search engine will then search its database looking for all the webpages which contain those two words.

■ Any sites which have both of the words, or have a high occurrence of either of the words will be listed near the top of your results. However, you may also get sites that have got the word "tragedy" in them, but have nothing to do with Shakespeare, and nothing to do with drama either!

3.1.3 How Many Search Engines are on the Web?

- There are hundreds of search engines on the web, and they all have different sites in their database.

- Because they are all different, it is sometimes worth using more than one to find the information you are after. And things change – a year is a long time on the Internet. Before the previous version of this book had been written, Google was a fairly new search engine that not many people had heard of. At the time of writing now, it is the biggest and most well known. By the time you read this, maybe some other engine will be the next big thing.

3.1.4 Some Common Search Engines

You can just type in the URL of a search engine to use it.

Often you will find that search engines give you predominantly American sites, so there is often a UK version which will let you search for UK sites.

Search engine name	Global version	UK version
Google	www.google.com	www.google.co.uk
Yahoo!	www.yahoo.com	www.yahoo.co.uk
Excite	www.excite.com	www.excite.co.uk
AltaVista	www.altavista.com	uk.altavista.com

3.1.5 Getting to a Search Engine

1. *Click into the Address bar*

2. *Type in the address of the search engine, e.g. www.google.co.uk*

3. *Press Enter*

   or

   Click on the Go Button

3.1.6 Searching for Words or Phrases

1. *Go to the search engine page*

2. *Type the words you want to search for into the Search box*

3. *Click on the Search button to show a list of possible sites*

4. *Click on the website that you require*

Google

Web   Images   Groups   News   Froogle^{New!}   **more »**

fish chips yorkshire   [Search]   Advanced Search
                                    Preferences

Search: ⦿ the web ○ pages from the UK

Web   Results **1 - 10** of about **87,700** for <u>fish</u> <u>chips</u> <u>yorkshire</u>. (0.24 seconds)

The Wetherby Whaler **Fish and Chip** Restaurants **Yorkshire**
Chain of West **Yorkshire Fish** and **Chip** restaurants - information on branches and
menus. Contact details.
www.wetherbywhaler.co.uk/ - 10k - <u>Cached</u> - <u>Similar pages</u>

> The Wetherby Whaler **Fish and Chip** Restaurants **Yorkshire**
> AThe Wetherby Whaler **Fish** and **Chip** restaurants **Yorkshire**.
> www.wetherbywhaler.co.uk/newsletter/ - 30k - <u>Cached</u> - <u>Similar pages</u>
> [More results from www.wetherbywhaler.co.uk]

SKIPTON WEB: search for Takeaway
... food takeaway **fish chips**] 31 Water Street, Skipton, North **Yorkshire**, BD23 1PQ
... food **fish chips** takeaway] Westmoreland St, Skipton, North **Yorkshire**, ...
www.skiptonweb.co.uk/directory/ preset.asp?keyword=Takeaway - 23k - <u>Cached</u> - <u>Similar pages</u>

Use phrases

To search for an exact phrase, put quotation marks around it. For example, if you wanted
to find the phrase **fish and chips**, you would type in **"fish and chips"**

3.1.7 Advanced Searching

Some search engines let you put a plus (+) symbol before a word, to find all pages with this
word. Google does it automatically, so you don't have to – although it ignores common words
like "and" or "the", so if you want to find them, you'll need the plus sign next to them.

Put a minus (-) symbol just before a word to make sure the pages you find don't have that
word. For example, if you typed **fish -chips** into a search engine, you would find all pages
with the word **fish** on, and avoid any pages with the word **chips** on.

Any combination of the above can be used to really narrow your search down:

+"shakespeare plays" -sonnets   [Search]

This will find sites that included the phrase "Shakespeare plays" and would reject those
that included the word "sonnets".

CHAPTER 4

Viewing and Saving Webpages

What You'll Do

→ View and Save Webpages

→ Change Your Home Page

→ Create a Favourite

→ Add a Favourite to a Folder

→ Delete Favourites

→ Rename Folders or Favourites

→ Save Webpages

→ Open a Saved File

→ Copy Information from a Webpage

→ Hide Images

→ Switch Images Back On

4

4.1 Your Favourite Webpages

4.1.1 Changing Your Home Page

If you find a site that you really like or find particularly useful, you may want to set it as your home page. This is the page that Internet Explorer will open with.

1 *Click on the Tools menu*

2 *Click on Internet Options*

3 *Click on the General tab*

4 *Click in the Address box in the Home Page area*

5 *Type the address of the page you wish to set as your home page*

6 *Click OK*

4.1.2 What are Favourites?

When you find a useful site, you will often want to return to it regularly. If you make it a favourite, then going back is easy!

4.1.3 Creating a Favourite

1️⃣ *Go to the page which you would like to make a favourite*

2️⃣ *Click on the Favorites menu*

3️⃣ *Click on Add to Favorites*

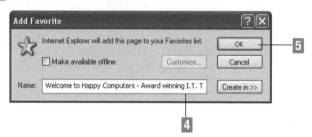

4️⃣ *Give your favourite page a name if required – type it into the **Name** box*

5️⃣ *Click OK*

Favourites/Favorites?

You may have noticed that the menu spells it Favorites (without the u) – this is because Internet Explorer is an American software product, and Americans and Europeans have never agreed on the spelling of certain words – favour/favor, humour/humor, etc. So in the UK we say favourites, but spell the menu/icon Favorites. Don't worry about it though, life's too short to get upset about things like that.

4.1.4 Adding a Favourite to a Folder

1️⃣ *Go the page which you would like to make a favourite*

2️⃣ *Click on the Favorites menu*

3️⃣ *Click on Add to Favorites*

4️⃣ *Give your favourite page a name if required*

5️⃣ *Click on **Create in***

6️⃣ *Double click on the folder you wish to add the page to*

    or

    Click on New Folder to create a new folder to put your page in

    Type in the name of the folder

    Click OK

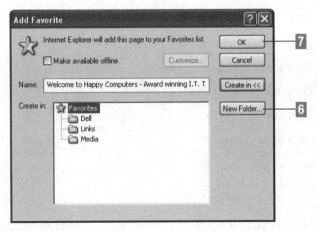

7 Click OK

4.1.5 Accessing One of Your Favourites

1 Click on the Favorites button – a list of favourites appears on the left

2 If necessary, click on the folder you wish to open

3 Click on the page you wish to go to

4 Click on the Favorites button again to remove the list

4.1.6 Deleting Favourites

1 Click on the Favorites button

2 Right click on the site you wish to delete – a new menu will appear

3 Click on Delete

4 Click Yes to delete the page

4.1.7 Creating Folders in Favourites

You can move favourites to different folders, rename, name, or create new folders at any time.

1 Click on the Favorites menu

2 Click on Organize Favorites

3 Click on **Create Folder**

4 Type in a name for your folder

5 Press Enter

6 Click Close

4.1.8 Renaming Folders or Favourites

1. *Click on the Favorites menu*

2. *Click on Organize Favorites*

3. *Click on the folder or page you wish to rename*

4. *Click on **Rename***

5. *Type in a new name*

6. *Press Enter*

7. *Click Close*

4.2 Saving Webpages

4.2.1 Saving to the Hard Disk

1. *Go to the page you wish to save*

2. *Click on the File menu*

3. *Click on Save As*

4. *Change the **Save in** box to the folder you wish to save in*

5. *Choose the type of file you want to save – web page, text file, etc.*

6. *Type a file name for your page, if required*

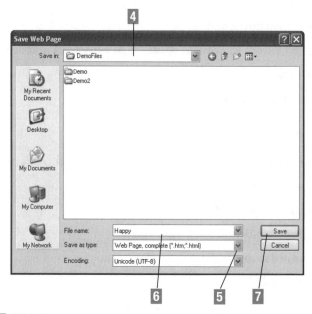

7. *Click Save*

Why do extra folders appear when I save a page?

Often when you save, you will end up with extra folders as well as the file. These are usually to hold any graphics that come with the webpage. If you do not want to see the graphics, you can delete them.

4.2.2 Opening a Saved File

1 *Click on the File menu*

2 *Click on Open*

3 *Click on Browse*

4 *Change the **Look in** box to the folder where your file is saved*

5 *Double click on the file you wish to open*

6 *Click OK*

My Address bar doesn't have a web address!

Your Address bar will now have the pathname of the file you have just opened. AutoComplete won't work and neither will some of the buttons (e.g. Back). Type in a web address or click on Home to return to the web.

4.2.3 Copying Information from a Webpage

1 *Select the information you want to copy (text, images, etc.)*

2 *Click on the Edit menu*

3 *Click on Copy*

4 *Go to the program you want to copy the information to (Word, Notepad, etc.)*

5 *Click on the Edit menu*

6 *Click on Paste*

4.3 Images

Images take a long time to download!

If you stop your computer from downloading images off the web, then you will massively speed up the download process.

4.3.1 Hiding Images

1 *Click on the Tools menu*

2 *Click on Internet Options*

3 *Click on the Advanced tab*

4 *Scroll down until you see the Multimedia options*

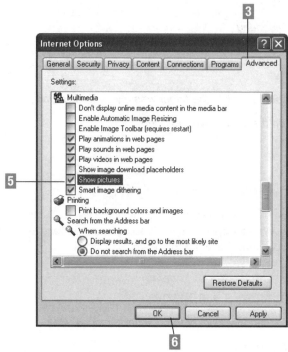

5 *Remove the tick next to* **Show pictures**

6 *Click OK*

Images will now appear as icons on any new sites you go to

Any pages that you have previously visited may still show pictures, as they are still stored in your computer's memory.

4.3.2 Seeing Images Temporarily

If a webpage is not making sense without its images, you can turn them back on temporarily . . .

1 *Right click on the picture you would like to see*

2 *Click on Show Picture*

4.3.3 Switching Images Back On

1. *Click on the Tools menu*

2. *Click on Internet Options*

3. *Click on the Advanced tab*

4. *Scroll down to the Multimedia Options*

5. *Click in the box next to **Show pictures** so that it is ticked*

6. *Click OK*

4

CHAPTER 5

Printing

What You'll Do

→ Print a Page

→ Print Certain Pages or Text

→ Print More Than One Copy

→ Print Frames

→ Change Page Orientation

→ Change the Margins

5.1 Printing

5.1.1 Print Preview

Note: this feature is not available in Internet Explorer 5 and below.

1 *Click on the File menu*

2 *Click Print Preview*

3 *Click Close to go back to the page*

5.1.2 Printing a Page

 Click on the Print icon

5.1.3 Printing Certain Pages or Text

A web page may not necessarily be just one sheet of A4. You might want to print certain pages, or even just a piece of text you have selected.

1 *If required, select the text you want to print*

2 *Click on the File menu*

3 *Click on Print*

4 *Click on the General tab*

5 *Type in the pages required in the Pages boxes*

Or

Click on Selection to print the selected text

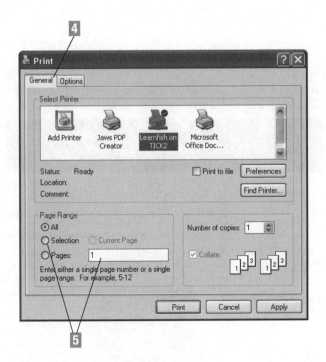

5.1.4 Printing More Than One Copy

1. *Click on the File menu*

2. *Click on Print*

3. *Click on the General tab*

4. *Change the number of copies to the number you require (see below)*

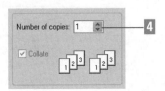

- Use the up and down arrows to change the number of copies, or click into the box and type in the number of copies you require.

- Tick Collate if you require the copies to come out in the order page 1,2,3, page 1,2,3, etc.

- Do not tick Collate if you require the copies to come out in the order page 1, page 1, page 2, page 2, etc.

5. *Click OK*

5.1.5 Printing Frames

Sometimes you may not want to print the webpage as it appears on the screen, but just a selection of it. You can do this if the page is divided into separate sections, or frames. This page has at least two frames – you can tell by the number and location of the scroll bars.

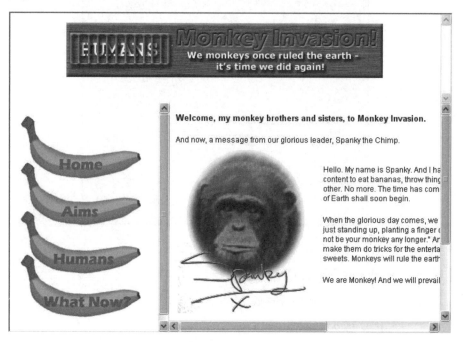

1. *Click your cursor anywhere in the frame you wish to print (but not on a link!)*

2. *Click on the File menu*

3. *Click on Print*

4. *Click on the Options tab*

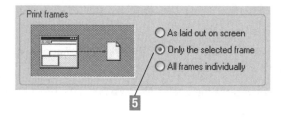

5. *Click next to the option you require*

6. *Click OK*

How can I tell if a page has frames?

Sometimes there will be scroll bars but more often the page will just have different sections that are separated by lines or that just look different. If the page doesn't use frames, the **Print frames** area will be greyed out.

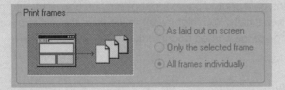

5.2 Page Setup

You can change various things about the way that Internet Explorer prints your pages, such as whether the page has landscape or portrait orientation. Any options that you change will remain set for all the future pages that you print out, as well as the current webpage. You can change the page setup options as many times as you like.

5.2.1 Changing the Page Orientation

You can choose whether to have the page printed vertically (portrait) or horizontally (landscape). For example, a webpage might look better when printed landscape if it is wider than it is long.

1. *Click on the File menu*

2. *Click on Page Setup*

3. *Click in the circle next to Landscape*

   or

   Click in the circle next to Portrait

4. *Click OK*

5.2.2 Paper Size

1. *Click on the File menu*

2. *Click on Page Setup*

3. *Click on the drop down arrow next to the Size box at the top, in the Paper section*

4 *Click on the paper size you need*

5 *Click OK*

5.2.3 Changing the Margins

There are four margins on a printed page: top, bottom, left and right. Internet Explorer will set these for you automatically. You might want to increase these if you want more white space around the edge of the printed document.

1 *Click on the File menu*

2 *Click on Page Setup*

3 *Click in the box for the margin you wish to change*

4 *Change the margin to the amount you require*

5 *Repeat steps 3 to 4 for any other margin you wish to change*

6 *Click OK*

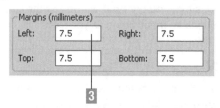

Check the unit of measurement

Look at the text next to Margins in the box to determine the unit of measurement being used. One inch is a lot bigger than one millimetre!

CHAPTER 6

Getting Started with Outlook

What You'll Do

→ Get Started with Outlook

→ Understand Email

→ Understand Email Security

→ Open and Start Outlook

→ Discover the Components of Outlook

→ Display the Outlook Bar

→ Open the Inbox

→ Use Help in Outlook

→ Change the View

→ Show and Hide Toolbars

→ Show or Hide the Preview Pane

→ Show or Hide the Folders List

6.1 Understanding Email

6.1.1 What is Email?

As well as using the Internet to look at websites and webpages, you can send and receive text messages called email. This is short for electronic mail.

Just like the Internet, you need a modem and an Internet Service Provider to use email. You need either email software (like Outlook, Outlook Express, Eudora, Thunderbird) or an Internet-based email account (like Gmail, Yahoo or Hotmail), which lets you read and send mail through your Internet browser.

6.1.2 Advantages of Email

You're not limited to text messages in email – it is possible to attach files (like documents or pictures, for example) to send things to other people.

Email is fast and cheap, and if you use a web-based account you can read your email from any PC in the world.

6.1.3 Email Addresses

Email addresses are usually made up of four parts. Let's use fredbloggs@johnsons.co.uk as an example.

- The first part is usually the user name, or full name of the user.

- The second part (johnsons) is either the company name, or the name of the ISP.

- Like Internet addresses, the last two parts refer to the organisation type and country (co meaning commercial business, uk meaning United Kingdom). Also like Internet addresses, these can vary enormously. See page 453 for more about this.

6.1.4 Email Etiquette

- Emails are not letters, so keep things fairly short and to the point.

- Try not to type everything IN CAPITAL LETTERS, AS IT IS CONSIDERED SHOUTING! KEEP YOUR VOICE DOWN!

- Make sure you ask permission before sending someone an attachment. Unless you know them well – they may not want it.

- Every email should have a subject line so that the person receiving it knows what it is about – and don't just put "urgent" or "important". The subject line should relate to the content of the email.

- Spell check your emails before sending them.

- Never send an email in anger – it is far too easy to send off a quick reply when you're angry, and you could regret it later. Wait a day, and see how you feel then.

- Last, but not least – please, please, please write properly. You don't have to have perfect English, but saying things like "plz snd files kthxbye" can be irritating to the other person. If you can't even be bothered to type the full word, why should they bother replying? On a similar note, putting thousands of exclamation marks after every sentence is really annoying!!!!!!!!!!!!!!!!! See???!! And it makes your email look like Spam (see next section).

6.2 Email Security

6.2.1 Spam

Sometimes you will get email from people you don't know. They'll offer you amazing deals, or free things. There will also be lots of capital letters and way, way too many exclamation marks, LIKE THIS!!!! FREE!!!!!!!! Usually, they'll be about extremely naughty things, and will involve naked people.

This is spam (the email, not the naked people).

They don't always have your email address. Sometimes they guess email addresses, sometimes they get them from web sites, sometimes they buy lists of customers.

Spam is any unsolicited email. Do not – ever! – reply to spam, or click the "Unsubscribe" link. This will just tell the spammers that your address is real, and they will then deluge you with more.

It's called spam after the Monty Python sketch, where everything on the menu is served with SPAM (the luncheon meat made by Hormel Foods), and a song about the meat eventually drowns out all conversation.

6.2.2 Viruses

A virus is a nasty program written to waste your time or damage your PC. It may come in the form of a file attached to an email – never run or open any files that you are not expecting, even if they're from a friend. Check that the friend really sent them – they may be suffering from a virus too.

6.2.3 Virus Hoaxes

If someone emails you telling you to email everyone you know about a new, scary virus, or to delete a file from your PC, don't. Check a virus library first – never forward these hoaxes, that's what the hoaxer wants. Hoax virus alerts waste time and fill up mailboxes.

Check with the virus library first at http://www.viruslibrary.com

6.2.4 Digital Signatures

A digital signature is a way of letting people know that an email from you is really from you.

You can set them up in your email software, so that if anyone receives an email supposedly from you, they'll know that only the digitally signed ones are real.

6.3 Opening Outlook

6

6.3.1 Starting Outlook

1 *Click on the Start button*

2 *Click on All Programs*

3 *Click on Microsoft Outlook*

Microsoft
Outlook

Or

From the desktop, double click on the Microsoft Outlook icon

6.3.2 Closing Outlook

1 *Click on the File menu*

2 *Choose Exit*

Or

Click on the X on the top right of the title bar

6.4 Outlook Screen

6.4.1 The Outlook Screen

The Outlook screen looks different depending on which component you are in. The picture below shows the Inbox screen.

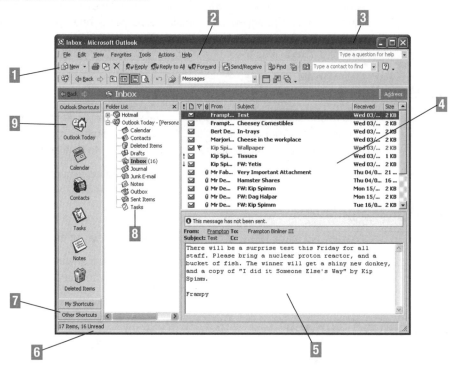

1 Standard Toolbar

2 Menu Bar

3 Title Bar

4 Viewing Pane with messages

5 Preview Pane

6 Status Bar

7 Groups

8 Folders List

9 Outlook Bar

6.4.2 What are the Components of Outlook?

Outlook has several different components. Each component allows you to perform a different kind of task. This list below names the components and gives a brief description of what each one is for.

Outlook Today

Inbox (15)

Calendar

Contacts

Tasks

Notes

Deleted Items

Journal

1 *Outlook Today* This is an introductory screen to Outlook. It shows you any appointments or events booked in your calendar for the coming week. It also shows you any tasks you have set for yourself, and whether you have email messages waiting for you in your Inbox.

2 *Inbox* The Inbox stores the emails you receive.

3 *Calendar* The Calendar allows you to book out times for appointments, or meetings, just like a normal diary. You can also use the calendar to schedule meetings with other people.

4 *Contacts* This is just like an address book. It holds information about all the people you are in contact with.

5 *Tasks* A bit like a to-do list. Use it to keep track of all the things you need to do.

6 *Notes* Just like Post-it notes. You can stick them to your computer screen as a reminder.

7 *Deleted Items* The same as the Recycle Bin in Windows. Use it to throw away any unwanted information.

8 *Journal* This keeps track of all the programs and files you have opened in a day.

6.4.3 Displaying the Outlook Bar

The Outlook bar runs down the left hand side of the screen and shows the components listed above. To turn it on or off . . .

1 *Click on the View menu*

2 *Click Outlook Bar*

6.5 Opening the Inbox

6.5.1 What is the Inbox?

The Inbox allows you to send and receive emails. The Inbox can be viewed from the Outlook Shortcut Bar or the My Shortcuts bar. A list of the emails you have received is shown here. Outlook does not limit you to sending only text messages; you can also send pictures and other formatted files.

6.5.2 Opening the Inbox

Click on the Inbox icon on the Outlook bar

Or

 Inbox (15)   *Click on the Inbox in the folder list*

6.6 Using Help in Outlook

Outlook comes with a Help feature which works in exactly the same way as the help in Word – see the Help section in the Word chapters on page 46 for more details.

6.7 Changing the View

You can customise the way your Inbox screen looks by changing your view, displaying folders and a preview pane, and showing or hiding toolbars.

6.7.1 Outlook Toolbars

Toolbars give you quick access to commands. There are three toolbars in Outlook: Standard, Advanced and Web.

6.7.2 Showing and Hiding Toolbars

1 *Click on the View menu*

2 *Click on Toolbars*

3 *Click on the toolbar you wish to show or hide*

Toolbars are on when ticked

If there is a tick next to the name of the toolbar in the Toolbars menu then it is on the screen. Toolbars are hidden when not ticked.

6.7.3 What is the Preview Pane?

This is a small window which lets you read a message by just clicking on it once.

6.7.4 Showing or Hiding the Preview Pane

Click on the Preview Pane icon on the Advanced toolbar

Or

1 *Click on the View menu*

2 *Click on Preview Pane*

6.7.5 What are Folders?

Folders are used to organise the messages you receive, send, save, and give you access to other components of Outlook. You can also create your own folders to store your messages.

6.7.6 Showing or Hiding the Folders List

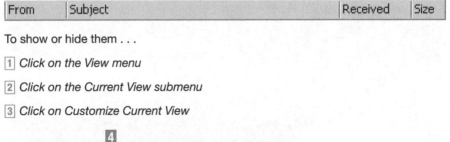   *Click on the Folder List icon*

Or

1 *Click on the View menu*

2 *Choose Folder List*

If the Folder List is displayed, then this will hide it – if it is hidden, then this will display it.

6.7.7 Inbox Headings

These are the grey headings above the emails – Subject, From, To, etc.

From	Subject	Received	Size

To show or hide them . . .

1 *Click on the View menu*

2 *Click on the Current View submenu*

3 *Click on Customize Current View*

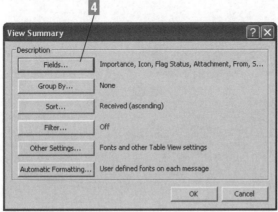

4 *Click on Fields*

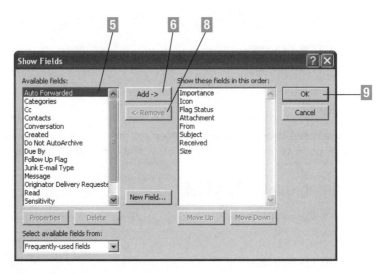

5   *Click on the field you want to add*

6   *Click on Add*

7   *Click on the field you want to remove*

8   *Click Remove*

9   *Click OK*

10   *Click OK*

CHAPTER 7

Working with Email

What You'll Do

→ Work with Email

→ Create an Email

→ Send an Email

→ Save a Message

→ Flag Mail Messages

→ Receive an Email

→ Read Mail

→ Close an Email Message

→ Forward and Reply to an Email

→ Delete Text

→ Send and Receive Attachments

→ Move and Copy Text

→ Check Your Spelling

→ Print an Email

7.1 Creating a Message

7.1.1 Creating an Email

[1] *Go to the Inbox (if you are not already there)*

[2] *Click New*

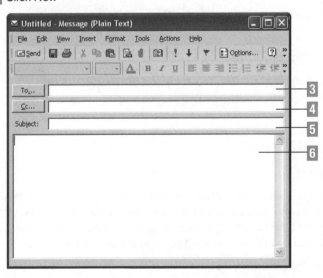

3 Type in the address you wish to send the email to in the box next to **To**, e.g. fredbloggs@fishface.com

4 If required, type in the address(es) you wish to send a copy to in the box next to **Cc** (**C**arbon **c**opy)

5 Type the subject in the box next to **Subject**

6 Type your message in the white space underneath

Don't forget the subject!

The subject line appears in the recipient's Inbox before they open the email.

I want to send an email to more than one person

Separate the addresses with a semi-colon,

e.g. marymiggins@pies.com; jobbo@spetetoot.com

7.1.2 Blind Copy

If you want to send a copy of your email to someone, but don't want everybody else to know that they have been sent it, you can send a blind carbon copy (bcc).

1 Create a new message

2 Click on the View menu

3 Click **Bcc Field** – a new box will appear under the **Cc** box

4 Type in the address(es) next to the **Bcc**

The Bcc field remains

You will still see the Bcc box for your future messages. To turn it off, click on the View menu and then click on **Bcc Field**.

7.1.3 Sending an Email

   Click Send

The message goes to the Outbox if you **are not** connected to a network or the Internet. It is sent immediately if you **are** connected to a network or the Internet. Unless you are connected to a network, or the Internet, your message will go to the Outbox and will sit there until you do connect. To send your message from the Outbox . . .

   Click on the Send/Receive icon

7.1.4 Saving a Message

If you start to type a message, and then don't send it, you can save it in your Drafts folder.

 Click on the Save icon – the message is saved in the Drafts folder

To get back to your message . . .

1 *Click on the View menu*

2 *Click Folder List*

3 *Click Drafts*

4 *Double click on the message you require*

7.1.5 Flagging Mail Messages

You can indicate how urgent an email is by flagging it. A symbol will appear next to the message in the recipient's inbox, so they can prioritise their mail.

1 *Create your message as normal*

 2 *Click on the Flag icon*

3 *Click the drop down arrow next to **Flag to** and choose the subject for the flag*

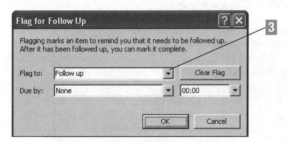

4 *Click the drop down arrow next to **Due by** and choose the response date for the email*
Or
Click Clear Flag to remove the flag

5 *Click OK – a flag message will appear above the email*

7.1.6 Making Your Message Important

You can let people know that your message is important – it will be marked with a red exclamation mark in the Outlook inbox. Similarly, you can mark the message as not important, so that if they are busy they can safely leave it for a while.

1 *Create the message as normal*

2 *Click the **Importance: High** icon* ❗ *or the **Importance: Low** icon* ↓ *– the icon will appear "pushed in" when you have clicked on it*

They didn't read my important message!

Just because you have flagged a message as important, it doesn't mean that Outlook will force the other person to read it. Shockingly, many people will sometimes still ignore emails, no matter how many flags or red things you stick on them... If it's really, really important, it might be better to phone them, or, better yet, meet them.

7.2 Receiving Email

7.2.1 Receiving an Email

If you are connected to a network or the Internet, you do not have to do anything!

Your messages will just appear in your Inbox when they have arrived. As they are arriving, you should see a message at the bottom of the screen saying something like "Receiving message 1 of 3".

If you are not connected to a network or the Internet, just click on the Send and Receive icon. When you click it, a box will appear:

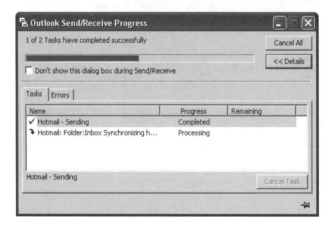

When this box disappears, Outlook has finished sending and receiving. If you don't have any new mail, then nobody has sent you any. Don't worry, I'm sure you'll get some soon.

7.2.2 Reading Mail

How do I know if I have mail to be read?

There are several ways in which Outlook will indicate if there is new mail:

- The number of unread messages appears in brackets next to the Inbox icon and the Inbox in the folder list

- A closed envelope appears next to unread messages, and the text will appear in bold

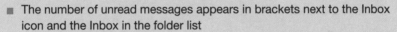

- There is a message at the bottom left of the screen telling you how many unread messages you have

To read your message, double click on it. The message will open in a new window. Or you can click once on the message, and it will appear in the preview pane.

How do I know if I've read a message?

Once a message has been read, the envelope will look as if it has been opened, and the text will no longer be in bold.

Marjorie PindleWindle   Cheese in the workplace

7.2.3 Marking a Message as Unread

Once you have read a message you can make it look as though it still hasn't been read to draw your attention to it.

1. *Click on the message in the Inbox, or select the messages you want to change (use the Shift or Control key to select multiple emails)*

2. *Click on the Edit menu*

3. *Click on Mark as Unread*

   Or

   Click on Mark as Read to make it look as though you have read the email, without having to open it

7.2.4 Closing an Email Message

1. *Click the X on the title bar of the email message (**not** the one on the Outlook bar!)*

Or

1. *Click on the File menu of the email message (not the one in the main Outlook window)*

2. *Click on Close*

7.3 Forwarding and Replying to Email

7.3.1 Forwarding a Message

Sometimes you might want to send a message on to someone else – this is called forwarding.

[1] *Go to the Inbox*

[2] *Select the message you wish to forward*

 [3] *Click Forward – a new message window will appear*

[4] *Enter the email address of the person you wish to forward the message to in the box next to **To***

[5] *Enter any text in the message area*

[6] *Send the message as normal*

7.3.2 Replying to an Email

[1] *Select the message you want to reply to*

[2] *Click Reply – a new message window will appear*

[3] *The address will already be filled in, and the original text of the message will appear*

[4] *Type in your message*

[5] *Send the message as normal*

> ### The sender gets their message again!
>
> When you reply to a message, your reply will include the text from the original message. See the section after the next one to learn how to delete this text.

7.3.3 Replying to All the Recipients

If the message you are replying to was sent to more than one person originally, you can reply to all of them.

[1] *Select the message you want to reply to*

[2] *Click **Reply to All** – a new message window will appear*

[3] *The addresses will be filled in, and the original text of the message will appear*

[4] *Type in your new message*

[5] *Send the message as normal*

Be careful with Reply and Reply All . . .

Before using Reply All, make sure you really, really need all the recipients to see your email. Does everyone on the list need a copy of your reply if it just says something like "me too", or "haha!"? Make absolutely sure you know who you are replying to! Careers have been damaged and lost by careless use of the Reply and Reply All buttons . . .

7.3.4 Deleting Text

You may want to delete some text when you are forwarding or replying, if you do not want the whole of the original message to be included – particularly if the email has been replied to or forwarded several times.

⬚1 *Select the text you wish to delete*

⬚2 *Press the Delete or Del key on the keyboard*

7.3.5 Not Including the Original Message

It's often useful to include the original message, so that the person you are replying to knows what they said to you in the first place. However, you can turn this feature off . . .

⬚1 *Click on the Tools menu*

⬚2 *Click Options*

⬚3 *Click on the Preferences tab*

⬚4 *Click Email Options*

⬚5 *Click the drop down arrow next to **When replying to a message***

⬚6 *Click **Do not include original message***

⬚7 *Click OK*

7.4 Sending and Receiving Attachments

An attachment is a file that you send with an email. The attachment can be any sort of file – a Word document, an Excel spreadsheet, a film, a picture, etc. It is an easy way of sending someone a file. Always check with them first, so they know it is coming, and don't send anything too large – 500K is usually the maximum.

7.4.1 Sending a Message with an Attachment

1. *Create a new email as normal*

2. *Click on the Insert menu*

3. *Click on File*

4. *Change the **Look in** box to the folder where the file you require is saved*

5. *Click on the file you require*

6. *Click Insert – the file will appear in an Attach box*

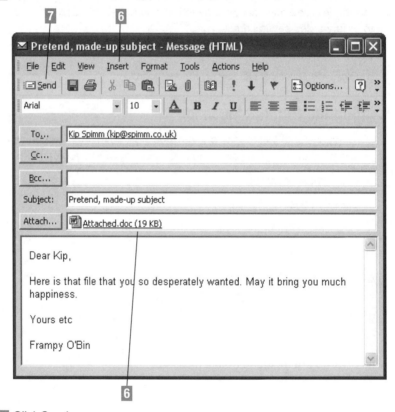

7. *Click Send*

7.4.2 Receiving an Attachment

If your message has an attachment, you will see a paper clip symbol next to it in the Inbox.

✉ 0 Mr Fabulous   **Very Important Attachment**

To open the attachment . . .

1. *Double click the email you wish to open*

2. *Right click the attachment icon in the message*

3 *To open the file, click **Open***

or

*Click **Save As** if you wish to save the file onto your computer before you open it*

Or

1 *Ensure the preview pane is displayed (see page 476)*

2 *Click on the email that contains the attachment you wish to open*

3 *Right click on the file at the top of the preview pane*

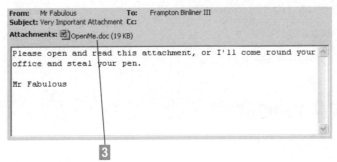

4 *To open the file, click **Open***

or

*Click **Save As** if you wish to save the file onto your computer before you open it*

I can't open my attachment!

If the attachment was created in a program which you do not have on your machine, you may not be able to open it. For example, if someone sends you a Word XP document and you have Word 6, you will not be able to open it. You must obtain the software, or ask the person who sent it to you to send it in a format which you can open.

Beware – Viruses!

Be careful with attachments! If you are not sure that your attachment is completely virus free, check for viruses before opening the attachment. Most virus checkers will allow you to right click the attachment and scan it with the virus checking software. Do this even if it is from someone you trust – they could be infected without realising!

7.4.3 Deleting an Attachment from an Email Before Sending

If you attach the wrong file, it is easy to delete it.

1 *Click on the attachment icon in the email – it will become highlighted*

2 *Press the Delete or Del key on the keyboard*

7.4.4 Deleting an Attachment from an Email in a Folder

You may want to delete an attachment from an email in your Inbox or another folder. For instance, this might be to save space if you no longer need the attachment, but want to keep the message. Or, you may have already saved the attachment somewhere on your computer.

1. *Open the email with the attachment*

2. *Right click on the attachment icon in the email*

3. *Click Remove*

4. *Click on the File menu*

5. *Click Save*

6. *Close the message*

7.5 Moving and Copying Text

7.5.1 Why Move and Copy Text?

If you have text that you need to repeat, there is no need to retype it – you can simply copy the text to anywhere in that email, or into another email. If you decide that the text needs to be somewhere other than where you have typed it, it is easy to move it as well.

You may also have text in another Windows file, such as a Word document, that you want to use in your email. Moving or copying this text to email will save you the effort of retyping it.

7.5.2 Moving Text in a Message

1. *Select the text you would like to move*

2. *Click on the Edit menu*

3. *Click on Cut*

4. *Go to the email or document you want to move the text to*

5. *Click on the Edit menu*

6. *Click on Paste*

Editing a message

If you cut text from an existing message, you will have to let Outlook know that you want to edit that message before it will let you. Remember to save the changes before you close it, or the text will still be in the message when you close it.

7.5.3 Copying Text in a Message

1. Select the text you would like to copy

2. Click on the Edit menu

3. Click on Copy

4. Go to the email or document you want to copy the text to

5. Click on the Edit menu

6. Click on Paste

7.5.4 Moving or Copying from Other Documents

1. Select the text you would like to move or copy in the document

2. Click on the Edit menu

3. Click on Cut or Copy

4. Go to the email you want to move or copy the text to

5. Click on the Edit menu

6. Click on Paste

7.5.5 Switching Between a Message and the Inbox

Once you have opened a message (or created a new one), you can switch back to the Inbox without closing the email. This is useful if you want to move or copy text, or just read something in another message. To go to the Inbox, click on the Inbox button on the task bar. To return to the message, click the button for the message on the task bar.

Outlook opens a new window for each message

When you open a message, Outlook opens it in a new window with its own button on the task bar. If you have several messages open, they will each have their own button on the task bar. The subject of the message appears on the button so that you can tell them apart!

7.5.6 Opening More Than One Message

1. Open the first message

2. Click on the Inbox button on the task bar

3. Open the second message

4. Repeat steps 2 to 3 for any more messages you wish to open

7.5.7 Switching Between Messages

You can have several messages open at the same time. If you have opened more than one message you can also switch between the open messages. Just click the button for the message on the task bar to switch over to it.

Untitled messages

If the message does not have a subject (for example a new message you have just created) it will be called **Untitled**.

7.6 Checking Your Spelling

7.6.1 Spell Checking Messages

You can spell check any messages that you compose – Outlook comes with a spell checker which works in exactly the same way as the one in Word – see the Spelling and Grammar section in the Word chapters for more details.

Note: To start the spell checker in Outlook, you must be in the message part of an email – the big white box at the bottom of the email. Then click on the Tools menu, and click on Spelling. If you are not in the message part, then the Spelling option will be greyed out.

7.7 Printing Email

7.7.1 Print Preview

1. *Select or open the email*
2. *Click on the File menu*
3. *Click on Print Preview*
4. *Click on the main page preview to zoom in and out*
5. *Click Close when you have finished*

7.7.2 Printing Email

1. *Select or open the email*

 2. *Click on the Print icon*
   Or
   Click on the File menu
   Click on Print
   Click OK

7.7.3 Email Printing Options

1. *Select or open the email*

2. *Click on the File menu*

3. *Click on Print*

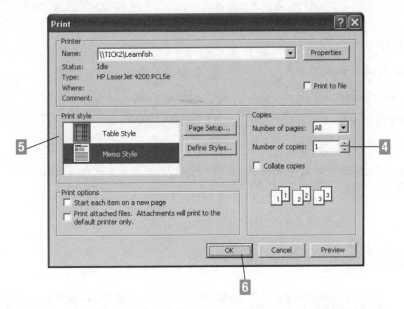

4. *To change the number of copies, click the up or down arrows next to the "Number of copies" box, or click inside the box and type a new number*

5. *Choose the style you want from the **Print style** box – **Table Style** prints the list of emails in your Inbox, while **Memo Style** prints each email more or less as it appears on screen*

6. *Click OK*

7

CHAPTER 8

Organising Your Emails

What You'll Do

→ Organise Your Emails

→ Display the Folder List

→ Close the Folder List

→ Create Your Own Folders

→ Move and Copy Emails to a Folder

→ Delete Folders

→ Sort Emails

→ Delete Emails

→ Use the Deleted Items Folder

→ Find Messages in Your Inbox

8.1 Organising Your Emails

The more emails you get, the more you will need to organise them. Delete old emails, and create folders to store emails of a similar type or from the same person.

8.1.1 Email Folders

Email is stored in several different folders within Outlook. The list below gives a brief description of what these folders do:

Inbox	Contains messages you have received
Drafts	Contains messages which you have written, but not yet sent
Outbox	Contains messages waiting to be sent over your network, or the Internet
Sent Items	Contains messages which you have sent

8.1.2 Displaying the Folder List

1. *Click on the View menu*

2. *Click Folder List*

3. Any folders shown in bold contain new messages.

8.1.3 Closing the Folder List

⚀ *Click on the View menu*

⚁ *Click Folder List*

Or

   Click the X at the top right of the folder list

8.1.4 Switching Between Folders

   Click on the folder you require from the list – the contents are displayed on the right

8.1.5 Creating Your Own Folders

⚀ *Click on the File menu*

⚁ *Click New*

⚂ *Click Folder*

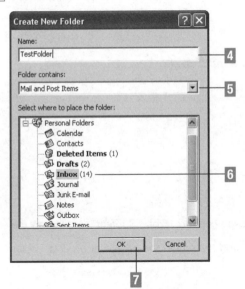

4 Type a name for your folder into the **Name** box

5 Click on the drop down arrow underneath **Folder contains**, and choose what the folder will be used for – usually you can leave it set at **Mail and Post Items**

6 Click on the folder which will hold the folder you are creating, e.g. **Inbox**

7 Click OK

8 You may be asked if you want to create a shortcut – click **Yes** if you wish a shortcut to appear on the Outlook Bar

8.1.6 Moving Emails to a Folder

1. *Click on the email you wish to move*

2. *Click on the Edit menu*

3. *Click Move to Folder*

4. *Click on the folder you want to move the email to*

5. *Click OK*

8.1.7 Copying Emails to a Folder

1. *Click on the email you want to copy*

2. *Click on the Edit menu*

3. *Click Copy to Folder*

4. *Click on the folder you want to copy the email to*

5. *Click OK*

8.1.8 Deleting Folders

1. *Click on the folder you want to delete*

2. *Click on the Edit menu*

3. *Click on Delete*

4. *Click Yes*

8.1.9 Sorting Emails

1. *Go to the folder you wish to sort*

2. *Click on the grey message headers (From, Subject, etc.) to sort the emails*

3. *Click on them again to sort the emails the other way around*

From	Subject		Received	Size

8.2 Deleting Email

8.2.1 Deleting Emails

You can delete email from any of your folders.

1. *Click on the email you wish to delete*

2. *Press the Delete or Del key – the email is sent to the Deleted Items folder*

8.2.2 Deleted Items Folder

The Deleted Items folder stores all the messages that you have deleted. The number in brackets next to it indicates how many messages it contains.

📄 **Deleted Items** (1)

8.2.3 Opening the Deleted Items Folder

Deleted Items

Click on the Deleted Items Folder icon from Outlook Shortcuts

Or

Click on Deleted Items from the Folders list

📄 **Deleted Items** (1)

8.2.4 Retrieving Messages from the Deleted Items Folder

Messages that have been deleted and are still stored in the Deleted Items folder can be retrieved by moving them to the Inbox, or one of your folders.

1. *Open the Deleted Items folder*

2. *Click on the message you wish to retrieve*

3. *Click on the Edit menu*

4. *Click Move to Folder*

5. *Click on the folder you wish to move the email to*

6. *Click OK*

8.2.5 Deleting a Message from the Deleted Items Folder

You can delete messages from Deleted Items, but be warned: once you have done this, there is no way of getting them back. Ever! So make sure you really, really want to delete it . . .

1. *Click on the email you wish to delete*

2. *Press the Delete or Del key*

3. *Click Yes*

To delete all the messages from the Deleted Items folder . . .

1. *Click on the Tools menu*

2. *Click on **Empty "Deleted Items" Folder***

3. *Click Yes*

8

8.3 Finding Messages

8.3.1 Finding Messages in Your Inbox

1 *Go to the Inbox*

2 *Click on the Find icon – a new pane will appear at the top of the Outlook screen*

3 *Type in words to search for in the box next to* **Look for**

4 *Click* **Find Now** *– any found messages are displayed*

5 *Double click on a message to open it*

To start a new search, or to display all your messages again . . .

Clear *Click Clear*

To close the Find pane . . .

Click on the X at the top right of the Find box

8.3.2 Advanced Searching

1 *Click on the Tools menu*

2 *Click on Advanced Find*

3 *Click on the Messages tab*

4 *Enter the words you wish to find in the box next to* **Search for the word(s)**

5 *Click the drop down arrow next to* **In***, and choose the area you wish to find the words in (subject, message body, etc.)*

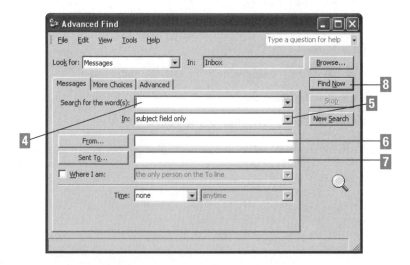

6 *If required, click **From** to look for messages from particular people – double click their name, then click OK to come back to the Advanced Find box*

7 *If required, click **Sent To** to look for messages sent by particular people – double click their name, then click OK to come back to the Advanced Find box*

8 *Click **Find Now** – any found messages appear at the bottom*

9 *Double click a message to open it*

8.3.3 Finding Messages Based on Time

1 *Click on Inbox from the Outlook Bar*

2 *Click on the Tools menu*

3 *Click Advanced Find*

4 *Click on the Messages tab*

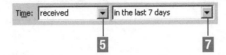

5 *Click the drop down arrow next to the **Time** box*

6 *Click the time you wish to search, e.g. received, sent, etc.*

7 *Click the drop down arrow next to **anytime***

8 *Click on the specific time you wish to find, e.g. yesterday, today, etc.*

9 *Click Find Now – any found messages appear at the bottom*

10 *Double click the message to open it*

8.3.4 Closing the Advanced Find Box

Click the X at the top right of the box

8

Addresses

What You'll Do

→ Create Contacts

→ Use Contacts for Email

→ Edit a Contact

→ Delete a Contact

→ Use a Personal Distribution List

→ Create a Personal Distribution List

→ Send an Email Using a Personal Distribution List

→ Edit a Personal Distribution List

→ Delete a Personal Distribution List

9.1 Creating Contacts

9.1.1 What are Contacts?

Contacts contain information about the people and businesses you are in touch with. You can store all sorts of information about a person, such as . . .

- Email address

- Postal address

- Phone number

- Job title

9.1.2 Getting to the Contacts

Click Contacts on the Outlook Bar

Or

🖼 Contacts   *Click Contacts in the folder list*

9.1.3 The Contacts Screen

1 *Contacts are shown in the big white area in the middle*

2 *Click a letter tab on the right hand side of the screen to move to the contacts that start with that letter*

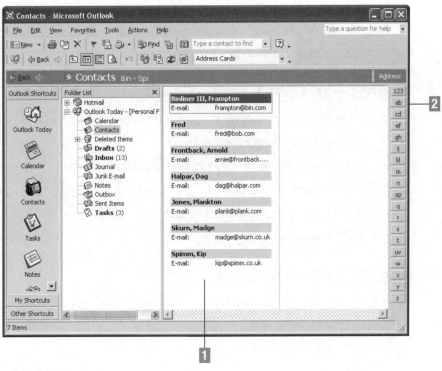

9.1.4 Creating a Contact

1 *Go to the Contacts*

2 *Click New*

3 *Click on the General tab*

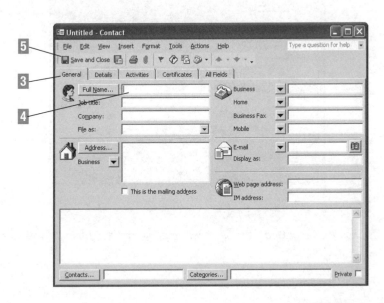

    4 *Fill in the information you require – make sure to add their email address, or the contact won't be much use in Outlook!*

    5 *Click Save and Close*

9.1.5 Creating a New Contact from an Email

When you receive an email, you can add the person who sent it to you as a new contact.

    1 *Open the email from the sender*

    2 *Right click on their email address with the right mouse button – a menu will appear*

    3 *Click Add to Contacts*

    4 *Enter any more details that you wish*

    5 *Click Save and Close*

9.1.6 Using the Contacts for Email

You can use the contacts to add the address quickly . . .

    1 *Create a new email*

    2 *Click the To button*

    3 *If necessary, click the drop down arrow next to **Show Names from the** and choose the address book you wish to use*

    4 *Click on the name you wish to use from the left hand side*

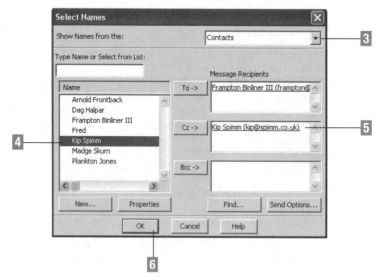

    5 *Click **To**, **Cc** or **Bcc** – the name will appear on the right, in the relevant box*

    6 *Click OK*

    7 *Send the email as normal*

9.2 Editing and Deleting Contacts

9.2.1 Editing a Contact

1. Go to the Contacts
2. Double click on the contact you wish to change
3. Make any changes you require
4. Click Save and Close

9.2.2 Deleting a Contact

1. Go to the Contacts
2. Click on the contact you wish to delete – it will go blue
3. Press Delete

9.3 Using Personal Distribution Lists

9.3.1 What is a Distribution List?

A distribution list allows you to group a set of email addresses together (e.g. all the people in the personnel department). When you want to write to everyone in that group, you can use the distribution list instead of typing out all the individual addresses.

9.3.2 Creating a Personal Distribution List

If you want to create a distribution list

1. Click on the File menu
2. Click New
3. Click Distribution List
4. Type a name for your list into the Name box
5. Click the Select Members button
6. Select a contact to add
7. Click Members
8. Click OK
9. Repeat steps 4 to 8 for everyone else you wish to add
10. Click Save and Close

9

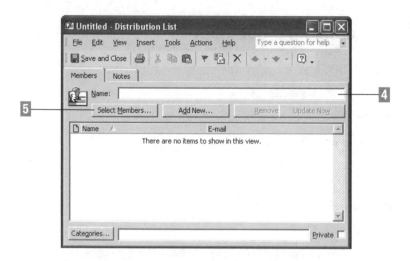

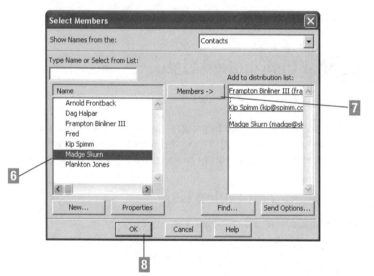

9.3.3 Sending an Email Using a Personal Distribution List

1 *Create a new, blank email*

2 *Click the **To** button*

3 *Click on the distribution list you wish to use*

4 *Click **To** or **Cc***

5 *Click OK*

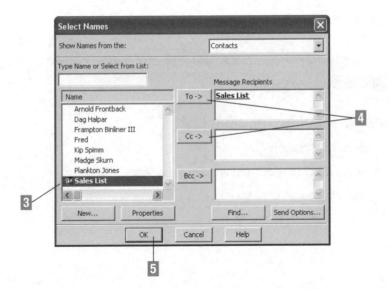

All the addresses in the distribution list will be visible to the recipient . . .

When a recipient receives a message using a distribution list, every name on the list appears in their message window. So the members of your distribution list cannot be kept secret from other members.

9.3.4 Editing a Personal Distribution List

1 *Go to the Contacts*

2 *Double click the Distribution List you want to edit*

3 *Select the person you want to remove*

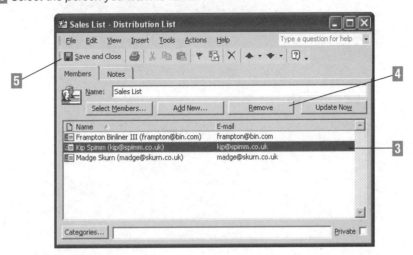

4 *Click Remove*

Or

Click Select Members to add a new member from your contacts

5 *Click Save and Close*

9.3.5 Deleting a Personal Distribution List

1 *Go to the Contacts*

2 *Select the Distribution List you want to delete*

3 *Press the Delete or Del key*

Quick Reference

What You'll Do

→ Get a Quick Reference to Web Jargon

10.1 Web Jargon

10.1.1 A Web Browser

- This is the software that you need to look at the World Wide Web.

- Internet Explorer is a browser. Other popular browsers are Mozilla Firefox, Opera, and Safari

10.1.2 The Modem (Modulator-Demodulator)

- The modem is a piece of hardware that connects your computer to the telephone socket.

- It converts digital information which is stored on your computer into analogue information that can pass down the phone lines.

10.1.3 Internet Service Provider (ISP) and Servers

- Just as you need a telephone service provider to give you your telephone service, you need an **Internet Service Provider** to give you access to the Internet.

- ISPs have **servers** – high capacity computers that can store a lot of information. The servers hold webpages and work like the post office for emails – storing and sending letters around the Internet.

- ISPs provide you with your email address and space to store any webpages you create on their server.

10.1.4 URL (Uniform Resource Locator)

- This is the term used for the address of a webpage, e.g. http://www.happy.co.uk.

- You type URLs into your browser so that your ISP knows where to get the information you require.

10

10.1.5 Webpages, Websites and Home Pages

- **Webpages** are the pages of information you can see over the web.

- Each webpage is stored as a file on a server.

- A **website** is a collection of files stored in the same folder on the server.

- The **home page** is the first page you see when you connect to a website. It works a bit like the front cover of a magazine, telling you what information you can find on the webpages inside that site.

Example Website

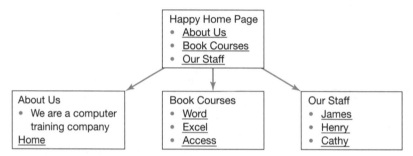

10.1.6 Hyperlinks

- These are the links in webpages that take you to other webpages, so that you don't get stuck at the same page forever.

- They are usually underlined text or pictures, and your mouse will change to a pointing hand when you position it over one.

10.1.7 HTML (Hyper-Text Markup Language)

- Every webpage is written in the computer language called HTML.

- You do not have to know HTML to use the web, because the browser translates it into pictures and text.

- HTML is essentially made up of tags and codes that instruct your browser what to show. For example, there is a tag called <strong> that instructs your browser to make something bold. So "<strong>Kermit the Frog</strong>" would appear as **Kermit the Frog**.

10.1.8 HTTP (Hyper-Text Transfer Protocol)

- This is a set of rules that all computers connected to the Internet have agreed to abide by. This means that HTML means the same to all browsers.

- When http:// appears at the beginning of a web address it is saying that it agrees to bide by the rules of HTTP.

10.1.9 Email Software

- Email software allows you to send mail over the Internet.

- Email software usually comes free with your browser.

- Some common types are Outlook, Pegasus, Eudora, and Thunderbird.

10